ONLY YESTERDAY

Only Yesterday

Times of My Life

Richard Baldwyn

Kendal
&
~~Dean~~

Copyright © Richard Baldwyn 2008
First published in 2008 by Kendal & Dean
18 Seaford Road, Wokingham, Berkshire, RG40 2EL
www.onlyyesterday.co.uk

Distributed by Gardners Books, 1 Whittle Drive, Eastbourne, East
Sussex, BN23 6QH
Tel: +44(0)1323 521555 | Fax: +44(0)1323 521666

www.amolibros.com

British Library Cataloguing in Publication Data
A catalogue record for this book is available from the British Library.

ISBN 978-0-9556719-0-6

Typeset by Amolibros, Milverton, Somerset
This book production has been managed by Amolibros
Printed and bound by T J International Ltd, Padstow, Cornwall, UK

CONTENTS

(The dates in brackets represent either the actual year of the event or the period of years during which I was involved.)

Preface

I AM VERY FORTUNATE in that from both sides of my family I have inherited memorabilia of all kinds which enable me to look over my shoulder and understand a little more about life in the nineteenth and early twentieth centuries. Photographs, letters, newspapers and cuttings, writings, menus, a detailed family tree reaching back to the twelfth century and a family sampler dated 17th March 1798, have excited me, my family and friends for very many years.

Modern technology does not encourage letter writing – it has virtually replaced it – and the future will be the poorer for the absence of character in computer communication.

Trunks, drawers, boxes in attics are redundant; they are no longer needed as treasure chests safeguarding evidence of our past. Secrets and mysteries are supposedly safe within the rigidity of the computer and its satellites. Chance is no longer an option.

It was soon after my eightieth birthday that I started scribbling down events in my life which persisted invading my psyche. There was no particular order as these memories jumped erratically to and fro over some eighty years and that is why the chapters in this book are not chronological. Whatever else such ramblings may achieve, I hope they paint a picture for future generations of what life was like to one human being living through the twentieth century into the twenty-first.

These fragments of memory are autobiographical, but only selectively, for they embrace few of the most intimate events in my life. My very dear Canadian and American families, my myriad Australian relatives, and my closest living friends, still journey with me and would be very much part of a full autobiography were I to have the talent, courage, and inclination to write it. Therefore, dear family and friends, please understand that little or no mention of you does not signify lack of love and affection. Good autobiography is very rare precisely because weakness and guilt is not easy to acknowledge and I would need to delve more deeply into the shape and motivation of my life before embarking on such a venture. Thomas Carlyle wrote: 'A good written life is almost as rare as a well spent one!'

Richard Baldwyn

Dedication

May 2006

My dear Harvey,

Before I explain why I am dedicating this odd collection of memories to you, I want to be quite sure that our other seven grandchildren, Phillip, Sally, Lucy, James, Ben, Dan and Grace, are aware that I love them just as much. It is quite simply that as I write these words, you are by far the youngest member of the family, laughing your way through your second year while I, in my eighty fifth year, am by far the eldest. We seem to get on quite well and it occurs to me that very often infancy and old age come full circle; the infant at first relatively helpless and gradually straining to gain independence, while the elderly are straining not to lose their independence. There is, therefore, a time when these two extreme states inevitably entail the burden of responsibility on others. The infant is unaware of that burden, while the elderly adult is only too aware and the wise one will strive to accept that inevitable dependency as gracefully as possible.

So, Harvey, we could boast we are completing the family circle – at least for the time being; but beware! Families are strange things, you know. Hugh Kingsmill wrote 'Friends are God's apology for relatives' – a trifle cynical may be, but there is substance in those words. I tend to subscribe to the feeling in the line from Dodie Smith's play *Dear Octopus* – 'The family, that dear octopus, from whose tentacles we never quite escape, nor in our innermost hearts never quite wish to.'

Your great-great grandfather, the Reverend Leonard Baldwyn researched the family genealogy and one day I am sure you will enjoy studying the family tree which he prepared, tracing your ancestors (on your mother's side) back to the thirteenth century; at present it hangs in our dining room and, incidentally, needs to be brought up to date. You will also come across the two brief, but precious albums my mother (your great grandmother) prepared and gave me on my fiftieth birthday; a labour of love, written in her very distinctive handwriting and carefully assembled with photographs to complement the theme of a mother's love for her son. (I hasten to add that her devotion was entirely undeserved.) I hope these albums survive because they are family history and history of any kind contributes to what each one of us is today. However, though relevant, those albums are in no way similar to the stories I am dedicating to you. Each chapter is my memory, my judgement, my prejudice, my query, my excitement and my disappointment. It will be many years before you read these lines and when you do, I will long ago have journeyed to that 'undiscovered country from whose bourn no traveller returns'.

You will read of the manifold happy and sad times that I have had during my life and I am grateful for all that I have been blessed with – though I regret very much my immaturity during those early decades. I tremble when I think of my arrogance and audacity in the theatre, my impertinence and assurance in running a business during my middle decades, when I had had no training for such work and my seeming ability to persuade others that I had qualities which were, in fact, illusory. I feel I have been a jack of many trades but master of none; how I wish I could have done but one thing very well – play the piano, paint a picture, teach. Could I have become a great actor? Could I have written a meaningful book? Had I understood as much about the value of education when I left school at sixteen as I did when I got my degree with the Open University at the age of seventy-three, would my life have been very different?

As you get older you accumulate more and more memories which rescue experience from disappearance. Obviously we only live in the present but we must not be hooked on it or suffer from amnesia, forgetting that the present is made up of the past; it is only by remembering we can attain fulfilment. To quote John O'Donohue, 'We need to retrieve the act of remembering for it is here we are rooted and gathered. Tradition is to the community what memory is to the individual.'

Time slides by unnoticed and it is not until middle and old age that we realise what has happened; and when realisation dawns, it is as well to remember how different the world is now, compared to, say fifty or seventy five years ago. You will not experience the world I experienced in my youth or even the world your dad lived through in his young days. Our world has changed more in the last hundred years than in the previous five hundred and that is why the elderly should be wary of giving advice to the young. So many of the things which did or didn't work when I was young will be irrelevant when you grow into manhood. I have touched upon my childhood and having wasted so much time. Horace wrote 'Carpe Diem'. (Seize the day.) I am sure you will do just that, Harvey.

I hope you get some enjoyment out of the adventures, descriptions and stories I relate in this collection of memories. If you do become interested in the genealogy of the Baldwyn side of the family, you can always visit St Andrew's Church at Chinnor and hack your way to the eastern end of the churchyard where eventually you will find the graves of your great-great grandfather, your great great grandmother, your great grandfather, your great uncle and even more distant ancestors! And if you go into the church you will find the stained glass window on the southern wall, in memory of your great great grandfather, the much loved Rector of Chinnor from 1902 to 1934.

You can also find your great grandmother's stone in the churchyard of St. Michael's, here in Bray and even the Horn's king-size grave just inside the churchyard gate in Lemsford, near Welwyn Garden City. But if you really want to see a plethora of ex-Baldwyns, then go to the tiny church of St. Barbara (the only St. Barbara in the country) in Ashton-Under-Hill in Gloucestershire and there you will find your ancestors buried and commemorated not only in the churchyard but also on the walls in the church and even under the stone floor!

So there it is, sweet Harvey. Have a good and happy life. You could not have had a better start with such loving parents. Work and play hard. Be strong but gentle and whether you believe in him or not, May God bless you.

Love

Dabbers

Acknowledgements

THANK YOU, KIM, FOR your patience and for spending hours typing onto the computer and then producing the hard copy and disc for onward transmission to the publisher; and thank you, Steven, for undertaking the first proof reading and as a result, introducing me to the great 'comma' debate which I never knew existed; and thank you, Michael and Julian, for guiding me through the technical jungle by answering my silly questions, and, of course, Helen and Les for their considerable contribution and enthusiasm.

My thanks, too, to Jane Tatam for her invaluable advice and fearless comment throughout the process of publication.

I should also like to thank Georgina Glover for permission to include the poem 'Mrs Malone' in the chapter on Eleanor Farjeon.

The Millennium

'Time, like an ever rolling stream, bears all its sons away.'

Isaac Watts

KIM AND I CHOSE to celebrate the passing of the old Millennium in Hartland, our second home; we wondered if 'celebrate' was the right word for saying farewell not only to a thousand years of undoubted material progress but also of horrific slaughter and cruelty. I suppose it was natural to choose a village in which to reflect on who and what had gone before as I have always felt more at home in a rural environment, despite my professional involvement in the theatre and in business.

We stayed at Beckland, our adopted farm, and had with us our beloved dogs, Cider and Rosie. Cider, the yellow Labrador, was born in Welcombe some five miles south of Hartland just over twelve years before. Rosie, the King Charles Cavalier spaniel, was approaching her thirteenth birthday. Both had enjoyed wonderful holidays with us in Devon and we were thankful they were still with us to greet the new Millennium.

New Year's Eve was overcast. An Atlantic mist had settled over the peninsula and with it, a gentle rain. But we had a wonderfully full day, visiting friends, walking with the dogs and enjoying a farmhouse supper before setting out for the festivities in the village. There were to be fireworks on the opposite side of the valley and the village brass band was to play in the square until midnight. Crowds were assembling on the muddy recreation ground to watch the display but, as lighting up time approached, it was evident that, in the mist and drizzle, little would be seen across the valley. The sound of one or two test rockets could be heard and a glimpse of a brave firework flickered in the mist but the master of ceremonies told us through his megaphone that the display would have to be moved from the other side of the valley into the recreation ground itself and there would be a delay of at least half an hour. There were no complaints as three pubs and the British Legion bar filled up, the fish and chip shop was enjoying its busiest fry-up in its history, and the Pavilion dispensed cups of coffee and mince pies. The fireworks were eventually greeted with delighted cheers and clapping from the umbrella- and raincoat-shrouded villagers shuffling around in the fading millennium's mud.

The band could be heard in the distance playing music from bygone days, intermingled with the last twentieth century chart toppers and, as the fireworks finished, the crowd drifted to the square. Kim and I held hands as we sheltered under the old church wall watching this extraordinary assembly dancing, chatting, and parading in costumes, carefree in anticipation. The band, under its hastily erected awning over the bandstand, was floodlit, and coloured spotlights around the square pierced the mist, producing silhouettes and shadows. Excited children, singing and laughing, flitted in and out of the darkness; the elderly stood quietly watching and remembering.

As midnight approached, I felt I was in a time warp. The elements wrapped individuals in shrouds. No one was recognisable. The past seemed to merge with the present and the celebration could have been for the relief of Mafeking, Armistice Day 1918, VE day in 1945, or Queen Elizabeth II's Coronation. I felt tears in my eyes as I squeezed Kim's hand, for, amongst that damp but happy assembly, I could see the father I had never known, my grandfather who had died sixty-five long years before, my mother who had been dead for sixteen years, my brother, killed in 1942, and countless others whom I had loved. I was glad that there were young children playing on the war memorial only a few feet away. The band fell silent as Big Ben heralded the New Year, the new millennium.

We slipped quietly away, returned to the car and drove slowly to the cliffs above Hartland Quay. I switched off the car lights and lowered a window so that we could hear the Atlantic rollers. We sat quietly for a few minutes and I kissed Kim and gave her a present. Silently, we drove back to the farm, our thoughts embracing what had gone before and the passing of the century rather than the future and the new Millennium. The young folk were looking forward into the uncharted years ahead and all over the world there was a unity of hope and dedication.

We thought of our children and grandchildren on whose shoulders the future would be borne. Rightly, at that moment, they were happy and excited. And naturally, at that moment, we were grateful, somewhat nostalgic, and endeavouring yet again to embrace hope – even faith.

Surprisingly, we slept well that night, and when we awoke nothing had changed; only the date – 1st January 2000.

Prep School

'Headmasters have powers at their disposal with which
Prime Ministers have never been invested.'

Winston Churchill

I HAVE WRITTEN ELSEWHERE about the reasons for my despatch
to boarding school just before my sixth birthday. In those days,
psychology was less advanced and the effect on a small boy of being
sent away from home at so early an age was probably not even
considered. And, of course, the fact that Tony, my elder brother by four
years, was already at the school, removed any doubts there might have
been about such a move. I was not particularly stressed the day I arrived
because the headmaster's wife a small, round, fat lady seemed to like
me and I was assured that, as I was by far the youngest boy, I would
be well looked after and it was apparent that I was likely to be spoilt –
at least during the period of initiation. As things turned out, I was spoilt
– in both senses of the word – and, as a result, became a rather nasty
little boy, becoming unpopular not only with the staff but with most
of the boys as well.

I had a huge mop of curly hair and a 'sweet' face, and being the
smallest boy was immediately cast as 'Dopey' in the school production
of *Snow White and the Seven Dwarfs*, collecting 'oohs' and 'aahs' every
time I came on stage. And the following year (still the youngest boy
in the school) a musical piece called *The Dogs of Devon* was put on and
I was cast as the innkeeper who had to sing a song 'Apples and Cream'
standing between six girls (boys) chucking them under the chin as I
sang one verse to each of them. On the big night, when all the parents

4

came and the ballroom was packed, there was thunderous applause at the end of my song and Miss Head at the piano nodded to me for an encore. Poor Miss Head played me into the encore and, to her horror, but to the delight of the audience, I decided to sing all six verses again and she could do nothing to stop me. No wonder I was unpopular.

~~~~~~~~~

The headmaster was a cruel man and I will call him 'Mr Jessop'. He was feared not only by the boys and staff but also by his wife and son who, by the time I joined the school, was in his twenties and teaching at another school. Jessop had a dark, book-lined study and the only time boys were admitted was to be caned. He kept this thin, supple, weapon on top of the books, second shelf to the left of his desk. We had to bend over the left arm of his leather chair and wait while he reached for the cane and at the same time he would tell us the sentence – either three or six. Once he had uttered that single word we would close our eyes, clench our fists, and try to be brave. He was a strong man and would lift the cane high above his head. Most of us whimpered at the impact on our small bottoms and would stumble from that awful place when he shouted, 'Get out.'

For serious misdemeanours – I cannot remember what they were – the whole school, including the staff, would be summoned to the elegant ballroom to witness the execution. We were grouped in an organised circle waiting for Jessop's entrance. He would then call his victim to the centre of the arena, bend him over a wooden chair and carry out the sentence – never less than six strokes. On one occasion, surprisingly, it was my brother's turn. Surprising, because Tony was responsible, well behaved, and would later become head boy. Again, I cannot remember what he had done to deserve this special treatment, but his name was called and he bent over the chair. Jessop paused for a moment and looked round the assembly. 'Where is Baldwyn 2?' I was cowering behind my peers, my eyes closed. 'Come to the front at once.' I did as I was told. 'And open your eyes.' My brother remained silent as the sentence was carried out – he was always much braver than I.

Perhaps Jessop's cruellest act was perpetrated in the Fives Courts.

There were large cellars under the old house and wire cage traps were set to catch rats. When several had been caught and were still alive in the cages, Jessop would have them taken to one of the Five's courts and let it be known that the rats would be released during the morning break and the boys would be expected to watch their demise. A Fives court has a hard floor and tall concrete walls and there was no escape for the rats once they had been released from the cages. Jessop would then fetch his two small terriers and lift them into the Fives court. He would then release the rats and they would run wildly over the floor, desperately seeking freedom, shrieking as they tried to climb the sheer walls inevitably dropping back into the terriers' jaws. Within minutes the rats had been torn to pieces and blood ran over the floor. The boys dispersed to play in the courtyard and one of the gardeners scrubbed the Fives court floor in readiness for afternoon games.

But very occasionally retribution overtook Jessop. One such occasion was on April Fools Day – always a fun day at school, one of the very few fun days in the whole year. Nearly every one of the sixty boys played tricks, or had tricks played on them, and most of the staff joined in too. At least that was the situation until April 1st 1929 when there was even greater excitement than usual.

Jessop was the only one who disapproved of such merriment but was restrained from intervening by his wife – nicknamed by the boys 'Ma Footyfat'. Mr Richardson, the Geography and History master quite enjoyed the frolics – he was a lovely man who spent most of the history lessons pinning up on the blackboard maps of the First World War battles and moving coloured pins to illustrate the advances, retreats and stalemates of the opposing armies. Mr Lock, the small round French master rather enjoyed it too, as did, surprisingly, Miss Poulson, the rather stern Maths mistress. She was greatly mocked by the boys because of her very definite moustache but was respected because she was constant. The swashbuckling English master, Mr Lang, who was a hero because he owned a Talbot car, always came up with a mega trick and even shy little Miss Griffiths, the Scripture teacher, dared a gentle trick or two. The Matron, Miss Haslam, was always upstairs and too starchy to play tricks because her father was a bishop; none of us would ever dream of playing tricks on Tyler, the sweet and very gentle handyman, who, amongst many other jobs, cleaned our shoes and boots every day. We loved Tyler; tricks would be inappropriate.

~~~~~~~~~

We were in the middle of breakfast, swapping stories of what had happened already, chuckling about what was yet to come, and alert as to what might happen at any moment. April Fools Day breakfast was always the noisiest meal of the year and laughter was reaching a crescendo when Jessop roared into the dining room yelling, 'Silence.' His commands were always obeyed and silence was instant.

'The laces of all my shoes have been knotted together. The boy or boys responsible are to stand up immediately.'

We all looked round eagerly to see who the hero might be but no one stood up. We all knew that Mr Jessop had at least six pairs of shoes and the thought of all these shoes being knotted together filled us with delight. We prayed that someone would stand up and confess, we would all have liked to carry the culprit shoulder high through the long, stark corridors, applauding his courage and invention.

'I will wait another ten seconds and if no one stands up, the whole school will be punished.' We could all feel the tension; Jessop was sweating with anger as the seconds slipped by. 'Right,' he snapped. 'The half holiday is cancelled and no one will watch the match against Downsend. Indeed there will be no more half holidays this term until the boy owns up.'

He stormed out. There was silence for several seconds and we were all finding it difficult to suppress our delight. Gradually muffled conversation ensued, we finished breakfast and went to our classrooms for the first lesson of the day. As we passed the locker room, we could see Tyler trying to untangle the knotted laces of our headmaster's shoes. No one was down-hearted. The loss of an half holiday was a small price to pay for such a daring and momentous trick.

But there was anti-climax at the end of the mid-morning break. The boys were assembled in the courtyard and we were told that the half-holiday had been re-instated. It was as simple as that and it was difficult to concentrate on the two lessons before lunch. If a boy had owned up we would have known, for without doubt the school would have been summoned to the ballroom for a public beating. If it was not a boy, then who? Surely not Tyler? It was unthinkable. Ma Footyfat? Definitely not, she had no humour and little courage. Miss Haslam would never countenance such an untidy act. The staff would not discuss it and the great mystery of the best April Fools Day trick ever witnessed at the school was left unresolved.

It was some thirty years later that I found out who the culprit was. My son, also called Tony, went to the same prep school, Jessop having died many years before. But Mr Lock was still at the school, teaching French and at some school occasion something reminded me of that exciting day and I dared to ask Mr Lock, of whom I was very fond, if he knew who the culprit was. He smiled, paused, and then said, 'Three decades have passed and both participants are dead, so I think I would be forgiven for betraying a confidence. You had no idea who it was?'

'No, none of us ever knew.'

'It was Miss Poulson. She went straight to Jessop's study after breakfast and was overheard to say, 'It was me, Mr Jessop, April Fool!' She would never have allowed the boys to suffer. It seems that Jessop nearly had apoplexy and said that as he could not let it be known that the perpetrator was a member of staff, the half-holiday would still be cancelled. Miss Poulson told him that unless the half-holiday was reinstated, she would put a notice on the school board admitting that she was the culprit. Jessop had to agree, but insisted that only the staff would be told and we would be sworn to secrecy. She was at the school for twenty years you know. She despised Mr Jessop.'

Dear Miss Poulson. I was terrible at Maths and I mocked you as much as any of the boys. You so seldom smiled, and we couldn't help noticing your moustache but I wish we had known that it was you who did that wonderful thing. We would have tried so hard to make it all up to you.

Athens – Winter 1944

'Do your duty and leave the outcome to the gods.'

Pierre Corneille

I WAS ENJOYING A relatively busy posting on 254 Wing at Biferno on the Adriatic coast during the winter of 1944 when suddenly I was told I was being posted to Athens for a few weeks. I knew there was some kind of trouble there but I didn't expect the days ahead were to be the most exciting time of the war. The Germans had gone and were pulling back through Yugoslavia, but their departure led to Greek fighting Greek with British forces in the middle committed to upholding the elected right-wing monarchist government against the Communist-backed ELAS and EAM. A curfew was imposed at dusk and the city was bisected by the opposing factions – Athens was vibrant with anger – suspicion and sporadic gunfire could be heard night and day. The drama reached its climax when Churchill flew in at Christmas for talks with Archbishop Damaskinos, the head of the Greek government.

I made a particular friend with Bogden Mifelev, a humble aircraftsman, second class. In reality, Bogden was only humble in rank; he had a brilliant mind and was highly popular with the Greek girls. (After the war, he achieved international fame in the UK and America as Chan Canasta, with his quite extraordinary tricks and telepathic abilities.) Bogden took me to meet the most delightful Greek family in the middle of the city and we spent many evenings there, eating, chatting and watching Bogden perform. One of the simplest, yet to me most baffling, was when he placed a postage stamp on a coin with the minimum of lick, he would then toss it energetically so that it would hit the ceiling and then fall back into his hand. The stamp would always remain stuck to the ceiling!

Even though we were RAF personnel, we carried revolvers for our own protection – we were quite literally in the middle of a civil war – but when we visited the family in the evenings, out of courtesy we left our guns and holsters in the hall. There were two teenage daughters in the family and Dora, the youngest, was only just seventeen years old. She was highly intelligent and very attractive, making it quite clear that, though her parents supported the government, she was an ardent Communist. This, of course, made her even more attractive.

One evening, when Bogden was on duty, I visited the family alone and enjoyed the usual meal and relaxation. I bade the family goodnight at about ten o'clock having retrieved my revolver from the hall. As I was walking down the hill on which they lived, there was an outburst of fire which seemed uncomfortably close. I ran into a doorway and drew my revolver, checking it was fully loaded. It wasn't. It was empty and so was the holster. I knew instantly what had happened and, as soon as there was a lull in the shooting, I retraced my steps to the house and rang the bell.

Dora's mother answered the door and was obviously concerned for my safety. I reassured her and said that I had remembered a message for Dora from Bogden. After a minute or two, Dora appeared, with eyes flashing and head held high. Never had she looked so attractive. I spoke quietly:

'Dora, give me back my ammunition.'

From behind her back, she produced a jam jar full of water covering the bullets. I took it from her, emptied the water into a plant, and dried the bullets as well as I could in my handkerchief.

'Can you hear the gunfire, Dora?'

'Yes.'

'Do you realise I could have been killed?'

'Yes.'

'Don't you care?'

'Yes.'

'Then why did you do it?'

'It is my duty.'

'What would your mother and father say if they knew what you had done?'

'They wouldn't understand.'

'No, I don't think they would.'

'Will you tell them?'

'No.'

'Thank you.'

'I must go now. Perhaps you would see me out and say goodnight to your parents for me.'

Before opening the front door, she put her arms around me and kissed me on the mouth. As I walked down the hill, I decided it had all been worthwhile.

It is little known that at this time the only RAF HQ in the whole war was captured when British forces had landed back in Greece, following the Germans' departure. The Air Officer Commanding – I think his name was Air Commodore Hubbard, discovered a very attractive castle at Kifissia, a few miles outside Athens and well away from the airport where the RAF aircraft were based. He decided to make the castle his headquarters despite a warning from the Army Supremo that, once the civil war had started, Hubbard's HQ would be highly vulnerable and its safety could not be guaranteed. Hubbard, whom I never met, thought he knew better, assuring the army hierarchy the natives seemed very friendly and that he and his staff were quite safe.

One day, however, when Hubbard was in Athens for a meeting with other service chiefs, news came through that Communist forces had surrounded the castle and were demanding surrender. The RAF personnel in the castle consisted entirely of administrators, clerks, accountants, cooks, etc – not a combatant amongst them! Despite this, they put up a gallant defence with the few guns they had. All this was taking place in mid-winter and the ground was covered with snow. The army could not divert forces from the civil war in Athens and there was little the RAF could do with their fighters on the airfield. For a whole night, and for several hours of the next day, those brave ground personnel, who had never fired a gun in anger, fought on until they had no ammunition left. From his nest in Athens, the Air Commodore advised his men to surrender and this they did!

There were only some twenty or thirty of them and they were marched north in the snow escorted by half a dozen rather scruffy armed Greeks. The RAF flew sorties over the bedraggled column, dropping food and cigarettes which the guards appreciated as much as their prisoners. It appears that ELAS had made no provision for the men and the guards had no idea where they were going!

There had been no casualties during the siege but, tragically and farcically, there was one yet to come. On the second day of their forced march and during an airdrop of food, one of the containers burst open and its contents rained to earth. A tin of corned beef hit a clerk on the head and killed him instantly. Tragi-comedy indeed. I wonder what the lad's next of kin were told.

After two or three days, the guards lost interest in their mission, and well stocked with allied food and cigarettes, they wandered off into the blizzard – they probably wanted to go home. As for the little band of RAF personnel, they headed back toward Athens, fed and watched over by the RAF. They managed to find their different ways through the ELAS lines to rejoin their Air Commodore in the middle of the city!

It was shortly after these events that Bogden and I arrived in Athens.

Richard Briers, Freddie Truman and James Mason

'Talent develops in quiet places, character in the full current
of human life.'

Goethe

IT WAS IN 1987 that I started recording well known actors and actresses
reading books of all kinds and, occasionally, poetry. Some of them had
theatre backgrounds, some were film stars and others had earned their
fame in television. I also recorded Her Royal Highness The Princess
Anne reading *Riding Through My Life*, her own account of her love affair
with horses. The one politician was Harold Wilson, reading extracts
from his TV series *Prime Minister on Prime Ministers*. These spoken word
recordings were for the 'Listen for Pleasure' label in the MfP/EMI stable,
which was the forerunner of the multitude of 'Talking Books' recorded
today by individual publishers.

Most of the artistes had never before tackled any 'reading'; they had
been brought up on 'dialogue'. There is as much difference between
reading aloud prose and dialogue as there is between writing a book
and a play. With dialogue, an actor is 'fed' lines and responds to them
– even soliloquies are comments and responses to other characters or
situations. In a book, there is occasional dialogue, but the content is
mainly prose, and the actor is confronted with two or three hours of
his own voice, not only setting the scene, describing the characters and
carrying the plot, but also dealing with any dialogue and having to 'feed'
the lines to himself as he portrays the different characters. It was quite
extraordinary to discover how few of the artistes – including many of
the so called 'stars' – had not realised the challenge to be faced and

had done little work on the script before coming to the studio. Indeed, the fact that 'lines' did not have to be learnt, covered a multitude of mediocre readings and it was within a few minutes from the start of a recording, that I knew who were the real artistes. Whenever I recorded someone for the first time, I always tried to glance at their script while we had coffee. Too often, it was still a virgin script with not a mark or note in sight. I knew then I had a hard day's work ahead. A crumpled, heavily noted and underlined script more likely foretold a good reading.

There were two glorious exceptions however, one involving a virgin script – the other no script at all! I had never recorded Richard Briers before and we were due to start work at 1.30 p.m. It was a children's compilation of stories but I cannot remember the title. Richard was reading half the stories, hence only an afternoon in the studio – and just before the set time he came through the door eating fish and chips out of a newspaper. Scruffily attired and beaming happily, he held his sticky hand out: 'Hello Richard, I'm Richard.' Then he greeted the studio staff whom he obviously knew well and turned back to me 'Shall we start then?' and disappeared into the recording booth, still contentedly eating his fish and chips. The engineer and I moved into our part of the studio, sat down, and through the glass partition, I watched Richard put his food down on the desk and then pull the script out of his coat pocket. The intercom was switched on and we could hear him humming and, between hums, talking to himself about the lines he was about to read. From what he said, it was apparent that he knew the story well and had probably read the script once or twice but had done little more. Once he was settled, I asked him to read a few lines for 'levels' and then, still beaming happily, he asked me if I was satisfied and, if so, suggested we start. We did – and to my astonishment, he continued to eat his fish and chips as he read. I looked at the engineer and he shrugged. I strained to hear interference in his delivery or rustling from the newspaper – but to no avail. He read perfectly, in his inimitable style, and surely has to be the only actor in the world who could record and eat fish and chips at the same time. Here was a true professional indeed!

Neither had I met Freddie Truman, the legendary Yorkshire and England fast bowler. He had written his biography entitled *Ball of Fire* and though books on sport tended not to sell well, I decided that if I could persuade him to read it himself, with his abrasive Yorkshire accent and notoriously direct personality, it would prove popular. He jumped at the offer and travelled down from Yorkshire on the overnight train. I had arranged for us to breakfast together near the studio in Soho and, when we met in the café, I noticed he was carrying nothing and I assumed he had gone to an hotel to deposit his suit case and I hoped he had not forgotten to bring his script. He hadn't. It transpired that he had received it but hadn't even bothered to read it because he knew the book so well and had therefore left it in Yorkshire, assuming we would have several spare copies! I ordered breakfast, found a photo-copying service, and left my script with them, pleading for a quick turn round.

As we ate breakfast, I was regaled with hilarious stories of Fred's escapades both on and off the cricket pitch and we collected his script on the way to the studio. I didn't even attempt to warn him that reading an abridgement of his book for the first time might be difficult; I had never been in this situation before and I felt that to suggest there might be problems would only compound the situation. Here was a character who never countenanced defeat and, in two extraordinary sessions, there was little need for direction and only the occasional plea to read at a slower pace. He found this as strange a request as if I'd asked him to become a slow bowler. We finished early and he told me that he thought the two-hour abridgement was much better than his book – it had cut out all the crap! 'Mind you,' he said, 'it wasn't my crap!'

The tape didn't sell well but those who bought it thoroughly enjoyed it and I treasure my copy, not only for its content, but also because the recording itself was quite unique.

Our 'Listen for Pleasure' series proved so successful that when we moved offices to Hayes, alongside the warehouse which distributed our LPs and cassettes, I realised there was ample room to build a small recording studio – the cost saving would be considerable. Most of the warehouse staff were packers and, of these, the majority were middle-aged women. Whenever we had 'big names' coming to record, I would always notify the staff and try to arrange for a walk-about with our visitor during the coffee break. It was most unusual for the celebrity to turn down such exposure to the general public!

James Mason came down to record and I felt quite nervous meeting this 'legend' of the film industry for the first time. I never considered him a 'great' actor because his range was somewhat limited and his voice, which was a considerable part of his attraction, was strangely clipped on delivery. However, he was undoubtedly one of Hollywood's great stars, thoroughly deserving the accolades showered upon him for so many of his performances.

James Mason had been living in Switzerland for several years by the time of this recording (1982) and when he arrived at Blythe Road, he was wearing an old raincoat and looked rather sad and weary. He carried nothing but the script from which he was going to read and was clearly as nervous as I was. I led him to the studio where we had coffee and chatted about the day's programme. When I asked him if, in the morning break, he would be willing to walk around the warehouse with me so that the staff could see him, much to my surprise, he quietly declined, insisting he didn't think he would be of any interest since he had worked so little in recent years. I told him I was sure the staff would be disappointed, but as we were just about to start recording, I didn't want to pressure this obviously shy man.

The session went well and we broke for coffee soon after eleven o'clock. By this time he was plainly more relaxed so I decided to risk raising the topic of 'walkabout' again, telling him that the staff knew he was in the building and would wonder why they had not had a chance to see him. He hesitated, and then very reluctantly agreed – but 'only for a very few minutes'.

We walked out into the middle of the warehouse and, to my astonishment, and to Mason's even greater surprise, there was a crescendo of shrieks and we were immediately surrounded by some forty to fifty women. For one awful moment I thought they were going to tear off his clothes, but they started applauding and calling out the titles of the films he had starred in and the names of his co-stars – *Seventh Veil*, Orson Wells, Anne Todd, etc., etc. They were holding up pieces of paper for him to autograph and I found myself separated from him but could still see his face through the mêlée. He was plainly dumbfounded as he tried to answer some of the questions shouted out to him. He had a very quiet voice and was finding it difficult to be heard.

It was when I saw tears running down his cheeks, I pushed my way back to his side and waved my hands to quieten the staff, explaining to them we had to return to the studio. Everyone immediately moved back, forming a corridor for us to walk through, applauding him as he walked by.

Inside the studio, Mason shook his head in disbelief. 'Extraordinary,' he said, 'quite extraordinary.' I didn't tell him it had been by far the biggest reception given to any of the visiting actors. For the rest of the day, he was a happy man – he seemed to have been released. When he left at the end of the day, he shook my hand and said, 'Thank you Richard, it's been a wonderful day.' I was able to tell him it had been a memorable day for me too.

Briers, Trueman, Mason – three men, each of quite different stature. An actor from the theatre, a sportsman, and a film star. Three human beings who, unknowingly, displayed their true colours through relatively unimportant recording sessions in a small 'spoken word' studio.

Gin, Cappoquin and my Nearly Profession

"My salad days, When I was green in judgement...'

William Shakespeare

I HAD NEVER BEEN to Southern Ireland before and when I was asked to join a company touring four plays early in 1938, I jumped at the chance. We were to visit some ten venues, most of them 'smalls' but starting with Wexford and Waterford. The company was headed by Colin Morris who, after the war, wrote a very successful farce, *Reluctant Heroes* – which ran for years at the Whitehall Theatre in London. Colin had minimal resources and we were all on low salaries, performing plays with small casts – *French Without Tears, Poison Pen, Dracula,* and *I Killed the Count.*

We started our tour at the Theatre Royal, Wexford – quite the grandest date we played. It was a beautiful old theatre and I remember revelling in the ambiance of the place. The contrast to some of the places we were destined to visit was considerable and I was not prepared for the 'halls', 'boat houses' and faded cinemas, we were to play in. However, we were all young, the countryside was beautiful and the people were friendly; we had little to grumble at even though sometimes Colin couldn't pay our wages but always paid our digs. We visited Waterford, Cashel, Mitchelstown, Innes, Gorey, Cappoquin and many other 'smalls' – our adventures were legion.

On arrival in Wexham, Colin was tipped off that, if we had a suitable play, there was business to be had in the many theological colleges in Southern Ireland. Accordingly, we hurriedly rehearsed *The Merchant of Venice* (to be played in modern dress!) and submitted our repertoire of plays to the college circuit. To our astonishment, the three colleges which engaged us to perform, all chose *I Killed the Count*, a murder mystery and quite the sexiest play on the list! We never performed *The Merchant* and we were quite relieved – we were all playing two or three parts and even though we were presenting it in modern dress to save the cost of costume hire, none of us had suitable clothes and couldn't afford to buy!

I was by far the youngest member of the Company but had parts in all the plays as well as being assistant stage manager. I was still an innocent and drank very little. I was fortunate in this regard because not only did it save me money but I discovered I needed very little alcohol to make me happy. We moved on to Waterford after Wexford. Waterford is a delightful town but the theatre was, in fact, a large hall. On the evening before the opening night and after a long day's dress rehearsal, several of us assembled in the bar of the hotel and I was enjoying a gin and tonic. An attractive young lady joined us at the bar and seemed to take a particular interest in me. I bought her a drink and as the evening wore on, I consumed several more gins, far more than I had ever downed before. As I was sitting on a stool, I was unaware how the drink was affecting me and only conscious of my euphoria and confidence in my progress with the young lady.

My last memory of that fateful evening was suggesting to the girl that we leave the bar and go for a walk. I remember standing up and wondering where my legs had gone. I encircled her with my arm and using her as a prop, I led her through the door onto the waterfront, proceeding down the waterfront. I remembered no more. But apparently we had gone less than fifty yards, when thankfully I collapsed on the ground in a drunken heap and had to be carried to my digs where I was put to bed and stayed all the next day and following night, missing the opening performance.

It was only when I was on an even keel again that my colleagues told me the full story, confessing to the 'practical' joke which had been perpetrated on me. The 'young lady' was not in fact a young lady at all but the company's male juvenile lead and with the entire cast's connivance, had dressed and 'made up' to test the maturity of the 'baby' of the company. They had not only set me up in the bar, but had then followed us out of the bar and onto the waterfront. They were devastated when I collapsed, not out of concern for me, but because the entertainment had been so abruptly terminated before any climax had been reached. I dread to think what fate I might have met had I not passed out and can only thank God for being so good to me and bringing retribution on the conspirators by necessitating them to search out an amateur to speak my few lines on the opening night. Meanwhile, I lay in my digs very sick and miserable!

It is hardly surprising I have not touched gin for nearly seventy years. I've never been back to Waterford but when ever I sniff a waft of gin when pouring one out for Kim or guests, I not only feel nauseous but I am transported back to that stool in the bar and the very fresh air as we weaved down the quayside. I do remember the name of that juvenile lead but I'm sure it is wiser not to mention it because he could still be alive and approaching ninety years of age. He wasn't a very good actor but he certainly gave a convincing performance on that night of gin in 1938.

Cappoquin was certainly one of the more unusual venues of that summer. Stunningly beautiful, it was only a village with a river running through it. The 'theatre' was the boathouse and the auditorium was where the boats were stored in the winter and repairs carried out. For our visit, the area had been cleared and some eighty chairs installed. The lucky eight in the front row had just enough room to sit with their knees just above the level of the eighteen-inch stage. The actors had to use the whole width of the building – there was no room for 'wings'. Entrances therefore had to be made either through a door stage right straight onto the bank of the river, or through the only other door stage left which opened straight onto the river itself. A boat, therefore, had to be moored alongside so that actors could leave the stage in as dignified way as possible, stepping out into a somewhat unsteady craft. If the playwright had insensitively arranged for the actor to make his next entrance from stage right, he would have to ferry himself round the back of the boathouse to the bank. I can't remember how the dinghy then got back to its very vital mooring – perhaps there was a spare one.

For our last performance on the Saturday night, we were all very excited because Lord and Lady Cavendish had booked all eight chairs in the front row. (Was it Lismore Castle they lived in?) Lady Cavendish had been Adele Astaire, Fred Astaire's sister, and had left the stage when she married. We had been warned that His Lordship was a very heavy drinker but we had not expected to find him asleep when the curtains parted. Even worse, he was snoring and only two minutes into the play, he stretched his legs onto the tiny stage so that we had the choice of going round them or stepping over them. Despite these little difficulties, the evening went well and we learnt later that not only Lady Cavendish but all Cappoquinians would have been surprised – even worried – had his Lordship behaved in any other way. He would be awoken at the end of each act and would join the applause before making the most of the intervals and then returning to his slumbers for the next act.

We had our usual quota of practical jokers in the company and it was inevitable that one of them would indulge on that evening. Mind you, it could be that the perpetrator of the incident that evening was a village local but somehow I doubt it. No one owned up so we shall never know. It happened just before the end of the play when a male member of the cast had to make a dramatic exit left. He opened the door and swept off. There was a loud splash. The boat had been removed. Fortunately it was a comedy that night and laughter was in the air. The audience knew exactly what had happened and even his Lordship had removed his feet from the stage at the final curtain as rapturous applause and calls of 'encore' echoed through the village. Those on stage were desperately trying to be professional and control their laughter as the curtains parted for the first call. The audience insisted on more calls, shouting for the missing member of the cast. Eventually the victim, soaked and dripping with river, crept on stage to join the line but even then the mob wasn't satisfied. He had to take a solo call before the rest of the cast returned for the final curtain.

The Cavendishes insisted on staying and plying us with drink from the local bar as we struck the set in preparation for our departure in the early hours of Sunday morning. His Lordship regaled us with stories of the number of touring shows he had slept through in the boathouse. Could it have been that it was his butler who…?

One week, we played in a very small town, Gorey. It had but one street, rather like the Wild West, with houses and shops down either side. Our theatre was a disused barn in a nearby field in which cattle still grazed. The barn had been partially converted and was used for village activities. I lodged with the local undertaker and his wife – a sweet couple whose house was spotless – and I'm sure that Gorey's deceased and their mourners were very sensitively looked after. I was fed bountifully with a substantial meal before I left for the evening performance and a snack and hot drink after the show.

On the Saturday morning before our last matinee and evening performances, my landlady knocked on my door and asked if she could come in and ask me something. I was mystified when she quite simply asked me if I would mind having my main meal after the evening performance because they wanted to make it a special occasion to celebrate my stay with them. I thanked her and said I would look forward to it. On my return from the barn, I found the dining room had been decorated as if it was Christmas and the meal was sumptuous. We talked of Gorey and they asked me about my family and my plans for the future. We had just finished the pudding when my host cleared his throat and I thought he was going to make a speech. I suppose he did in his own way for he had certainly prepared the content of the words he spoke.

He said that they hoped I had enjoyed my stay with them as much as they had enjoyed having me. He then said that I had probably gathered they had no children and that they had a thriving business which would certainly prosper because Gorey was likely to expand. We then had coffee before he told me they had a proposition to put to me. It was this: 'When you have finished your tour and returned to your family in England, would you consider coming back to us here in Gorey to train in our profession? We feel sure you would do well. We are not getting any younger and in time you would inherit our business.'

I was too young and immature to be moved by their affection and trust; and I suppose I might even have felt it was somewhat comical to be propositioned as an undertaker, particularly because I was supremely confident that soon my name would be lighting up the West End! All I can remember is saying, 'Thank you, but why me?' I shall never forget the answer: 'You have the perfect undertaker's face.' I can only hope I was gracious in rejecting their offer. They were such a gentle couple.

All that, of course, was nearly seventy years ago. It would be interesting to return to Gorey sometime to see what might have been!

~~~~~~~~~

We returned to England exhausted but content, completely unaware how close we were to World War II and the undercurrents which were gathering in Southern Ireland at that time.

Louis v Schmeling

'Boxing's just show business with blood.'

Frank Bruno

I HAVE NEVER BEEN a pugilist yet have always found world heavyweight fights quite irresistible to watch. I was too scared to box when I was at school and on the only occasion at Malvern College, when I was forced into the ring to box for my House (replacing a boy who was sick), I feigned injury in the first round – I think 'lie down' is the right expression. As a boy I would listen to the wireless and watch extracts on newsreels in the cinema and, when television invaded virtually every home in the country, I watched on the little screen, first in black and white, then in colour. Ah yes, colour greatly increased the excitement – the smokey venue, the spotlights focussing down on the ring, the vivid shots of the contestants in their coloured shorts and, most dramatic of all – the red blood.

The only professional heavyweight contest I have ever been to was, perhaps, one of the most dramatic. Henry Cooper – 'our 'Enry' – the British Heavyweight Champion, was fighting Cassius Clay, later Mohammed Ali, at Highbury, the Arsenal Stadium. I had come to know a Dr Lewis Davies, who had been helping my first wife Peggy through a difficult time and he had told me he used to box when he was a young man in Wales. He insisted on being called 'Sam' and was very short, with one cauliflower ear. I wanted to thank him for helping the family and could think of no better way than taking him to the big fight. Cooper, sensationally, knocked Clay down in the fourth round, and, against all the odds, was ahead on points in the fifth round when he had to retire with a deep cut immediately above his right eye. For me, the drama of the fight itself was heightened by noticing Sam's clenched hands punching the air throughout the contest!

Ironically, my fixation with heavyweight fights began when I was at Malvern. It must have been 1936 that Joe Louis, the American Heavyweight Champion of the World, fought Max Schmeling of Germany for the first time. Schmeling was the German Heavyweight Champion of Europe and the pride of Hitler and the Nazis. (Schmeling himself was never a Nazi.)

The fight took place in New York and unbeaten Joe Louis was the hot favourite. I was still a junior in my House (No 5) and knew there was a wireless in the Senior Common Room and that the fight would be broadcast on the BBC in the early hours of the morning. Accordingly, a few of us, all juniors, set our alarm clocks under the bedclothes and crept down to the Common Room trusting that the seniors themselves had not had the same idea.

All seemed to go to plan. The Common Room was dark and empty; we switched on, tuned in, and settled down. We enjoyed all the preliminaries but, alas, just before the bell sounded for the first round, the door opened and in marched the seniors. We were summarily told to get out and go back to our beds, not knowing until next morning that Schmeling had sensationally taken the title from Joe Louis. (The following year, Louis went to Germany and, much to Hitler's fury, knocked out Schmeling in the early rounds.)

We were, of course, all thrashed that same day. The prefects always used a heavy gym shoe and would take a run at the victim when landing the blow. It was extremely painful. The victim would be called by name, the prefect shouting the surname down the long, dark corridor. The walk to the prefects' room would follow, passing the boys' studies on the way. Doors were always left slightly open so that the innocents could hear and count the number of strokes, listening for any reaction from the victim. Doors closed quietly for the long walk back!

Happiest days of our lives, eh?…

Balls

'All animals are equal but some animals are more equal than
others.'

George Orwell

IT WAS BLACKPOOL EARLY in the war and a score of RAF recruits
were lined up in a draughty hall to be medically inspected. I was one
of them and we were all naked. As we waited for the medics to arrive,
there was embarrassment for some, titters from others and hilarity from
the end of the line because No 20 was sporting a considerable erection.
I felt somewhat miserable for I was not an hairy man and felt sure that
my genitals must be the most insignificant on parade.

Three RAF doctors arrived and the sergeant stood us first to attention
and then at ease. Whether or not the erection obeyed the latter
command, I never knew. Each doctor examined a recruit from head
to toe exploring every inlet and protrusion to be found. I was No 4 in
the line and when the MO reached me and was feeling my testicles,
he suddenly looked up and asked, 'Any problems?' I told him I wasn't
aware of any, sir, and started to feel a little uneasy as he continued to
finger me. Panic started to take hold when he called to his nearest
colleague, who immediately let go of whatever he was holding and
joined me and my examiner. The two medics held a conference,
crouched in front of my testicles, until the second doctor started
fingering me whilst the first doctor summoned the third doctor from
the end of the line to come and join the fun. He in turn had a good
feel, and, after another short conference, they rose and faced me. To
my astonishment, they were all smiling and held out their hands for

me to shake. The doctor who had started it all said, 'Congratulations, Baldwyn.'

'Why, sir?'

'Are you not aware you have three balls?'

'No, sir,' I replied as quietly as possible.

'Well, you have,' the doctor said cheerily, and almost shouted 'Congratulations' again.

Uproar ensued. Laughter, cheering and even applause erupted and for one sickening moment I thought there was going to be a free-for-all to examine the freak. The Sergeant roared for order to be restored and I detected a look of pride in his eyes that I was one of his 'men'. I was known as 'Three Ball Dick' at Blackpool thereafter and didn't regain my dignity until I was posted away. Later on I was nicknamed 'Windyballs' but that is another story. It had something to do with my surname – I hope.

For the record, you have my assurance I am not superman – nor ever have been – I do not have three balls. It seems that when I was a small boy, I had an operation for an undescended testicle and in forcing it down to its proper location, the testicle was distended into a figure of eight shape, giving the impression I had been blessed with two for one. But no, I'm just plain ordinary.

Padre and Madre

'I hold this to be the highest task for bond between two
people: that each protects the solitude of the other.'

Rainer, Maria Rilke

ONCE UPON A TIME there was a charming, early Victorian, rectory
in the Oxfordshire village of Chinnor, at the foot of the Chiltern Hills.
With its grounds virtually filling the centre of the village, it stood
opposite St Andrew's, the parish church. Sadly, in the middle of the
twentieth Century, when the Church Commissioners were trying to
balance their books, it was decided that the rectory and most of its
land had to be sold. Though a new, modern rectory now stands in the
old walled kitchen garden, the lovely old building in which I grew up
was demolished and replaced by an estate of pleasant detached houses.
Only in the last twenty years have the stables and coach house virtually
fallen down and been replaced by a village hall, public meeting rooms
and a community centre.

My paternal grandfather, Leonard Baldwyn, was Rector of Chinnor
and Emmington from 1902 until he retired in 1934 and, for the last eight
years of his incumbency, he was Rural Dean of Aston Rowant, a deanery
embracing a dozen or so villages in the surrounding area. He was a
small, quiet man, an uninspiring preacher but a true fisher of men,
content with the simpler things of life and unimpressed with fame and
fortune. He was loved and respected and knew the names of every one
of his several hundred parishioners. He had attended a theological college
in Salisbury and, after four years at Exeter College, Oxford, he held a
curacy at St Peter's in Weston-Super-Mare until he moved to Chinnor.

He was a passionate organist and, within three years of arriving at St Andrews, he had installed a new organ, the casing of which still stands today nearly one hundred years later. He insisted on playing the organ himself at every service, despite the evident fact that by doing so, the congregation had to wait while he slithered off the organ seat to reach the lectern, pulpit or his desk. Nobody seemed to worry too much and perhaps in those days there was little need to hurry and certainly the services were very well attended. I remember him as a 'back door man' for, on his visits round the village, he would push open the back door without knock or ceremony and walk in. He enjoyed his drink and would always include the five village pubs on his calls. He would never stay too long at any one bar, buying or accepting a beer without fuss, and he kept a well stocked cellar under the rectory.

I remember my paternal grandmother, Jeanne Louise, as a rather private person who found it hard to express emotion. She was a formidable character, courageous and hard working. She was tall and had a classically beautiful face. Definitely a front door woman, she was always carefully dressed with a long skirt and noticeable hat. She carried out her parish duties conscientiously and was respected rather than loved. She did not have Leonard's natural warmth and informality and therefore had to work much harder to perform her many duties but, most certainly, she fulfilled them. She would never talk of her childhood or blood family even when, toward the end of her life, she lived with Peggy and me at Coulsdon.

It was only after her death in 1952 that I found a document amongst her papers dated 31st July 1946, which at least told us as much as she herself knew of her first few hours in this world. (The Baldwyn Family Tree, which Leonard prepared, states that my maternal great grandfather was Professor J Goetz-Smith and that Jeanne Louise was born to his first wife.) I quote the document:-

I, Jeanne Louise Baldwyn of Russell Close, Chinnor, in the County of Oxford, widow, do solemnly and sincerely declare as follows:

1. I have always understood and do verily believe that I was

born on the 2nd October 1867, in the town of Rouen, France and for that reason was named 'Jeanne' after 'Jeanne d'Arc'.

2. At the date of my birth, my parents who were both British subjects, were travelling from Italy to England and I was born during the journey, at Rouen, aforesaid.

3. I have never been able to trace any official record of my birth, although I have frequently attempted to do so, and I believe the records of my birth were destroyed or lost during the Franco-Prussian War.

4. I have always understood and verily believe, that at the time of my marriage to Leonard Baldwyn on 2nd day of October, 1886, I was 19 years of age, and I am the person named 'Jeanne Louise Smith' in the Certificate of Marriage now produced and shewn to me, marked 'A' and I am therein stated to be 19 years of age.

5. I depose as above from my own personal knowledge and from the tradition which has always existed in my family during my lifetime, and I make this declaration conscientiously, believing the same to be true, and by virtue of the provisions of the Statuary Declarations Act.

Signed ...L. Baldwyn
Witnessed by: Edward L. Lightfoot, Commissioner of Oaths, Thame

In many ways, they were a strangely odd couple. By friends and relatives, they were known as Padre and Madre and indeed that is how they addressed each other. Tony, my brother, Joan my sister, and I always called them Gampy and Ganny. They were certainly very supportive of one another but maybe that was as much duty as affection and perhaps I was too young to understand their relationship. Madre slept in a large comfortably furnished south-facing room, with two single beds. Padre occupied a very small almost cell-like room facing north. I cannot recall seeing him in, or even near her bedroom, neither can I recall ever hearing rows or disagreements between them. Those were the days of primitive loos and portable baths and though there was a relatively modern loo on the ground floor of the rectory, Padre never used it. He had his own 'privy' in the woods to the north of the house and whatever the season and whatever the weather, he would go out after breakfast carrying the newspaper, cross the drive and disappear into the woods down the darkened path. At the time I never wondered why he patronised such a cold inconvenience outside; maybe Madre had banished him, or perhaps he simply liked being close to nature. He seldom came into the drawing room, preferring to stay in his large, book-lined, pipe-smoked study with its open, and usually lit, fireplace. It was only at meal times in the large, elegant dining room that they were always together with the family (and now they have lain together for over fifty years in the same grave, in the overgrown eastern end of St Andrew's churchyard).

I was too young, of course, to appreciate the tragedy in their lives of having lost both their children; perhaps it shaped their relationships not only with each other, but with all the family. Hugh (my uncle) died in 1906 when he was only eighteen years old. A midshipman on Queen Alexandra's flagship HMS *Exmouth*, he contracted appendicitis when the fleet was sailing south of the Bay of Biscay. He died before they could reach land and was buried in Villa Garcia, in Spain. It seems he was a brilliant young man and we treasure the exquisite examples of his skills as a calligraphist and artist still in our possession. Their second son, Cecil (my father) died from First World War wounds when he was twenty-nine years old. He had been an Oxford running Blue (quarter mile) just before the war, joined the Worcestershire Regiment and was mentioned in despatches. (His notation was signed by the war minister of the time one Winston Churchill.) Demobilised (rank of Captain), he was warned not to over-exert himself due to a small piece of shrapnel still lodged near his heart, but as a school-master teaching English at Bedford School, inevitably he became involved in sports. He contracted pneumonia which caused septicaemia to set in, inflaming the war wound, and he died on 26th November, 1922, three days after my first birthday.

I suppose I remember Padre as 'the gentle one'; maybe he was weak, but I was too young to know. I remember Madre as a stern, assertive character. It seemed to me he always wandered around the village, whereas she strode; he often smiled, she was seldom light-hearted. He was calm and easy going, she was a disciplinarian. With Kate the cook and Elsie the maid, he was entirely informal, she was very definitely mistress of the house, but always fair. With William the gardener (Willum to Tony, Joan and me) he was a friend; she, again, the mistress. But maybe Padre could not have been what he was without Madre balancing his ministry in her own way; he certainly could not have entertained his clergy and friends so well and enjoyed his food and drink so evidently, had Madre not been so proud. I remember so well she insisted on cleaning and refilling the many paraffin lamps herself, immediately after breakfast, in the pantry each morning – and she was always busy. She rested and slept in the drawing room at 2.00 p.m. each day and always sneezed vociferously at 2.20 p.m. exactly – a moment eagerly awaited – telling us we had but ten minutes to wait before resuming normal activity.

My memories of those years are legion. We had moved to the rectory in 1926 when my mother, Vi, had to fight for a war widow's pension which was her only income. Padre and Madre, therefore, paid for Tony, Joan and me, to go to boarding schools – my mother also went to boarding schools as Matron, enabling the four of us to be together at Chinnor during school holidays. My mother was always close to Padre, but found Madre too rigid a character. Tony was a very responsible person and Madre adored him; he probably reminded her of the sons she had lost. I certainly gave her good reason to be wary of me and I took every opportunity to play tricks on her. The rectory had a very good grass tennis court, and she, Vi, Tony and Joan, all good players, often played doubles in the summer holidays. I was too young to be serious about the game and Madre never hid her displeasure when very occasionally my mother insisted that I make up a four. I would delight in being my grandmother's partner because when I served, she would always go to the net, giving me the opportunity to aim the ball directly at her backside. Occasionally I scored a direct hit, but she always spoiled my delight by pretending that she hadn't even felt it.

Our holiday lives were full and reasonably social. We were involved in church work, delivering magazines and notices, helping with fêtes and attending village functions. The rectory was always a hub of activity with parish and family visitors; I have vivid memories of the choir singing carols in the conservatory and staying for mulled wine and mince pies, of the village fêtes in the rectory fields, of the scouts parading in the backyard, and of tennis and croquet parties in the summer. The rectory gardens were a playground paradise; trees to climb, woods to hide in, and a drive and stableyard large enough not only to ride and race our bicycles but also to learn how to drive a car. Gampy (a terrifyingly bad driver) taught Tony, and Tony taught Joan and me. Willum had a large asparagus bed in the kitchen garden and we tormented him by using it as our favourite 'Hide and Seek' area but as he had a very gammy leg, we could always escape when he spotted us. Mind you, Willum was our friend and would never betray us. Sometimes in the middle of our games, the church tenor bell would toll and we would stop for a moment because we knew a villager had died and we wondered for whom the bell tolled. My mother, Tony, Joan and I, would have the most wonderful bicycle rides around the neighbouring villages, often taking picnics with us and climbing Chinnor hill. We were even allowed to ride on the footplate of the GWR High Wycombe to Watlington branch line engine quite simply because we were the rector's grandchildren! This happened when we were travelling to and from boarding school via High Wycombe and Paddington. This line is still open, not as part of the railway network, but as a tourist attraction.

I think I was closer to Padre than Tony or Joan simply because I was the youngest and we seemed to have an unwritten and unspoken affection for one another. For a time, I was the leading treble in the choir when I was at home during the holidays and, as his beloved organ was such an important part of his life, perhaps he was pleased we shared the music to that degree. After dinner at night, he would often go to the church and play the organ and I well remember lying in bed during the winter evenings, listening to the distant sound of his music. The church was less than a hundred yards from the rectory and my bedroom faced the woods which bordered the road and churchyard, and when the wind blew, the music ebbed and flowed through the trees. Though it was renovated in the last decade of the last century, the organ that Gampy installed and played over eighty years ago, still looks and sounds the same to me as it did when I was a small boy.

I have written of the relationship between my grandparents but perhaps a small incident illustrates just how that relationship appeared to me, a small boy not ten years old. As leading choirboy I headed the procession (with another boy) from the vestry at the west end of the church, up the centre aisle, up the one step into the chancel and then wheeling back into the choir stalls. Because the rectory was so near to the church, I tended to leave my arrival at the vestry until the last moment and, in doing so, one Sunday I did not have time to change into outdoor shoes, arriving at the church as the five-minute bell was tolling its last sixty seconds. I flung on my cassock and surplice, thanking God (with due reverence) that the length would almost certainly hide my bedroom slippers.

The Sunday School children sat at the west end of the church under the very strict control of my grandmother; this then was the first hurdle to clear. Would she notice that I was an inch shorter than usual? As we processed up the aisle, there was no evident reaction and I felt confident I could relax until the return journey at the end of the service. I was wrong; for as I took the one step into the chancel, the boy immediately behind me trod on the back of my slipper and it came off. Obviously I could not stop and pick it up; there would have been a calamitous shunt of choristers and clergy. Limping, I carried on, wheeling back into my usual seat which happened to be the one nearest the chancel step. The choir cleared the step and then, as was the protocol, there was a small gap before the curate processed into the chancel followed by my grandfather, the rector. To my dismay, I could see my slipper sitting right in the middle of the chancel step, in full view of the congregation and, of course, my grandmother. The curate passed over it gracefully and, as Gampy approached, I stared at him imploringly. But he wasn't looking at me, he was looking at the step and, as he passed over my slipper, with as deft a side-kick as I have ever seen on a soccer pitch, he kicked it into touch just behind the lectern.

Before the end of the service I had removed my other slipper and tucked it into my belt under my cassock so that when I led the procession down the church, I would at least be on an even keel. I managed an innocent smile at Ganny as I passed her and once the church had emptied, I retrieved my slipper from near the lectern and crept back through the woods to the rectory kitchen door and entered unobtrusively. I never knew whether or not Gampy realised it was my slipper; I suspect he did but he would never have mentioned it to me nor, of course, to Ganny. It was our secret.

How vividly I remember the hunt ball at the Brooke-Popham's mansion in a village near Thame, or perhaps I remember it for what occurred immediately afterwards. The Brooke-Pophams had grandchildren of about our age, that is six to ten years old and were therefore including other children as guests to keep them company at the ball. Gampy would never countenance attending such an occasion – not because he disapproved, but because he would have been bored stiff, preferring his social intercourse to include as little ceremony as possible. He was very low church. Our party consisted, therefore, of Ganny, Vi my mother, Tony, Joan and me, and, as my grandmother did not drive, my mother took the wheel of Gampy's Overland. The occasion was full of splendour and I remember driving back the nine or ten miles, tired but contented, just after midnight. The rectory had a long drive through the trees and the front door was up some stone steps leading into a large conservatory. There were then large glass inlaid doors opening onto the long hall at the end of which was a beautiful winding staircase leading to the main bedrooms.

The car pulled up and I jumped out, ran up the steps into the conservatory, through the doors and into the hall. I stopped in my tracks, for there, standing at the sideboard near the foot of the staircase was my grandfather in his nightshirt and nightcap with a glass in one hand and a bottle in the other. I closed the door behind me and shouted a warning whisper, 'Gampy!'

He spun round and then, still holding the bottle and glass, turned away and hurled himself up the stairs, wending his way out of sight and into his bedroom. We all went to bed and so far as I knew, no word was ever spoken of this incident.

And I recall another incident – I must have been eight or nine years old – of which I feel heartily ashamed, but I recount it because it typifies my relationship with Ganny. We went on holiday in the late 1920s taking her with us. We rented a moored houseboat on the River Arun at Burpham, just outside Arundel and my grandmother slept in the farmhouse at the top of the track which led down to the river. The Arun is very tidal, and rises and falls as much as ten feet. The boat was therefore moored to a stage with poles and rings that slide up and down with the tide. At high tide, one would step straight onto the boat from the stage but, at low tide, one had to climb down a wooden step ladder and then step onto the boat.

Ganny would join us after breakfast, bringing a newspaper and any post; and on this particular occasion, the tide was halfway down, which meant that she would have to climb down the ladder before stepping on to the boat. She would put the newspaper in her mouth and free her hands to grasp the ladder and would rely on us to shout when she was level with the boat. I decided it would be rather fun to let her make her own judgement as to when she reached water level and I kept silent as she descended the ladder. She was wearing her usual long skirt and it was not until she was knee deep in the water that she realised what was happening. She had too much dignity to scream and, in any case, had she done so, the morning post would have fallen into the river. She calmly ascended the three submerged rungs, stepped onto the boat, handed me the paper and said, 'How stupid of me.' She knew perfectly well I was responsible for her 'wetting' but once again denied me the pleasure of my cruelty by refusing to acknowledge I had had anything to do with it. Ashamed, I watched her take off her shoes and stockings and borrow a skirt from my mother. She wrung out her own long skirt out and placed it in the morning sun to dry.

My grandparents retired in 1934 and bought a house, The Gables, in The Close of Gampy's beloved Salisbury Cathedral. He would be able to play the organ and enjoy his last years. St Andrew's was full to overflowing for his last service. After thirty years of devotion to his parish, the village wanted to express their gratitude and show their affection for their Rector. The Bishop of Oxford preached the sermon and Gampy played his organ for the last time.

At the end of the service, my grandfather gave the Blessing, taking rather longer than usual. He then turned back to the altar and knelt. He got up to the swell of the organ and the congregation rose to its feet. The choir started to file from the stalls as Gampy moved down the altar steps. He had reached the last step when he stopped, turned slowly back to the altar, knelt, and then prostrated himself up the steps which he had just descended. He lay there motionless as the choir started to move down the chancel. The last choir men had seen what had happened and stopped, thinking that he had collapsed. They were just about to go to his aid when he lifted his head, kissed the top step, rose slowly to his feet and walked down the chancel and aisle, as if nothing unusual had occurred.

Sadly he lived only a few months in retirement. My mother, Tony, Joan and I were going to spend Christmas with Gampy and Ganny in Salisbury, but the night before we were due to travel down, he became very ill and our visit was cancelled. He rallied however, and the four of us drove down for New Year but on arrival we were told to be very quiet because he had had a relapse. Later that evening (New Year's Eve 1934), he sent down a message that he wanted to see his three grandchildren and individually bless them. Tony went upstairs first and was with him for three or four minutes, followed by Joan and then I went up to the lamp-lit bedroom. He was lying peacefully on his back with his arms outstretched outside the bedclothes and he smiled as I approached the bed. I knelt beside him as he gently raised his right hand to bless me. He held my hand for a few seconds and then I stood up and started to move away but he put pressure on my hand to stop me. He inclined his head on the pillow and said, 'You rescued me that night of the Hunt Ball, and I forgot to thank you.' He squeezed my hand and whispered, 'God Bless.' Still smiling, he let my hand go and closed his eyes. I left the room quietly and he died four hours later. It was 1st January 1935.

After Gampy died, Ganny left Salisbury and bought a flat in Weston-Super-Mare. Kate, dear Kate, the rectory cook at Chinnor, joined her there. The war came and Tony, now a doctor in the RAF, visited her to say goodbye before he departed for the Middle East. Only a few months later, he was reported 'Missing believed killed'. At the time I was in Blackpool, in the RAF, training to be a wireless operator/air gunner, when my mother telephoned me from London where she was working; in her typical and unselfish way, she told me to try and get leave and go straight to Ganny in Weston to break the news. She knew how devoted Ganny was to Tony.

I was given compassionate leave and embarked on the long train journey to Bristol, where I arrived too late to catch any connections to Weston. I decided to try and walk the twenty miles, hoping to hitch a lift on the way; but in those times, however, there was little traffic on the road, there were no street lights, and the houses were blacked out. The few vehicles that did pass, had headlights that were sharply dipped and, although I was in uniform, no one stopped and I arrived in Weston-Super-Mare as dawn was breaking at seven a.m. I had breakfast in the town and walked up Bristol Road to the flat. She was not, of course, expecting me but the moment she saw me, I think she knew why I had come, for when I spoke the words she was completely controlled. Kate burst into tears; Ganny tried to comfort her all day and I felt almost surplus to requirements. She had lost both her sons, her husband, and now her favourite grandson but it was as if she had anticipated and already accepted her fate.

Bristol had had several very heavy air-raids, but Weston-Super-Mare, being primarily a holiday resort, was not considered a likely target for the Luftwaffe. But on the second night I was there, the sirens sounded and soon anti-aircraft fire could be heard, followed by the familiar drone of bomber engines and then explosions. Ganny told Kate and me to get under the dining room table and we did as we were told. I made room for my grandmother to follow, but she walked out of the dining room and I heard her open the front door. I got up and ran after her. She had gone up the path, opened the gate, and was standing in the middle of the road, looking upwards shaking her fists above her head, shouting through the gunfire and explosions, 'You devils! You devils!' With difficulty, I propelled her back into the house.

She lived for another ten years. At the end of the war, she moved back to Chinnor, building a bungalow, Russell Close, only a few hundred yards from St Andrews and Kate lived with her. She then joined Peggy and me at Coulsdon where she died in a nursing home in 1952. She had never seemed a happy person to me, and, after Tony was killed, she seemed to retreat into herself even further. My mother, Vi, had lost her husband aged twenty-nine years and her son at the age of twenty-three years – but she was never bitter. I suppose Ganny had lost even more, but I wish I had known her full story and been able to understand this enigmatic person and I wish I had treated her better when I was a small boy. Whatever else, my grandmother was quite a lady.

There is a stained glass window in memory of my grandfather, on the southern wall of St Andrew's. I wish it could have been dedicated to my grandmother as well. For thirty years, as the Reverend and Mrs Baldwyn, or Padre and Madre, they did their duty to their parishioners and friends and for at least ten of those years as Gampy and Ganny, they loved and cared for their three grandchildren. I never heard them speak of the sons they had lost.

The Ledder

'Know ye not that they which run in a race, run all, but one receiveth the prize.'

The Bible, 1 Corinthians

I HAVE WRITTEN ABOUT Malvern College elsewhere. I went there after leaving my Prep School, Southey Hall, and I disliked it just as much – so maybe the fault lay with me rather than the schools. I never felt motivated to work and was always near the bottom of the class. I failed my School Certificate (equivalent to GCSE) and only just scraped through at the second attempt. I disliked team games, but enjoyed squash and fives, playing for my house and the school colts in the latter game. I left Malvern when I was sixteen, having learnt little and achieved nothing.

However, I did enjoy cross-country running and maybe it was because I was free and away from school boundaries and completely in control of my own destiny for an hour or two – beholden to no one else. It so happens that Malvern boasts one of the stiffest public school cross-country runs in the country and it starts at Ledbury, a small town some seven miles distant, across fields and tracks, then over the considerable Malvern Hills before descending the last mile into the school grounds, onto the cricket pitch and specially prepared finishing line. There was no route marked out and runners were only allowed to cross roads, not run along them. Obviously, there was a generally recognised 'quickest' route, though there were alternative gates, tracks and fields and as many opinions as to their merits. If there had been a lot of rain and the fields were muddy (or in racing parlance 'heavy'), then a longer route using tracks would be chosen; but such decisions were entirely up to the runners themselves, though competitors from the same 'House' would generally confer, since as well as the individual prizes, there was a cup presented to the House with the most points.

It was indeed a strenuous race, not only because of the actual distance, but also because the sixth mile involved the severe climb over the Malvern Hills. Boys had to be sixteen years old to enter and pass a serious medical test. There was usually a field of some seventy runners and the first nine to finish were presented with a green Ledder cap which they were allowed to wear instead of their House cap until the following year's race. I considered this was by far the most illustrious and prestigious cap in the school, not only because of its splendid colour, but also because it represented 'aloneness' and what could be achieved without bat, ball, racket, glove, club or stick. I hero-worshipped those boys who wore those green caps during my few years at Malvern and it was the one halo I would have liked to adorn my head. However, I was only just sixteen when I took part and I finished twelfth out of a field of sixty-seven – I think it was the only time I was ever complimented about anything by my housemaster!

The race started in a Ledbury field and the runners sprinted up a slope to a stile over which they climbed before settling to their varying paces down a track. Obviously minutes elapsed between the first and last climbing over the stile, and the race could be won or lost at this early stage. However, there were usually two or three boys who were outstanding cross-country runners and however they were placed over that Ledbury stile, one of them would surely win the race. The 'start' was always at a fixed time and it was therefore known, to within a few minutes, when the winner would cross the finishing line. The whole school would assemble on the cricket field some fifteen minutes before the leaders were expected – waiting in anticipation to welcome the runners as they came through the school gates. Cheers and clapping could be heard in the distance, signifying the approach of the contenders. It was similar to the expectancy in an Olympic stadium when the crowd awaits the lead marathon runner to appear from the tunnel and start the lap to the finishing line.

Many years before I ran in the race, there was a 'Ledder' sensation and the story is well worth telling. In this particular year, there was one boy who was such a good cross-country runner that it had been taken for granted he would easily win the race. Crowds had assembled in the usual way several minutes before the favourite – I shall call him Morris – was expected, when to everyone's surprise, there was clapping and cheering near the entrance gate. A communal gasp could be heard as through the gates came one of the youngest and least renowned runners – I shall call him Ashcroft. As he ran on to the cricket pitch to cross the line, uproar ensued as his house mates shouted and threw their caps into the air. Officials around the podium were very confused and conferred with the master who had started the race at Ledbury Ashcroft had definitely been seen sprinting toward the stile which the runners had no option but to clamber over before setting out on the six miles to the Malvern Hills. As the course only crossed one small road (and in the 1930s there were not many cars about) Ashcroft could not have hitched a lift without being seen and in any case, he was not, apparently, a deceitful boy but something of an extrovert with an enthusiasm for life in general.

When Morris, the favourite, appeared through the gates pursued by two other boys, he held his arms above his head to acknowledge the applause he did not get. He was quickly made aware of the winner's name and walked over to face the rather slight boy, some two years his junior. At first everyone thought that congratulations were going to be offered in the usual public school way but instead Morris almost hissed 'How the hell did you get here?'

Ashcroft, now relatively rested, smiled and said, 'Same way as you Morris, I ran.'

'You're a liar.'

'I'm telling the truth. I ran every stride of the way.'

By the time the last runners finished, chaos ensued. The sports master then announced that the award ceremony would be deferred in view of objections raised by some of the runners. The 'winner', Ashcroft, was told to bathe, change, and then go to his housemaster's study where he would be questioned about the race.

An hour later Ashcroft knocked on the study door, was bade enter, and found himself confronted by his housemaster, the sports master and the chaplain. I should like to think the following dialogue ensued.

'Sit down, Ashcroft,' his housemaster said, and then, after a long and very searching look, went on, 'I've always thought of you to be a truthful boy and we all heard you tell Morris that you had run the whole way. Quite simply, that cannot be the truth.'

'It is, sir.'

The chaplain leaned forward. 'The Bishop confirmed you not so very long ago, Ashcroft, and I had always thought that the occasion was important to you. If that is right, surely you would not contemplate deception so soon after the laying on of hands.'

'No, sir.'

Seeing that his companions were not progressing too well, the sports master decided to try practicalities. 'Ashcroft, you finished nearly ten minutes ahead of the best cross-country runner in the school, over a seven-mile course. I am sure you will agree with me that this at least seems highly improbable.

'Yes, sir.'

'Then how do you account for it?'

'Perhaps I found a quicker route.'

'There isn't a quicker route.'

'There are choices, sir. We use different fields and tracks.'

'Yes, Ashcroft, but none that would make a significant difference. The recommended course is mapped out virtually as the crow flies from, Ledbury to the college. The only alternative route would be to go around the Malvern Hills. That would add at least three miles to the course and twenty to thirty minutes to a runner's time. No, Ashcroft, there is only one possible route. Ledbury, over the Malvern Hills, and down to the finish in college. There cannot be a shorter route.'

'Excuse me, sir, there is.'

'What do you mean?'

'Well, sir, you said "over" the Malvern Hills.'

'I did, Ashcroft, I did. They happen to be there. To reach the college, you have to go over them and, as I have already told you, to go round them would add miles to the route.'

'Yes, sir.'

'Well?'

'There is a third way, sir.'

43

'What are you talking about. If you don't go over them or round them…. How?…

'Under them, sir.'

'Under,' the Chaplain repeated – and this made Ashcroft feel he had to come to their rescue.

'Yes, sir, under.'

There was more silence during which there were glimmers of dawn penetrating the minds of the three adults. The housemaster eventually dared, 'But Ashcroft, there is only a railway tunnel under the hills.'

Ashcroft nodded. 'Yes, sir, it's a track, a railway track.' There was an even longer silence. Again, Ashcroft felt he could help. 'There is nothing in the rules against it, sir.'

The housemaster tried to help by saying, 'Ashcroft, that is the main London to Hereford Line.'

'Yes, sir, I had a torch.'

The Chaplain joined in again: 'You could have been killed.'

'I was very careful, sir.'

The sports master felt he had to get the facts straight. 'You had a torch and you ran through the railway tunnel and you don't think that that was cheating?'

'Not really, sir, we're always being told to use our initiative, and I think that is what I was doing. I was taking a risk.'

'Of being punished?'

'No, sir, of being killed. An express train did come through when I was halfway through the tunnel which was a bit scary. But at least I now understand all that business about there being light at the end of the tunnel.'

Morris was declared the winner of course, and the establishment nailed poor Ashcroft on the illegality of trespass. He didn't even get a green Ledder cap. Instead he became a legend. At the so-called inquiry, he defended himself stoutly, emphasising that apart from the start and finish lines and the prohibition on running along roads, there was no delineation of the route and that, therefore, in view of the fact that he didn't enjoy running up hills, he had every right to choose another route if he so wished. He only accepted the findings of the inquiry because it had been pointed out that, if his trespass had been reported to the Great Western Railway, there would have been a heavy fine which his parents could ill afford to pay.

The school authorities were wise enough not to punish him. Instead, they let things be and changed the Ledder Rules. Ashcroft did not enter the race again simply because he did not enjoy running up big hills. He remained a hero until he left Malvern College two years later. I could never find out what happened to him, but I would guess he became a Captain of Industry.

The Tree

'I shall be like that tree. I shall die at the top.'

Jonathan Swift

WE WERE LIVING IN a pleasant cedar wood house in Pound Hill, a development on the outskirts of Crawley, and why I should remember this incident so vividly, I really don't know. Perhaps such mishaps run in the family – you will read how Kay drove the car through Great Uncle Will's garage early in the last war – in neither case was it funny, yet I can't help chuckling.

It was summertime and I was working for Paul Hamlyn in London. The offices had just been moved to Drury Lane and we occupied the top floors of Drury House, immediately opposite the stage door of the Theatre Royal. (The building has long since been demolished and replaced with another office block.) I used to drive up to work every morning and park comfortably nearby. The year must have been 1965 or 1966. Tony was away at the time, either in Israel on a kibbutz or maybe he had just started his training in the police. Peggy was at home and Jenny was a daygirl at Kingsley school in Horley. I would sometimes drop her there on my way to London, and this is what I was going to do, and did, that fateful morning.

Now Jenny was a lively girl (still is, as a matter of fact) and had always enjoyed adventures – her own or other people's. Adventures are either planned or just happen and this one fell under the latter heading. Mind you, there's a very thin line between adventures and disasters but happily this particular occurrence didn't quite cross the line from the one to the other. Both Tony and Jenny had learned to drive cars early in their teens even though they never had the long rectory drive to practise on which my brother Tony, Joan and I had at Chinnor. I used to let them steer the car on minor roads in Devon and then get behind the wheel on Bursden Moor near Hartland. The roads were visible for miles and we could always see when a car was approaching.

I had a Singer Gazelle at the time and we were all in a good mood that summer's day because I was exchanging the Gazelle for a Daimler V8 when I got to Drury House. We were getting ready to leave the house and Jenny shouted up the stairs asking if she could back the car out of the garage. Why not? She had done it before and, as we lived in a six-house close, there was no passing traffic. I shouted back my assent and about three minutes later, just as I was leaving my study, there was a not inconsiderable bang from outside. I tore down the stairs, through the hall and out of the open front door to find Peggy standing with her hands to her face and the back end of the Gazelle firmly embedded in a young and innocent fir tree which stood at the side of our very short drive – just where Jenny should have reversed to the left (our left, her right). Jenny sat rigid in the driver's seat, in shock I suppose. I ran to the back of the car to survey the damage. The damage to the car was considerable, to the tree, terminal.

All these years later, Jenny tells me I was strangely calm – maybe like my frightening Great Uncle Will – but it seems Jenny was doubly scared precisely because I didn't seem to be too concerned. I found the situation intriguing. The tree had somehow got between the boot lid and the bumper and of course the impact had made a deep and lasting impression on both. The tree had snapped and we were faced with a car that seemed to have a fir tree growing between its rear body parts. I could see that to try and remove it would only cause further damage and as the car was still drivable, I quickly seized a small saw and some secateurs to prune away the greenery and protruding branches as well as I could. As we drove away with the tree several feet high like a mast – I should have hoisted a flag – we left Peggy incredulous, and Jenny mourning her last ride in the Gazelle and still wondering why I was so calm.

I don't remember what happened when we got to the school except that I dropped Jenny in the usual place. Parents and pupils must have noticed a tree growing out of the back of a car, and there must have been some reaction; giggles, astonishment or may be as Jenny was notorious for her escapades, such an occurrence was the norm. Would they, I wondered, when I turned up next morning in a beautiful new Daimler, even consider what kind of people we were and anticipate Jenny's arrival the morning after that on the pillion of a motorbike?

I drove on to London, waiting for a police car to pull me in. The tree wasn't tall enough to make me worry about low bridges but I was relieved to arrive undisturbed in Drury Lane. A Mr Jackson was general manager at Hamlyn's, responsible for all matters to do with transport and when I told him to come out and take delivery of my Singer Gazelle, I thanked God he was a sweet man unlikely to come between me and my Daimler. When he saw the union of car and tree, he said, 'Good God' and roared with laughter!

The Daimler was a beautiful car. British racing green, with lots of real wood inside. I drove it home that night feeling a little guilty and when I swung into the driveway, I lowered my head as I passed the tree stump. Jenny did not ask to get the car out next morning.

Marathon

'I survived.'

Emmanuel Joseph Sieyes (when asked what he did in the French Revolution)

KIM AND I MOVED to Bray in Berkshire in 1970 and our house, Cannon Lodge, stands a few hundred yards from the parish church, St Michael's. During the first ten to fifteen years of our lives in the village, Kim and I were quite involved in local activities. Kim started the playschool in the village and I was chairman of the village hall for a number of years. For three consecutive years I produced a topical Christmas revue, which combined carols with sketches I had written lampooning various characters in the village. I started the Thursday Club (which is still in being), members of which met up every Thursday evening in the annexe of the hall to play snooker and drink at the bar. (Now the annexe has been completely renovated with a relatively luxurious bar and lounge – even poker has been introduced!) Neil Howells was the vicar and I used to read the lessons from time to time.

The eight church bells were set in the upper chamber of the tower immediately above an empty chamber which in turn was above the ringers' chamber. Inevitably, the weight and action of the bells so high in the tower weakened the structure and over the centuries alarming cracks were appearing. Accordingly, it was decided that action had to be taken; the eight bells were to be moved down into the empty chamber below thus lowering the weight from the top to the middle of the tower. It was a mammoth and costly job and the bells were silent for many months as the work was skilfully and lovingly carried out. Eventually the bells rang out again from their lower base in the tower.

St Michael's also needed a new roof and this was going to be an even more costly job and would take several months through the spring and summer of 1982. I was asked to be on the fund-raising committee but, never having been a good committee man, I declined the invitation and set about thinking how I could raise money for the fund by my own efforts. The first London Marathon had been run earlier in the year (1981) and though, in those early years, there were no 'fun' runners as such and there were only 18,000 participating, a lot of the amateur runners were taking part to raise money for various good causes and projects. As I had run cross-country and the mile at Malvern and in the RAF, I wondered if at my age (sixty-one) I would be able to run well enough to complete the twenty-six-mile course. It was still summer time and, hoping no one would notice, I jogged around the village and, as a result, decided it was at least worth applying and if accepted, 'having a go'. I felt sure I could raise a few hundred pounds from family, friends, contacts in the record industry, and from my friend and employer at the time, Paul Hamlyn.

The 1982 Marathon was to be run early in May and I started training in September with modest runs in and around the village, increasing the distance marginally week by week. My office at Octopus Books was in Grosvenor Street and only a few hundred yards away, near Hanover Square, worked an old friend of mine and former employee, Tony Morris.

He was managing director of Polydor Records and I knew he had a shower in his office suite. He kindly allowed me to use it at any time and accordingly, on most weekdays, I would walk around there at lunchtime, change into my running gear, head for Hyde Park past Claridges and the American Embassy in Grosvenor Square, cross Park Lane into the park – and then run the circuit alongside Rotten Row. I would vary my return route to Hanover Square, shower, then walk back to my office for the afternoon's work. The 1981 winter was very hard and there were weeks of snow which made training on roads and pavements slippery and dangerous. I would often get up early, therefore, and run in the dark when the snow was still fresh and crunchy. I would see lights appearing in the houses and the milkman delivering his bottles. Sometimes I would run circuits round and round the cricket pitch timing myself on the clock over the pavilion.

Very boring, but safe. Indeed, running can be very boring, especially if one has to train on roads. As the winter wore on, I went further afield and was sometimes dropped off in villages several miles distant and would then run home, picking up bottles of water which I had left in hedges on my car journey out.

I had recorded Sebastian Coe that autumn, reading his book *Running Free* and when we were having lunch I asked his advice about tactics. Coe was not, of course, a long distance runner but he was a superb track athlete and he simply said that I should run my training pace and ignore everyone else, particularly at the start when most of the runners would sprint away. He warned me how tempting it would be to go with the crowd but assured me I would pass most of them later in the race if I was patient. How right he was! The longer the race went on, the more runners I passed, particularly on the Embankment only two or three miles from the finish when many of the runners became walkers!

I got myself into a panic a week or two before the race. I had been a bad sleeper for years – ever since I had left full-time work in the theatre, and had been taking Mogadon sleeping pills for at least twenty-five years. (I still do.) I was worried I wouldn't sleep the night before the race and as a result wouldn't be able to complete the twenty-six miles. Accordingly I went to see my GP, Richard Flew, who as well as his NHS work, ran a sports clinic. Should I take one, two or even three pills on Marathon Eve to ensure a good night's sleep? Richard laughed and assured me that if I didn't sleep at all, adrenalin would see me through and refused to give an opinion on my pill intake for the big night. I decided to take two pills and eventually fell asleep from worrying as to whether I was doing the right thing!

It was a pleasant morning on Sunday, 9th May, and I got up early to give a lift to another aspiring runner from Maidenhead. We had an easy drive up to London and I parked outside Charing Cross Station, catching one of the Marathon trains to Greenwich. The carriages were crowded with an assortment of all shapes, sizes, colours and ages –

but common to us all was excited anticipation, a degree of nerves and, without doubt, as Richard had forecast, adrenalin.

I eased my way through the thousands of runners to be as near to the starting line as possible and when the race started at nine o'clock, I swung into my training pace and ignored the hordes surging by. As we left the park and settled into the onlooker crowded streets, I felt exhilarated and confident that I would complete the distance. As I was running for the church, I had St MICHAEL'S in bold letters on the front and back of my running vest and suddenly I realised I was the cause of the chorus 'Good old Marks and Sparks' emanating from the pavements! This chant was to continue for the next four hours or so and I cursed myself for not asking Marks & Spencer for sponsorship; Octopus had a big turnover with them at the time and they were highly prosperous! After we had run round the Cutty Sark, I desperately wanted to pee. I had followed all the official advice about the intake of water prior to the start and therefore could not understand what was going on. I felt annoyed because I had been determined not to stop or walk. However I decided I had better get it over and done with so, at the next designated loo, I veered in and took up the conventional stance. Nothing happened. I waited for thirty seconds when a runner next to me said, 'Are you having the same problem I'm having?' I nodded and having decided my problem was psychosomatic, I shoved everything back into place and rejoined the runners. The urge vanished – I had obviously run through the problem and merrily snatched drinks from the 'stations' thereafter without any further pee problems.

The London Marathon must be one of the easiest to run. With no steep hills, runners are sheltered from any wind by the narrow streets and are enormously encouraged by the intensity of participation and enthusiasm from the crowds lining the route. Cheers, laughter, applause, music, and food being held out to snatch, makes it impossible for the runners to dwell on any physical distress or problem. I knew where my family would be and it was a wonderful moment when I spotted them on the north side of Tower Bridge.

It was a good moment to see their faces for, after Tower Bridge, the route turns eastwards and the runners head into the Isle of Dogs – then the bleakest part of East London. It had been heavily blitzed during the war and Dockland became a dead area. For eight to nine miles we ran through barren areas with few streets and no crowds. Today it is very different. Not only is the Dome there, but there has been extensive redevelopment and of course with the Olympics scheduled on the site for 2012, it is becoming not only built over but very fashionable. One and a half hours later, I was back at Tower Bridge, only a few miles from the finish. Another glimpse of the family, and, this time, Julian ran with me for a few hundred yards before I reached the carpeted cobbles along the Embankment. This was the stretch where I passed hundreds, if not thousands, of walking wounded and winded and I remember looking at my watch for the first time and calculating I was almost exactly on my scheduled time as I crossed Trafalgar Square. In those early years, the finishing line was on Westminster Bridge and I felt exhilaration as I ran down the Mall towards Buckingham Palace before wheeling left down Birdcage Walk to the finish.

I wanted to cry as a medal was hung around my neck and a silver cape wrapped around me to keep me warm as I proceeded to the clothing collection point on the south side of the river. I ached a little and my feet were sore but when I saw Tony approaching with food, drink and blankets, I felt happy, relaxed and exhausted at the same time. With Tony's help, I staggered to the car to meet up with the rest of the family, drove back to Charing Cross to pick up my car, and headed for home. I had completed the course in four hours and twelve minutes, a time within two minutes of my training schedule and, when the official placings were published, I was placed 11,012th out of over 18,000 runners. I was satisfied. There were fewer than one hundred runners older than me.

Quite by coincidence, I was due to read the lesson at Evensong that evening and I was determined to do so. I suppose the actor within me made me conscious of the occasion and I knew too that my mother would be at the service and would be a very important part of the congregation! When we got home, I had a glorious hot bath and surveyed my feet. Both my toenails were black and one of them dropped off the same evening. (I still have it in one of my drawers.) Though I felt very stiff, I had no blisters but I had lost half a stone since I got out of bed at dawn. We walked slowly and gently round to the church for the 6.30 p.m. service and I was able to stagger to the lectern on time. When Neil read out the notices, he made sure the congregation knew of my adventure and I got a round of applause! I had raised nearly £2,000 for the roof and bell fund and thoroughly enjoyed the process of doing so. I pondered on all the committee meetings I had missed as I lay in bed that night and forgot to take my Mogadon. I slept like a log!

23 and 24 Mecklenburgh Square

'Things won are done;
Joy's soul lies in the doing.'

William Shakespeare

MY MOTHER, WHO AT this time was in her mid-forties, ran a magical boarding house in Mecklenburgh Square from 1935 to 1940 when an unexploded bomb in the square right opposite the two houses, forced her to close down. Only two or three weeks later, five houses only a few yards down the terrace suffered directs hits with many casualties, several of them fatal.

Prior to 1935, we had all been living with my paternal grandparents at the Rectory in Chinnor, but when my brother Tony left Cheltenham College to train as a doctor at St Bartholomew's hospital, my mother had the seemingly crazy idea of renting a property not far from the hospital to 'take in' medical students and at the same time provide the family with a home. I say 'crazy' because she had never had any experience in business or catering, nor had she lived in London since the years just before she married my father during the Great War. She was, however, a lady of courage and determination and knew that Tony would lend support when it was needed. Tony was a very mature and practical young man for his seventeen years.

My mother found this beautiful Georgian house, 23 Mecklenburgh Square, which was already a boarding house, run in the traditional way with lace curtains and coloured paper on glass panelled doors with very sober furniture and fittings. It was full of middle-aged and elderly tenants and it was assumed that they would all leave when it became known that future lettings would be to medical students. This was the first of my mother's miscalculations.

When she took the place on, there were only two empty rooms and these were immediately filled by Tony's student friends. But not one of the remaining residents (whom we affectionately came to call 'the trouts') showed any inclination to jump ship. On the contrary, there was a unanimous excitement and ominous sign of rejuvenation. During the five years we were there, the intended transition from trout to student never fully took place and, as it happened, 'Meck' became a far more interesting place as a result. Within two years, my mother rented the adjoining house, No 24 and, when she was bombed out in 1940, there was still one little trout in the same room on the second floor of No 23, a sweet elderly lady and her name was Miss Broome. Medical students were in the majority, but in addition there were lawyers, drama students, art students, pilots and there was even a Rothschild!

Soon my mother made another miscalculation – and this time it was not such a happy one. When she took over, the staffing arrangements were not satisfactory – there were no 'living in' staff – in those days casual staff were readily available. Accordingly, the cook and cleaning ladies had to be replaced and with the installation of an Aga and other modern equipment, a new regime was essential. There was no capital available and improvements were only made possible by my mother's ability to charm the bank manager.

It was at this point she found her 'treasures' – a cockney family living down Gray's Inn Road in nearby Kings Cross. I shall rename them – the Poultons. Mrs Poulton, happily plump, was in her fifties, her married daughter in her late twenties and her youngest daughter in her early twenties. They worked part-time during the week but not at all on Sundays. Mrs Poulton helped with the cooking whilst the daughters acted as housemaids and cleaners of the residents' rooms. They were always cheerful and soon came to be regarded as part of the family, arriving early in the morning down the area steps into the basement carrying their bags and paraphernalia, leaving at varying times during the day as happy and full of life as when they arrived. They always joined in the Christmas celebrations and when there were special occasions, they always added to the general enjoyment. They were indeed 'treasures'.

The purpose of the 'Meck' adventure was not to make money but to provide a home for the family, the means for Tony to study at Barts, for Joan to study at Kings, and to create a happy setting for residents. My mother succeeded admirably but as I have already mentioned there was little money available and she relied on Tony to guide her on practical matters, including finance. In 1938, although the two houses were always full, expenditure was perilously close to income, and this was hardly surprising because food was plentiful and second helpings were taken for granted. When thirty people were being fed breakfast and evening meal daily, such generosity can be economically dangerous. It seems that Tony was mystified by the lack of profit even taking into account second helpings! At his instigation and without staff involvement, it was decided to take daily inventories of all incoming food and household items, checking them against quantities actually used. This continued for nearly a month and involved a lot of very hard work. The figures were then checked and there appeared to be a gap between what was bought and what was actually used. A very considerable gap.

My mother and Tony consulted no one but could only come to one conclusion. For a week thereafter, from his balcony on the first floor, Tony watched the Poultons arrive in the morning, noticing that the bags they carried appeared to be limp and therefore empty. My mother watched them leave at duties' end, and saw them climb the steps with difficulty and bulging bags. It was decided that there had to be confrontation of a kind that could only be decisive. My mother was inclined to 'talk' with the Poultons first – after all, they were part of the family. Tony insisted, however, that immediate and drastic action was needed.

It was to take place on a day when my mother had done a big shop in Marchmont Street just around the corner and Tony knew he would be back from Barts before the Poultons left the house. They took up positions at the top of the area steps and waited for the family to come out. As Mrs Poulton started her ascent, my mother, formidable on the top step, said quietly, 'Mrs Poulton, will you please all empty your carrier bags?' Apparently, Mrs Poulton stared at the Baldwyns for several seconds totally dumbfounded. She must have realised very quickly that with

Tony standing immediately behind my mother, there was little chance of making a run for it and that she was going to find it difficult to account for the contents of their carrier bags. Accordingly, in true cockney style, she decided to be direct and told them to get out of the 'effing' way. My mother was shocked. She was not at all used to this kind of language and, in the 1930s, such words were considerably more outrageous than they are today. However, she recovered her composure and said quietly, 'If you don't do as I ask, I shall call the police.' Mrs Poulton, shrieking even worse obscenities, dropped the bags she was carrying and yelled at her daughters to do the same. My mother and Tony stepped aside to allow the Poultons their frantic departure and watched them running out of the square towards Gray's Inn Road, never to be seen again.

The bags contained tins of food, packets of butter and tea, cleaning materials and even meat and vegetables. It was nearly half the Marchmont Street shop that morning! Tony tried to calculate the thousands of pounds worth of produce the Poultons must have stolen over the years. He wanted my mother to go to the police – he was quite right of course – but she wouldn't. Perhaps she remembered the family motto 'Credo et Confido'. After all, she had done exactly that. But it cost her.

Early Days

'There is always one moment in childhood when the door opens and lets the future in.'

Graham Greene

SO MANY AUTOBIOGRAPHIES START with highly detailed memories of life at a very early age – say two, three or four years old. My memories at that age are vague both in the area of relationships and actual events. It wasn't until we moved to live with my paternal grandparents at Chinnor that I can recall vividly the patterns and shapes of life, the routines, boundaries and awareness of love and mystery.

My first memories were when we lived at 39 Sefton Road in Addiscombe, nudging the eastern side of Croydon. The road is still very much as it was eighty years ago – semi-detached three-bedroom houses lined up facing each other as if on parade. I drove by a few years ago and it had changed very little – though surely the houses cannot be over eighty years old? The environment is the same, however, and, though I was only four years old when I lived there, I can remember the layout of the house exactly and the small fenced garden at the back.

My mother had rented the house – she certainly had no capital. My father had died in 1922 when I was a year old, leaving her with three young children and fighting for a war widow's pension, having to prove his death was a result of war wounds received in the Great War. My elder brother Tony had started at boarding school – Southey Hall in Great Bookham, Surrey (my grandparents paying the fees) and Joan and I attended Woodside School, just next to East Croydon railway station. We walked down Sefton Road to catch a bus – or was it a tram?

There were certainly trams in Croydon at the time which we used to ride on when we had a special shopping day – Kennards and Father Christmas – but perhaps they didn't clang out as far as Addiscombe.

It was at 39 Sefton Road that my first vivid recollection occurred. Joan and I were setting off for school and we must have had a row of some kind because she ran ahead up the short garden path with me in hot pursuit. She opened the gate, slamming it as I reached out my right hand to follow. The gate closed on the middle finger of my right hand, cutting through the tip and nail. It hurt – and I let Sefton Road know it hurt, but at least I had something to show for my screams – plenty of blood spilling from a finger and its nearly severed tip! Joan, nearly three years older than I, was distraught; my mother, calm as usual, put my finger together as well as she could and walked us down to the doctor's surgery. I then experienced the first taxi ride of my young life to the Mayday Hospital where my finger was stitched and secured. I was back at school the next day but couldn't write for several weeks. (Eighty years later I still have a mildly deformed middle finger tip and nail!)

My other memory of 39 Sefton Road was emotional rather than physical. We had friends who lived in a very select part of Croydon, their name was Wickham-Jones and they had a large house and garden. We knew them because their children were also at Woodside and we were invited to their Christmas party – we bubbled with excitement. We seldom went out because there was so little my mother could afford and any parties we went to were the semi-detached Sefton Road kind of parties – great fun but not on the scale of a grand house in Croydon.

Joan and I found it difficult to control our excitement when the great day came. The fact that it was a miserably rainy day added to our euphoria – it was mid-winter and Christmas time – and the thought of lavish decorations, a magical Christmas tree, a log fire and surprise presents must have intoxicated us with excitement. We were not normally badly behaved children and I can't remember what we did in the morning that caused my mother to warn us that, if we didn't stop whatever we were doing, we would not go to the party. She was a kind and caring person and I suppose this made us childishly sceptical of her warning and we continued to fight, rush around the house and be generally unhelpful. Lunch was prepared, our party clothes laid out, but when a plate was broken halfway through the meal, my mother uncharacteristically burst into tears. She composed herself and warned us again that one more act of misbehaviour would definitely mean we would not go to the party. When, after lunch, Joan and I had a fight at the top of the stairs which resulted in us both falling to the bottom (without injury), my mother said not a word but put on her coat and told us she was going next door and would return within five minutes.

We sensed we had gone too far and, when she returned, she told us very quietly we were not going to the party. She knew the neighbours were going into town and she had asked them to cancel the taxi. She took off her coat and told us we could amuse ourselves in any way we liked but that she was going up to bed. When, a few minutes later we heard her sobbing, Joan and I crept upstairs and hesitated outside her room before opening the door. My mother held her hand out and we jumped onto the bed beside her. With the rain still pouring outside, the three of us cried together for several minutes – this I remember vividly. My mother must have been living on a knife edge of emotions at this time – we had never seen her cry before and we sensed how horrible we had been. It was certainly the first time in my life I had felt remorse and, as we lay hugging on that bed, the Wickham-Jones party didn't seem to matter any more. I can't remember whether this was before or after Joan had slammed the gate on my finger but these two episodes are the first memories of my childhood.

There is a sad postscript to the story of the party we didn't go to. One of the Wickham-Jones' children was a boy called Tony and much the same age as Joan. We must have left Addiscombe by 1926 and had no further contact with the family. Some twenty-five years later when I was acting in London, I bought the *Evening Standard* and read that a Sabena aircraft from Brussels had crashed on landing at Heathrow and amongst the fatalities was the young theatrical impresario, Tony Wickham-Jones.

Hartland – furthest from the Railway

'God made the country and man made the town.'

William Cowper

HARTLAND HAS BEEN AND still is a very special place to me and my family, and indeed to countless friends to whom we have introduced the village, its magical surroundings and fearsome but magnificent coastline. I want to set down the history of our involvement with this place and how Corner Cottage and Mount Pleasant became our second and third homes.

When I first visited Hartland, as one turned off the main Bideford to Bude road to reach the village some four miles from the sea, one was confronted with a large board on which was inscribed the words 'Hartland – the village furthest from the railway'. Presumably this was correct in the middle of the twentieth century but of course those days were before Beecham when so many small branch lines were closed. At the time, the nearest railway stations were at Bideford twelve miles away and Bude, in Cornwall, thirteen miles away.

I was directing a play, *The Lady and the Mortal Man* at the New Lindsey Theatre in London in1953, written by Parnell Bradbury, a close friend of mine. Parnell was a chiropractor, working and living in Hove. He was a dreamer and wrote plays; he had a vivid imagination and wrote flowing dialogue but, in a strange way, he was not of this world and his plots were often too whimsical. He was some twenty years older than I, but we worked well together and we wrote one three-act play *Between Ourselves* for which I provided the plot and Parnell wrote most of the dialogue. It was performed in several repertory theatres up and down the country and broadcast on the radio. I spoke at his funeral in the Forest of Dean and Kim and I remember that occasion well. It was a lovely day and the church and churchyard were in an idyllic spot. To reach the grave from the church, Parnell had to be carried down a track past the cars of the mourners. Jo, Parnell's partner, had left his dog in the car during the service and, as we walked slowly and silently behind the coffin past the cars, the dog started howling and continued to do so until Parnell was lowered into his grave. Parnell would have relished such drama!

It was Parnell who introduced me to North Devon and Hartland and I am eternally grateful. He told me of the place at rehearsals of the play at the New Lindsey and suggested that if I was free at the weekend, I should go with him to Hartland. An elderly patient of his had recently died and, because Parnell had helped her through the last years of her life, in gratitude she had left him her cottage – 'Gillan' – in Spekes Valley and he was going down to assess how much work would need to be done before he and his family could use it as a holiday home. I readily accepted his invitation and we drove down after the Friday rehearsal. This was of course many years before the M4 and M5 had been built and it took us nearly seven hours as we wove our way through Andover, Amesbury, past Stonehenge, then through Wincanton and Mere, Taunton, Wellington, Bampton, South Moulton, Barnstaple and Bideford. A glorious journey even though much of it was in darkness and we weren't going to see Hartland village that evening because we were branching off down narrow lanes to find a thatched cottage called Stitworthy less than a mile from the Atlantic Ocean.

I shall forever remember my first night in North Devon. Stitworthy is a thatched cottage, hidden from the lane down a winding track at the bottom of a small valley. (It is still there but I have not been inside since that night more than fifty years ago.) It was owned by an elderly retired naval commander who, with his equally elderly housekeeper, ran it as a B & B. We were welcomed warmly with supper – I wish I could remember what we ate – and then, contented and tired we went to bed. My room was quite enchanting with an iron bedstead and – ah me, it was wonderful – a feather bed! How well I slept and at daylight how eagerly I jumped out of bed and threw back the curtains to search the view down the valley and breathe in the pure sea air. After a full cooked breakfast, we drove the mile or so to Spekes Valley, turning left at the crossroads and, within a few hundred yards, reached our destination – Gillan. The valley is a very beautiful place leading down to Spekes Mill Mouth with its three-tier waterfall, forbidding cliffs and jagged rocks. At low tide there are narrow strips of sand; at high tide pebble and stone are hurled onto the ever-changing shoreline.

We were to spend many happy days at Gillan over the next few years but inevitably, I suppose, a time came, when, much as we loved Gillan, we fantasised the idea of finding a cottage of our own. We had very little capital but dreams don't need capital and so, towards the end of the 1950s, we bought the local paper to see if any cottages for sale appeared in the Hartland area. But no, there seemed to be nothing that compared to the romance of Gillan in the Spekes Valley setting. Besides, we lived over seven hours away and were not 'on the spot' to pounce on any bargains that might suddenly appear.

But one night at home in Redhill, I had an idea. I would write out a dozen postcards or so, outlining what we wanted and asking the addressees to contact us should they hear of any property becoming available. I enclosed a stamped addressed envelope and then set off for a one-night stop at Gillan to deliver my envelopes to all the farms in the Hartland area. This was in September and I returned home, hopeful but not optimistic. The weeks passed and we had almost forgotten our unlikely scheme when one November morning, through our letterbox came an almost illegible scrawl on one of our postcards: 'I have heard that Miss Dixon is selling her cottage in Elmscott. Don't tell anyone I told you.' I couldn't read the signature but it was from a farm in a nearby village called Eddison. I received the card on a Friday morning and the same evening I drove down to Hartland having phoned Parnell for permission to camp at Gillan yet again.

On the Saturday morning, I was up early to take a look at Elmscott, a hamlet just south of Spekes with two farms, five cottages and a youth hostel converted from the village school. I asked at one of the cottages where Miss Dixon lived and was directed down a lane between Elmscott and another hamlet, Milford. But before I dared knock on Miss Dixon's door, I was told that the cottage in question was the end one of three very old daub and wattle terraced cottages on the corner of the lane leading to Welcombe from Hartland. The walls were three feet thick and painted white and the middle cottage appeared to be derelict. The corner cottage was certainly empty and I peered through the windows noting the place had little else but character. I could see that the floors were stone and irregular and I could only see one electric light dangling from the ceiling in what I supposed was the kitchen though, apart from a very old sink, the little room was empty.

I was almost trembling with excitement when I knocked on Miss Dixon's door but was soon put at ease by this elderly lady who insisted I take tea with her. I came straight to the point, outlining our dream and telling her I had heard she might be selling her Elmscott cottage. She said yes, that was correct and then asked me how much I thought it was worth. An extraordinary feeling of guilt engulfed me but I was able to say quite honestly that, as I hadn't been inside the cottage, I had no idea. She gave me the key and asked me to go and inspect and then return and advise her. But as I walked back to Corner Cottage (that was to be its name whether or not we came to own it) I knew I would have as little idea as to its worth after I had been inside as I had before.

Miss Dixon had warned me that the cottage had been flooded a few weeks before and when I went inside, I found a layer of mud covering part of the flagstone ground floor. There was only one tap and the light I had seen through the window was, in fact, the only light in the cottage. There was a small walk-in larder, and the small living room with an open fire was potentially very attractive. The staircase led out of this room to three bedrooms, two of which could just manage a single bed, the third a modest double bed. I peered out of a window and a herd of cows passed by brushing against the walls, not interested in the stranger inside Corner Cottage. Little did they know that before too many milkings had passed, the stranger would get to know them quite well. Despite the damp, the mud and the emptiness, it was love at first sight and as I floated back to Miss Dixon, I hadn't the slightest idea what I was going to say to her.

It was dusk when she seated me in her cosy drawing room and offered me a drink. I dared to ask if she had whisky and she told me she always kept a bottle in the cupboard. It was a man's tipple, not like the gin she was going to have. We settled down and then came the moment I was dreading. 'Well, Mr Baldwyn, now that you've been inside, what do you think it's worth?' I dithered for a few seconds and then said, entirely without conviction "£500, perhaps?' Miss Dixon looked straight at me, her eyes widening and said, 'Good gracious! That sounds much too much.' I stammered something about neither of us knowing much about house prices (which was true) and perhaps we should get advice and then talk again. She promised I would hear from her and just as I got up to leave she said, 'I know who I'll ask. My brother is a solicitor. He's sure to know all about it.' My heart sank and I returned to Redhill cursing solicitors.

A few weeks later, I received a circular from a Bideford estate agent informing me that the cottage was to be auctioned. Even if the date had allowed us to attend, we would not have done so, because we felt sure the price would be too high and the journey would not be worth while. But miracles seem to crop up from time to time. A week or two after the auction date we had a letter from the same estate agent saying that he understood we had been interested in the property and, if we would increase our offer to £550, he felt sure Miss Dixon would accept! We did and she did! And so we became the proud owners of Corner Cottage. With the help of a grant from the council to install plumbing and make the place habitable, we decorated it and furnished it and by the spring had spent the first of many holidays in our second home. The water was plumbed in from a well across the road; our garden sloped away eastwards, boasting several fruit trees. We had a sturdy outhouse for coal and garden tools, and our neighbours across the road were the Rowe family. He worked for the farm further up the lane and Beth, his wife, became our caretaker, stocking and warming the cottage for our visits.

There were no snags. Yes, Corner Cottage was right on the corner without any pavement to ward off bumps and blows but I write of days many years ago, over fifty of them, when traffic consisted of tractors, the occasional car, delivery vans and herds of cows twice a day! But as the 1960s wore on, we found ourselves still dreaming, and, as financially we were slightly more secure, I wondered if there was another place near Hartland which was less exposed and had larger rooms.

We had had some wonderful years at Corner Cottage and it was some fifteen years since we had started to use Gillan for our holidays and we had made friends in Hartland. We had become ex-Grockles and felt we could quite reasonably make inquiries at the Post Office, at Huggins' garage, at Gifford the baker, at Jeffery's the store, about cottages which might be coming on the market. I think it was Mrs Gifford who mentioned Mount Pleasant to me. She told me it was down Ball Hill in the Pattard Water area. I had never heard these names nor knew the area north of the village but was given directions – only five minutes walk down the hill. The house was empty apparently and was owned by a family of two brothers and two sisters who were looking after it, their parents having lived there until their recent deaths.

That evening I pored over the ordnance survey map and located the area and house – it seemed to be in a perfect setting and there was a stream running through the garden. The next morning I drove down Ball Hill and turned into the lane in which Mount Pleasant stood. I passed a man carrying a bucket and stopped to ask him where I could find Mount Pleasant. He told me he was going there to feed the chickens and asked me what my interest was. He turned out to be one of the brothers – Mr Dayman – and led me another fifty yards and pointed to his left. There stood Mount Pleasant, tucked into the side of the hill, overlooking a most beautiful valley. The little stream raced round the cultivated garden and a paddock sloped up the side of the hill. There was a larger stream running down the centre of the valley between the fields – the setting was idyllic. The house itself was not pretty. It had been modernised between the wars but, from the moment I saw it and its location, I knew we had to buy it.

Everything slotted into place very quickly. The family wanted to sell quickly and a price was agreed. I sold Corner Cottage to our friends the O'Dells who had recently bought the cottage at the end of the terrace next to the chapel. They had also bought the derelict 'Tiddy' cottage in the middle, so called because potatoes were stored therein. With the three cottages, the O'Dells converted two into their own home and holiday let our Corner Cottage.

And so the Mount Pleasant era began in the late 1960s and lasted for nearly twenty years, bringing much joy to the family and many friends. One of the first decisions we made was to extend the front of the house to form a wonderfully long window overlooking the valley. By ridding ourselves of the old front door and altering the staircase, we were able to covert two small downstairs rooms into a most unusually shaped single room embracing virtually the whole ground floor except for the kitchen and bathroom. We also extended the area upstairs, turning a rather pokey little bedroom into a very large one with sensational views up and down the valley.

When we first moved in, Mr Middle was our neighbour. He kept a smallholding in the valley and would come down on his motorbike and sidecar every morning to tend to the animals. He was a VIP in the Hartland horticultural establishment and every year won prizes in the annual flower show. He insisted we exhibit our one redcurrant bush and mysteriously we won a third prize! His wife's name was 'Leafy' and they died peacefully in old age within three days of each other. Ray and Kathy Prouse (Kathy being one of the sisters who owned Mount Pleasant) bought Mr Middle's land and outhouses and built a bungalow into the hillside. They were dear neighbours but as I write this in 2005 they have recently sold Watermead and moved back into the village.

On the other side of the valley lived the Hadijas in a house called The Tucking Mill. Kosta came from Yugoslavia and was the most courteous and gentle man I have ever known. He had been a prisoner of war in Germany and, being an eye surgeon, had worked in a POW hospital. He met Joan when she went out to Germany at the end of the war as a nurse. Joan was a dear person too but with a formidable presence, tending to call a spade a shovel! They had a daughter, Alex, and the family moved to Uganda for a number of years where Kosta was the Senior Ophthalmic Surgeon in Kampala's main hospital. We met them when Kosta retired and they returned to Tucking Mill. They became very much part of our Hartland lives and Toto, their parrot, used to exchange calls with me across the valley.

Sadly Kosta died of a heart attack in the 1980s, followed only a few years later by Alex who had married and had two children, a girl and a boy. She lived in Cornwall and tragically died of cancer in her mid-thirties. Joan lived bravely on at Tucking Mill but was able to enjoy visits from her two grandchildren as they grew toward their teens until she too died in the year 2000, aged eighty-six. I spoke at their funerals; their ashes lie in the churchyard of St Nectan, Stoke (Hartland's parish church).

One of the glories of Mount Pleasant was watching the weather through the huge window, sitting in the comfort of our third home. Colours changed dramatically through the day even when there was a grey sea mist. At night the shades of darkness mingled with the animal noises from the adjacent woods, the paddock and the fields. The delights were bountiful with the peace of summer and the wildness of winter, the meals, the fires, visitors and the joy of just being there. We left Mount Pleasant after eighteen years, our sadness greatly softened by selling it to John and Peggy Jeffery who loved the place, transforming the paddock into a nature reserve. Sadly, John died ten years later but Peggy told us that those years were by far the happiest in their lives. It is warming for us to know that. We have always visited Peggy over the years but recently she has had to sell the house and move back into the village with her family.

Hartland is a unique parish, it occupies a promontory which faces the Atlantic to the west and the Bristol Channel to the north and can therefore be approached by land from the east and south. One has to divert from the Bideford/Bude road and it is therefore relatively isolated; hence its charm! The only land one can see from Hartland Point is Lundy Island, some eighteen miles across the Bristol Channel to the north. Locals swear they can forecast the weather by looking at Lundy. 'Lundy low, wet and blow', Lundy high, fair and dry'. Most certainly the island seems to change shape day by day, the only constant factor being the flashing light from the lighthouse on the cliffs.

Hartland has extraordinary character and my memories are legion – the wreck of the *Green Ranger* on the rocks just below the cliffs at Elmscott; I drove down the next day and climbed on board the stranded ship to find the vessel had already been stripped of its fittings! (the ship was carrying no cargo); the excellent quarterly publication, the *Hartland Times,* which faithfully publishes all the parish activities; Huggins' garage and, in our days, its owner the wonderful 'Taffy' who had inherited it from his uncle and auntie. Taffy was always prominent in the brass band and, in his spare time, rescued visitors from the treacherous cliffs; the stupendous carnival every year on the second Saturday in August; the annual flower show; the memorial service to Winston Churchill in the Methodist Chapel with the Brass Band nearly lifting the roof; fish and chips from O'Donnells, with the main item on the menu in the café at the back of the shop 'Anything with Chips – 1s 9d'; Winnie Tape, whom we knew as a schoolgirl at Elmscott and who moved to Hartland when she married – she used to look after Mount Pleasant for us and to this day makes outrageous appearances on one of the floats in the carnival year by year; the chair at the church at Stoke (a mile or two seaward from Hartland, near the Abbey) in which the Emperor Haille Selassie sat during his exile from Abyssinia when the Italians occupied his country during the late 1930s.

So many memories of peace and adventure, of happiness and sadness, of life and death. Hartland – a very special place.

Stella

'The mind is its own place and in itself can make a heaven
of hell, a hell of heaven.'

John Milton

I CANNOT REMEMBER HER real name – I shall call her Stella; it is possible she is still alive, but I doubt it for I am reaching back to the 1960s when I was forty-five years old or so, and she was only a few years younger. She was the daughter of close friends when we moved to Pound Hill near Crawley from Buckhurst Close in Redhill. Our friends lived in Reigate where they had a modern house on the hill (he was a builder) and we had met Stella on several occasions.

Stella was very severely mentally disabled. Her illness had apparently surfaced at puberty and had now reached a stage where she could no longer be cared for at home and was placed in Netherne Hospital on a permanent basis. It was on her occasional visits home that we met her but she never showed any sign of recognition.

Our friends were going to the continent on holiday and they asked Peggy to go with them. As they would be away for two weeks, I offered to visit Stella, though it was highly unlikely she would know me. At the time, we had a small bitch called Paddy who was a very loving dog and would follow me wherever I went and on the day I decided to visit Stella I took her with me. She would be quite happy sitting in the car for the short time I would be in the hospital.

I had never been to Netherne before and even though it was a very pleasant day, I felt apprehensive when I saw this huge, gaunt, grey building. I found somewhere in the shade to park and lowered the windows of the car a few inches so that Paddy would have plenty of air. I locked the car and walked through the large, forbidding doors which were open; I asked an attendant the way to the ward and was directed down a very long straight corridor. I felt overpowered by the strong antiseptic smell and then felt something brush against my leg; I looked down and there to my astonishment was Paddy. I must have left one of the car windows open just enough for her to squeeze through.

I picked her up; the lead was, of course, in the car. Should I go back and fetch it? Would a small dog in my arms pose any problem in the ward? Something told me to go on and I found the ward door being held open by a male nurse. He was talking to a colleague and did not see Paddy in my arms as I walked through the door. I found myself in a very large room full of light and all round its perimeter sat these sad human beings; they were all women and most of them were dressed in uniform overalls. There were some thirty to forty of them all swaying to and fro, uttering little sounds. As I walked into the centre of the room I tried to pick out Stella, but was unable to do so. I put Paddy down and told her to 'sit' at my feet.

As I did so, all the women rose from their chairs and started shuffling toward me, but they were all looking at the little dog; there were smiles on their faces and they held out their hands towards Paddy. I became surrounded by the women and quickly picked Paddy up in case she was trampled on; I need not have been concerned; they were gentle as their poor lost hands touched and stroked the somewhat bewildered little dog. I caught sight of Stella but she didn't know me as I stood marooned in the midst of this extraordinary outpouring of warmth and affection. A male nurse came in and eased his way towards me and when he saw Paddy in my arms, he smiled. The women shuffled back to their hard chairs and I remember saying an awkward goodbye as we left the ward. The male nurse locked the ward door behind us and as he escorted us along the long corridor, he said, 'They don't get many visitors and dogs are not allowed. Pity.'

As we drove home, Paddy sat on my lap; little did she realise how much she had given to those desolate souls.

London Blitz – 1940

'When there is no peril in the fight, there is no glory in the triumph.'

Pierre Corneille

DESPITE THE FALL OF France, Dunkirk and the Battle of Britain, the smell of war had not really permeated London until the late summer of 1940. A feeling of denial and make-believe hung in the air and then quite suddenly, in the space of a few minutes, Londoners were faced with reality. The daylight raids in August had centred on the East End of London, particularly the Dockland area. The City had been hit too, but it was not until early October that Goering changed his tactics – largely as a result of heavy aircraft and crew losses – and started the night blitz. Although the main areas of attack were still the East End, night after night the raids became more and more indiscriminate until virtually the whole of central London was affected.

I happened to be at home in Mecklenburg Square on the first night of that offensive; the BBC news was avidly listened to, not only in the UK but all over the world, and on that October evening, the six o'clock news contained the usual mixture of war/domestic/economic stories, none of which was particularly sensational for those traumatic times.

I think we had had supper and it was later in the evening when one of the residents rushed into our sitting room to tell us to turn on the wireless. We did so and heard that enemy aircraft in large numbers were approaching the South East of England and that their likely destination was London. Within a few minutes the sirens sounded and we all went out into the square to watch the searchlights playing on the eastern sky. We could hear distant ack-ack fire and then, ominously but with a strange sense of calm, the drone of bomber engines. We felt directly involved.

It wasn't until the distant sound of explosions prompted us to move indoors, that I realised that not one of the many people in the square that night seemed at all frightened, and it was only when we were back in the house that someone reminded us that we were not obeying the official advice to go down to the basement; we did so as the mêlée of noise got louder. As the kitchen was in the basement (ironically at least half its area extended outside the main building and had a flat roof and glass canopy directly exposed to any furies from the sky) cups of tea and snacks were plentiful and there was a general sense of confidence and companionship.

My mother, always the adventurer, whispered to Joan and me, 'Let's take a look from the roof.' We slipped away and climbed the five flights of stairs onto our relatively flat roof. The scene before us was truly sensational. We were looking toward the City and it seemed we were staring into a furnace. The sky was red, almost blood red, and buildings were starkly outlined against the cauldron sky; central to this throbbing backcloth was St Paul's Cathedral, silhouetted against the burning horizon like a huge indestructible rock. We stood stunned and motionless for several minutes; the action was evidently not immediately close to us, even though the noise was considerable. St Paul's was over a mile from Mecklenburgh Square and there appeared to be no fires between us and the Cathedral – the main target area was obviously the East End and the Docks. We held hands and I think my mother simply said, 'Oh dear.' I said, 'My God!' and then Joan added, 'Perhaps we had better go down.'

We returned to the basement and told the company what we had seen. We turned on the wireless and listened to commentators describing the scene which we had just witnessed from the roof. The drama continued for some fifteen minutes until there was a gradual lessening of noise from the guns, followed by an eerie silence. A few minutes elapsed before the 'all clear' sounded and no one knew quite what to say. The show seemed to be over for us, but we all realised it was continuing for thousands of others. My mother led the way back up the stairs on to the roof until there were some twenty of us standing in silence, watching London burn. Still no one seemed to show fear. We had waited for this to happen at night for many weeks and now we had tasted our first raid – it seemed dramatic but not terrifying. But that was the first night; tasting is not consuming.

The next morning, London was bathed in brilliant autumn sunshine as we read of the devastation in the City and the East End. Joan and I carried our bicycles up the area steps and headed for the East End. As we pushed our bikes up Ludgate Hill, we could see that St Paul's was untouched, but as we rode eastwards, we passed cordoned-off streets and we stood astride our bicycles, watching rescue crews, police and servicemen, digging and clawing and scraping their way into the rubble of little houses. We saw stretchers, ambulances and firemen; weeping men and women; dogs with their handlers searching the mounds of broken bricks and mortar. We saw total devastation and knew that there were hundreds of people under the rubble, many of them still alive.

There was a second raid the next night, and, having seen the devastation, this time we did feel afraid and this fear remained night after night for those who were still in London. A few weeks later there was a direct hit on five houses in the Square, on the same side as numbers 23 and 24; only four houses remained standing between us and the stricken buildings. Twelve people were killed. I was not in London at the time, but my mother had to evacuate our houses within forty-eight hours – there was an unexploded bomb lying in the square. There was damage to all the houses, but as my mother was only renting, the landlords were understandably not prepared to carry out repairs when nightly raids continued; she never returned to those two precious havens. She stayed in London, however, and throughout the Blitz she was warden of two houses in nearby Gordon Square which had been taken over by the council to house victims of the air raids.

I have photographs of 23 and 24 Mecklenburgh Square, with glorious creeper trailing from the first-floor balconies, and the square itself green and shadowed by tall trees and houses heavy with flowers in window-boxes. When you have time, go and look at that lovely square and you will notice numbers 23 and 24 are centre stage. The houses that were blitzed have been lovingly rebuilt.

New York, New York

'New York, New York – a helluva town
The Bronx is up but the battery's down.'

Comden & Green

IT MUST HAVE BEEN the early 1960s when I first went to New York and indeed I think it was the first time I had flown since I left the RAF in 1945. Paul Hamlyn was interested in adding to his book empire by importing low-priced art reproductions which were enjoying huge sales in America. He was flying out on publishing business and I was to go with him to investigate the print market and report on the feasibility of selling art reproductions in the UK. In those days, Pan Am was the biggest American carrier with its 707s but, on this occasion, Paul and I were booked on a Tristar which was, ironically a Lockheed aircraft, the same corporation which made the Ventura, the ill-fated plane of my Adriatic ditching. (You will read of this later.) I was, of course, excited, but not a little apprehensive at the thought of flying with hundreds of other people, over the sea, for seven hours or so. During the war, because I was involved with medium bombers, I seldom flew with more than four colleagues and the contrast in the size of the aircraft, was daunting. I remembered the air shows which toured the country in the 1930s. Alan Cobham and Scott were the pioneer airmen at that time, and one paid a few shillings for a ten-minute flight in a bi-plane, taking off from a field, sitting in the cockpit behind the pilot. No flying helmets were needed, and indeed the joy of the flight was the freedom of feeling the wind, looking down at the tapestry of familiar countryside and the sensation of solitude. And now, I was to be locked in to a machine which would enable me to travel in relative comfort, to be fed, watered, and transported across the Atlantic in a few hours, being cosseted by attractive air-hostesses. As I boarded the Tristar I wallowed in nostalgia and was glad to land safely in New York and be released from the cabined confinement.

If my research proved to be positive, I was to head up a new venture to be called Prints for Pleasure and during my visit to New York, I was to visit retail outlets selling the prints, and then contact the main publishers. We knew that 'pretty' contemporary subjects were popular, but we had also been told that some of the old Masters and Impressionists were proving big sellers, and artists such as Van Gogh, Rembrandt, Degas, Lautrec, Gaugin, Picasso, Pissaro, Utrillo, Seurat, Raphael, Durer, Vermeer, Renoir, Monet, Manet, Dufy, Matisse, Goya, Cezanne, Breughel and even Kandinsky and Klee were evident in displays and catalogues. Retail prices were incredibly low and the reproduction quality varied alarmingly. But the low price enabled a great many people who had never before been able to afford to purchase prints – particularly the young – to buy them.

We touched down in New York in mid-afternoon and after dinner in Greenwich with one of Paul's publishing friends, we went to our respective hotels, Paul to the exclusive Pierre, I to an entirely acceptable hotel, but less expensive! With jet lag and excitement, I had little sleep, rising early for breakfast in my room and then setting out on a gloriously sunny, late autumn, morning. The city sparkled, and carrying nothing – not even a brief case – just a street map in my pocket, I sauntered down 5th Avenue, feeling completely free, forgetting for a few minutes that I was a business man. The traffic, though 'hooter' noisy, was not dense and the pavements were busy but not crowded. I knew that the biggest print displays were in departmental stores, but I had not checked opening hours. I decided I would visit Macey's first, took my map out, and zigzagged my way toward Broadway.

I reached Macey's at about 8.40 a.m. and imagined that the store would open, at the earliest, at 9.00 a.m. I would be happy to pass the time exploring Broadway and admiring the window displays. I was surprised to notice that Macey's window displays were more 'Oxford Street' than 'Knightsbridge' and as I turned the corner of the building,

I could see a queue snaking into the store; I joined it, went in through a single door, moved along a corridor, losing some of those in front of me as they peeled off to the right and left. I followed a group through double doors straight ahead and found myself in what appeared to be a gift department – though dust-sheets were still being pulled off the counters and units. For the first time since touching down at the airport the afternoon before, I felt a very real sense of disappointment; this was not at all how I imagined the famous Macey's would operate.

I then noticed a large board indicating the floors of departments and, seeing that the picture department was on the sixth floor, I crammed into a lift of chattering men and women and was relieved to be spewed out onto the right floor. The print display was impressive, though somewhat casual, and several of the displays were still shrouded. I found a counter with a pile of prints uncovered and while I was sifting through them, I felt a heavy hand on my shoulder, I turned around to find two security men standing there. I bade them good morning but my good will was not returned. The following dialogue (or something like it, then ensued):

'Are you a Macey employee?'

'Good gracious, no.'

'Then what are you doing?'

'Looking at the prints.'

There was a pause as the two men looked at each other. Then,

'Where are you from?'

'England.'

'How did you get into the store?'

'Through a door with a lot of other people.'

'The store does not open for another fifteen minutes.'

'Oh!' I couldn't think of anything else to say.

'This way.'

I was then marched back to the lift and only after I reassured them I was not going to run away, the heavy hand was removed from my shoulder. The lift was crowded and the melee of people fell silent when they realised I was being escorted by security men; as we shot to an upper floor, I smiled weakly back at the several pairs of eyes staring at me and was relieved when we reached our destination. I was led down corridors with offices on either side until we stopped at a door marked 'Security Director'. One of the men knocked, and I was escorted in. A bespectacled man sat behind a very large desk.

'We found this man on the sixth floor.'

There was a long pause while the Security Director gazed quizzically at me.

'Why were you in the store?'

'I came to research your picture department.'

Another silence.

'The store doesn't open for another five minutes – how did you get in?'

'I walked in with a lot of other people.'

Yet another silence. Clearly this was an unusual situation.

'You're from England?'

'Yes.'

'You must have come in the staff entrance.'

'I think I must have done.'

I detected a glimmer of a smile as Macey's Director of Security told his two guards that they could go, and I just had time to thank them for their help as they left the room, hoping that it didn't sound like sarcasm.

'Sit down please.' I did so. 'Why were you on the sixth floor?'

'I wanted to look at your prints.'

'Are you in the picture business?'

'No, not yet, but we're hoping to be.'

'And so?'

'I am over here to meet print publishers and see as many retail outlets as possible. I only arrived yesterday afternoon and as I knew that Macey's print department was one of the biggest in New York, I came here first. Seems I was too eager.' My interrogator leaned across the desk and held out his hand.

'I'm John Driscoll.'

'Richard Baldwyn.' We shook hands.

'Have you had breakfast, Mr Baldwyn?'

'Yes, but it seems a long time ago.'

He got up. 'We'll go to the canteen.'

'That's very kind of you.'

'And I'll arrange for you to have a guided tour of the store. By the way, what's your schedule?'

'I have a lunch date.'

'Where?'

'At the Pierre Hotel. But until then, I make my own schedule. This is my first trip to New York, indeed to the States, so I have plenty to see.'

'Your first trip, eh! Macey's will look after you, Mr Baldwyn. We'll see that you get to the Pierre on time. Come on. Let's go.'

And so it was: I had become a guest of honour and was submitted to a real dose of American hospitality; I was fed, given small items of merchandise as souvenirs, shown a detailed analysis of their picture department, systems, sales figures, marketing strategies, and forecasts. As I was driven back to the Pierre in a Macey limousine, I realised that I had been given practically all the data about art reproductions that I needed in less than three hours. I had allotted a week for the task!

I like New York very much indeed – as much as I dislike Los Angeles. It is a beautiful city of tremendous character and it has some of the best museums and restaurants in the world. Its theatres and galleries are exciting and its people exude surprise and vitality. If John Driscoll is still alive, I would have liked to tell him that most probably he was responsible for me falling in love with his city.

Hammersmith Hospital

'Look to your health, and if you have it, praise God, and value it next to a good conscience; for health is the second blessing we mortals are capable of, a blessing that money cannot buy.'

Isaak Walton

QUITE ONE OF THE most distressing nights of my life took place when I was in my early seventies and had been admitted to Hammersmith Hospital for an operation to remove a small cancer growth just outside my back passage. I believe it was classified as skin cancer but in view of the fact that skin cancer is usually associated with sunshine, it was difficult to understand how I had contracted such a complaint in an area never exposed to the rays of the sun. But Kim was not surprised commenting, 'Everyone thinks the sun shines out of his backside!'

It seems that surgeons are loath to use a knife so near the anus because they risk harming very delicate muscles. I had, therefore, two or three radio-active, very small rods inserted in the affected area and these would burn away the cancer. I wasn't particularly nervous since such an operation was not life-threatening; on the other hand, I was not looking forward to a week in hospital. I knew that after the operation I would be in a room on my own – not because I was a private patient (which I wasn't) – but because I would be radio-active for a few days!

I was not, however, prepared for the one night I had to spend in a general ward before I was taken for surgery in the morning. Kim and Charlotte came with me in the late afternoon to deposit me in the hospital ward, and when they left, nothing had occurred to prepare me for the night that lay ahead. Indeed, before they left, we shared a bottle of 'Bubbly' to defy what we were each thinking. I settled down to read and was aware that opposite me was an Asian gentleman who was receiving a lot of attention from the nursing staff. The two of us were curtained off in a corner of the ward and, as the evening wore on, I became aware of bells ringing, cries for help and the increasing activity around my immediate neighbour.

I soon understood that I was not a priority in terms of the nurses' attention and it was later in the evening that I realised that I was in the cancer ward. Since I left theatre work, I have never been a good sleeper (I am sure this has something to do with having to learn lines in repertory) but the night ahead turned out to be one of the worst nights of my life. It was not because I was having an operation the next day – indeed as the night wore on, I found myself looking forward to it – it was hearing, smelling and feeling the suffering that was taking place around me. There was never silence and although I could not actually see all that was going on there was for ever a bustle, a noise of buzzers and bells, groans and whispers of comfort and reassurance. And perhaps worst of all, there was a smell – or was it an atmosphere? Certainly it was related to death.

I was glad when dawn broke and natural light invaded the ward. There was greater activity around the patient opposite and soon relatives were gathered round his bed. I was glad when the trolley arrived to take me to the theatre and I found myself looking forward to the sleep that lay ahead. I had had no contact with my fellow patients in that cancer ward and so had no farewells to say.

The room in which I awoke an hour or so later, was off the passage leading out of the ward in which I had spent the previous night. It was small and apart from the bed and side table, it had no furniture. There was no chair, presumably to prevent anyone from sitting near me; I was radio-active you see, even to the doctors, nurses and visitors. There was a screen, however, behind which visitors had to stand with only their heads visible above the parapet!

Physically I felt reasonably comfortable and greatly relieved that the operation was over and done with and that I was no longer in the cancer ward. I was on my own and it seemed there was no bell to ring but, as I was comfortable, I just lay and contemplated. I noticed that my personal belongings were stacked on the locker beside me but as my bed faced the door, I could not see what kind of view I had from the window. I didn't imagine it would be uplifting – the hospital itself and the area are both rather depressing – and Holloway prison is practically next door. When I was able to look out of the window, my fears were confirmed – I looked out onto a small courtyard and another grey wall of the hospital.

A cheerful Irish nurse breezed in and seemed delighted to find me alive and well. She took no notice of the screen and chatted away about her family, her work and her boyfriend and then picked up the bell which was lying on the floor under the bed. She told me that because of the possible radio-activity, nurses and domestic staff were told not to spend unnecessary time in the room; however, she thought this was a lot of nonsense, and, indeed, I was told by a doctor just before I left the hospital at the weekend that the precautions were sensibly extreme but that the chance of any kind of radiation transference in a case such as mine was infinitesimal. And through the week it was fascinating to note the difference in the attitudes of the various nurses toward the rules, and not one of the cleaners or catering staff seemed to have any regard for the possible danger to their health; I think they liked the privacy and used it in true cockney fashion to gossip and laugh.

I had lots of visitors from family and friends and Kim drove up every day, bless her. Children and pregnant women were not allowed but, as I had none of either category around at the time, there was no problem. My visitors had a full view of me lying in bed, of course, but I had an entirely original view of them – I could only see their head and feet. I slept a lot and read a lot. Jenny had given me Ben Pimlott's biography of Harold Wilson for my seventy-first birthday the previous November and I devoured this large book by the end of the week. I was still producing audio cassettes for EMI at this time (I hadn't told the company I was having an operation), and as I was due to go into the studio with Leo McKern to read one of John Mortimer's Rumpole books in less than two weeks, so I was able to work on the script during the last two or three days in hospital.

I was dreading the removal of the stitches. As I indicated above, the area involved is very sensitive and delicate, and the thought of having stitches wrenched out was quite frightening. The rods themselves apparently dissolve completely, but when I heard the doctor's approaching steps, I felt like the condemned man being summoned for his walk to the gallows. It was all very anti-climactic, however. The doctor chatted away and I was barely aware of the deed being done. Kim fetched me in the morning and the drive home reminded me of the feelings I had at the end of term leaving boarding school – the difference being, of course, that now I had a sore bottom. I write this some twelve years after the event and can happily report that the treatment seems to have been a complete success and I can only be grateful for the care and skill that was bestowed upon me. Our national health service is so often a target for criticism and even contempt but my experience over the years has been that of a more than satisfied customer. I marvel at the dedication and tolerance of staff and thank them for it.

'To be or not to be?'

'People ask you for criticism, but they only want praise.'

Somerset Maughan

THERE IS A GUILD of Drama Adjudicators, the members of which are qualified to adjudicate three-act or one-act plays in Amateur Drama Festivals throughout the United Kingdom. There are thousands of amateur groups in the country, nearly all of which compete in the festivals. I cannot remember what qualifications one needs to become one of these VIPs but I know that in the 1960s and 1970s I was a member of the Guild. I was, and still am, an Equity member but the majority of the adjudicators are certainly not stage professionals and, looking back on those times, I don't really think I was at all well qualified for such an onerous and thankless task. However, there were highlights which I would not have missed for the world and which, I think, made up for the agonies I suffered, particularly at one-act festivals. There is a yearly booklet published listing the names of qualified adjudicators, with their addresses and telephone numbers but I still don't know how the societies or festival organisers choose their adjudicator. I suppose he or she is often chosen because the locality is nearby and that would mean lower travelling and accommodation expenses which are paid on top of the miserable fee. Obviously, there are relatively few very well known, and sometimes notorious adjudicators, who are chosen for their skills and entertainment value.

Since it is some twenty-five years since I last adjudicated, I know little of the current fashion in adjudicators. Most certainly, when I was around, one was expected to wear a dinner jacket and was usually treated like royalty. Given anything one asked for, seated in isolation with facilities for making notes during the performance, one was plied with refreshments throughout the evening and occasionally wined and dined afterwards. Very often the Mayor was present at this annual highlight but even he or she was a second-class citizen compared to the adjudicator. To ensure one was not 'got at' by one of the competitors, no one was allowed access to the Adjudicator, except the person appointed as 'guardian' before, between and after the performances. One could feel the eyes of the society's supporters drilling into the back of one's neck and if one dared to leave the auditorium to prove one's humanity by going to the loo, the file containing notes and exclamation marks was never left on the table. As efficient as the organisers usually were, they were seldom able to provide the adjudicator with a separate loo; one prayed that no one would try to engage in casual conversation while nature was taking its course, or even slip a 'tenner' into one's pocket as a token of appreciation.

To adjudicate a one-act festival, it was necessary to make notes as the play progressed and in the fifteen to twenty minutes between the first and second play, summarise notes and possibly scribble a tentative mark. The same procedure would follow between the second and third play. After the third play, the poor adjudicator would complete his notes, try to remember all the detail of the first two plays, decide the result and then signal to the organisers that he was ready to ascend the steps on to the stage. Maybe twenty minutes was allowed for all this to happen and to enable the cast of the last play to grab seats in the auditorium to hear the verdict. The groups of competitors and entourages awaiting judgment reminded me of the European Song Contest grouped backstage as the scores were announced from the different countries.

The adjudicator's task would be so much easier if, as a rule, the standard of performances was at least within reasonable boundaries – and this applies particularly to one-act festivals; but I fear that in my experience this was seldom the case. There are many excellent amateur dramatic societies but there are probably just as many abysmal ones. Those in the second category should never enter festivals but are usually the first to do so. They have a perfect right to entertain themselves, relatives and local fans with their strange ways but they should be banned from torturing adjudicators! Somebody should tell them and, as you will read, one night I did. Often one would witness an extremely good production, an average production, and an abysmal one. One always tried to be constructive but how could one give just acclamation to an exceptional production without lambasting an appalling one? There was a choice of withholding plaudits, richly deserved, or softening condemnation desperately needed. On that unfortunate evening, I had to make that choice. I shall not quote the names of plays, performers, or even the festival location because, being a coward, I do not wish to be physically assaulted again, however much I might have deserved it then.

Adjudicators are always sent scripts of the plays they are going to see several weeks before the festival. Plays chosen are part of the adjudication and obviously part of the judgement is whether or not the play is suitable for the cast tackling it. On this particular evening, I knew none of the one-act plays submitted and on reading them I decided that two of them were interesting and that their effectiveness would depend entirely on performance. The third play was so melodramatic that even the RSC would be unable to rescue it. When, on arrival at the town hall where the festival was taking place, I was given the programmes to peruse, my heart sank on reading that the melodrama was written and produced by one of the cast and I didn't need to be a fortune teller to know that he would be the leading man as well. He was. This play had a cast of six – and four of them bore the same surname; only disaster could lie ahead. It is usually unwise for an author to produce his own play – a detached director nearly always adds to the perception of the piece and can expand and interpret – but red lights flash ominously when, in addition to direction, the author is not only acting, but also casting a sizeable part of his family as well.

The play was set on a river houseboat and there were six on board. The husband and wife (in real life too) didn't get on at all well and their two children (in real life also) aged about sixteen and twelve years, were understandably rather miserable because their mother was having an affair (on board) with a handsome young man who had come along for the ride because he knew how to navigate the boat and work the locks. I cannot remember exactly who the sixth member of the cast was, but I think she was somebody like a grandmother, who philosophised and tried to cheer everyone up if things went wrong – and they did go wrong. Halfway through the play, the twelve-year-old daughter had had enough and jumped overboard. Unfortunately she could not swim and was drowned which was a shame not only for the family in the play but for the company itself and the audience – she was the only one in the cast who could act!

When the time came to adjudicate, I had no doubt about the winner; the first play had been exceptionally well produced and acted and the company had succeeded in turning a mediocre play into a thoroughly enjoyable production. My houseboat drama was the second to be performed and the third play was adequately presented. I dealt with the last play first, then the opening production and finally came to the unfortunate family on the houseboat. There really wasn't very much I could be constructive about. I pointed out as delicately as I could the dangers of authors producing their own plays, particularly when the play itself desperately needed help from outside. I fear that I warmed to the subject and remember saying that no one could blame the young daughter from drowning herself, not only because of the shenanigans on board, but also because of the production itself; it would have been far better if she had stayed on deck and the rest of the cast had jumped overboard. My remarks got a big laugh and a round of applause but on looking back I confess I feel rather ashamed.

At the gathering afterwards, however, the author-actor-producer pushed through people around me, seized hold of my lapels and shouted he was going to sue me. Officials unhanded him and he was escorted from the hall; the committee members apologised profusely and then, much to my surprise, congratulated me. It seemed that this man and his family were the scourge of local festivals and the organisers had been waiting for years for an adjudicator who would have the nerve to be cruel in order to be kind. I was relieved of course, but I doubt if my remarks had any effect.

But such tribulations are sometimes balanced by highly enjoyable evenings, usually with three-act plays. I remember with much pleasure a festival I adjudicated in Northern Ireland many years before the Troubles escalated. These were productions in Londonderry and

Portadown and the final evening was at Queen's University, Belfast, who had chosen a very difficult play – T S Eliot's *Murder in the Cathedral*. This must have been in the late 1950s, which meant I was still in my thirties. I tremble to think how I had the audacity to make public comments on stage about such a play, let alone a performance of it. Some thirty-five years later, I was to appear in this play with the Liverpool repertory company in the Anglican Cathedral and, even then, I found some of the lines and passages quite difficult to understand. (Robert Donat played Archbishop Becket in the original production some time in the 1930s and I have a cassette of his recording.) The production at Queen's University was a worthy one and I adjudged them winners of the festival.

Without any doubt, however, the greatest fun I had as an adjudicator – and why shouldn't an adjudicator have fun? – was when I toured the country adjudicating the Royal Navy's three-act drama festival. I really don't know how I came to be asked to do it but there was not a dull evening. Some of the entries didn't take themselves too seriously, but they all provided a splendid evening's entertainment. The festival was spread over several weeks and involved visits to Rosyth, in Scotland, Haverford West, in Wales, Plymouth, Portsmouth, Chatham and Greenwich. I was dined and wined in all the locations and found myself rubbing shoulders with admirals and other high-ranking officers; the navy certainly knows how to entertain its guests.

Haverford West is a Royal Naval Air Station on the south-western corner of Wales. I drove down, arriving late afternoon, finding what can only be described as a nissen hut campsite with interiors which were luxuriously furnished. Having been checked in by the guardroom, I was pointed in the direction of the Mess and no sooner had I stopped the car than the commanding officer (I cannot remember his rank) sprang from the main doors and greeted me with, 'Come in and start drinking, old boy, it's our only chance of winning.' I suppose there must be Guild rules somewhere about bribery and corruption but nothing in the world would have stopped me from accepting the CO's invitation and I have seldom met such a happy collection of young servicemen; by the time we had had dinner, I was a very happy adjudicator! Their performance of a light comedy was quite the heartiest I have ever seen on either the professional or amateur stage and was uplifted by applause, cheers and boos from an audience of all ranks, male and female. The cheers and boos were nothing to do with the characters in the play – they were reserved entirely for the individuals playing the parts – and by the end of the evening, I had more than an inkling which members of the cast were popular, unpopular, or merely tolerated. There were prolonged ovations at the end for the cast of the play, and when I stepped on to the stage having made no notes, I was given an even bigger ovation. I told them that, though I didn't think they would win the festival, they had certainly provided me – and the audience – with an evening which would never be forgotten! By bed-time I had had a lot of drink and thankfully climbed between the sheets without disgracing myself. I was given an enormous cooked breakfast in the morning and was waved off by the CO and most of his colleagues – it really had been great fun.

The climax was at the Royal Naval College, Greenwich. I had dinner in the Painted Hall, sitting on the stage with all the top brass. The performance was in the theatre and a full house saw an impressive performance of Shaw's *Major Barbara*. It was a worthy winner of a Festival which had achieved its purpose, entertaining the audiences and enabling the participants to strive and expand, to risk and, to varying degrees, succeed.

I have never regretted leaving the ranks of drama adjudicators. It was hard work with low pay and the embarrassments just outweighed the fun times. On reflection, therefore, I have to be grateful to that houseboat family for making me ponder 'to be or not to be' (a drama adjudicator), and thereby helping me to make the decision.

The Boulestin

'Conscience. The inner voice that warns us someone may
be looking.'

H L Mencken

IT WAS EXPENSIVE AND old-fashioned but it was warm and friendly.
The Boulestin Restaurant was in Southampton Street, between The
Strand and Covent Garden. It was cluttered, richly shabby in deep reds
and, of course, the food was excellent. To reach it, one entered a very
stark and cold passage, walked down stone steps, through double doors
and into its faded splendour. Kim and I became very fond of it but,
alas, it is no longer there, which, I suppose, makes the incident I am
about to relate all the more shameful.

As I write this, sitting at my desk in the study, one of my pipes is
resting in a large deep red ashtray which belonged to the Boulestin. I
stole it. I did leave a large tip on the night of the theft and I mention
it, not as justification, but as confession and hope for forgiveness. And
I must admit that I have, over the years, taken other such souvenirs
from hotels and restaurants: nothing of great value but a little something
as a memento and celebration of joy or revenge for misery.

On this occasion, some time in the late 1960s, we had had a splendid
evening and I was puffing on my cigar over coffee. I nudged my ash
into this gorgeous ashtray and commented how right it would look on
my desk at home. Kim, knowing my past sins, retorted firmly and swiftly,
'Don't you dare!' I like a challenge, and those three words seemed to
me to be exactly that. I pondered. It was summer and I was wearing a
very lightweight suit with not very large pockets and I wondered whether

or not the ashtray would fit. After Kim had left the table to visit the 'Ladies' and the waiter had taken my card to prepare the bill, I acted swiftly. I emptied the ash into a smaller ashtray, checked that neither staff nor other diners were watching, and dropped my treasure into the left-hand pocket of my jacket. It only just fitted.

When Kim returned, I stood up and the weight of the ashtray caused my left shoulder to sag. I straightened up, and, standing smartly to attention, said weakly, 'Shall we go?' We were escorted to the double doors and thanked for our custom. As we ascended the stone staircase, I quickened my pace and Kim asked me if I was feeling all right. I confessed to her that my conscience was weighing on me in the shape of a heavy ashtray in my pocket and would she please not linger. Kim was furious and insisted we return it at once. I pointed out it would be rather difficult to convince anybody that such a heavy object had slipped into my pocket accidentally. Reluctantly, Kim took the point, and we hurried out into Southampton Street, heading for Covent Garden.

We had just reached the corner when we heard a shout behind us. Neither of us was suitably kitted to make a run for it so I turned very casually, looked back, and saw, to my horror, a waiter running after us, waving. We stood frozen to the pavement. As he came near us, he seemed to be smiling. But our hearts sank; we felt sure he was looking at the considerable bulge in my left pocket and was enjoying his moment of triumph.

Suddenly he waved an arm above his head: 'Madam left these on the table,' and he graciously handed Kim her white gloves. Ashamed, Kim said 'thank you, thank you so much.' I wished fervently that they had been my gloves so that I could have offered them to the waiter as a present. As it was, I slunk back to the car and deposited my souvenir on the back seat.

But now I come to think about it I don't feel too guilty, for, after nearly thirty years, the ashtray is still in use, loved and cared for. Had the restaurant still been open, it would surely have been replaced by now and most probably thrown away when the Boulestin closed. Yes, indeed, I've cheered myself up considerably by confessing.

Dick Turpin in Bushey Park

'A mixture of a lie doth ever add pleasure.'

Francis Bacon

READERS OF MY GENERATION will remember the early days of children's television from the BBC Lime Grove Studios in Shepherds Bush. The programmes were nearly all 'live' and one of the most popular series was a sixty-minute medley programme made up of ten- to fifteen-minute slots of playlets, serials, sketches, games, jugglers, puppets etc. It was called *Whirligig* and if I recall correctly, the producer was Michael Westmore. I think *Whirligig* will be remembered principally for Annette Mills and her puppet Muffin the Mule. Annette was John Mills' sister. Sadly she died of cancer a few years after the series finished. Like her brother, she was a lovely person.

I was involved in this programme in the early 1950s both as an actor and writer and one of my contributions was a series about Dick Turpin which was to run for ten, ten-minute slots. However, the budget was tiny and I was instructed that I would only be allowed ten out of the hundred minutes for location filming. The remaining ninety minutes would be in the studio where no horses were allowed. I was blithely confident at the time but, looking back, I cannot think how I had the audacity to be confident in writing a hundred-minute script about a highwayman who did little else but mount, ride, and dismount from a horse with only one tenth of the action on location. However, the script was approved and the serial was due to go out in March. The location shots had, therefore, to be ready several weeks before. Michael decided we could comfortably complete the relatively few minutes of location shooting in one day and chose Bushey Park, close to Hampton Court, as the ideal setting. With its avenues of trees and tracks, there should be no problem with coach and horses or Dick Turpin and his steed.

February was a cold, wet month and the chosen shooting day had to be cancelled because of the foul weather. Another day was booked but the weather was even worse leaving only one possible day on which to film if the deadline for the first programme was to be met.

Prior to these happenings, Michael had asked me if I knew a suitable actor to play the part of Dick Turpin. Obviously, he needed to be a reasonably competent equestrian as well as having competent thespian skills. I remembered an actor I had worked with in Rep and seemed to recall he had regaled the company with his experiences on horseback. He was a good actor and great fun to have around so I telephoned him at his flat. Sure enough, he was there and had been 'resting' for a few weeks. Yes, he would like very much to meet Michael Westmore and, yes, I had remembered correctly, he had spent many happy hours on horseback. I told him that most of the action was in the studio but there would be these few shots of Turpin astride Black Bess, bearing down on the coach. Jack (for obvious reasons I have changed his name) assured me there would be no problem. Michael gave Jack the part and studio rehearsal proceeded splendidly. Jack was in his element and became quite the most popular member of the cast.

Our day in Bushey Park arrived. We were to meet at The Crown at eight a.m. to don costumes and admire the coach and horses. Jack had been assured that Black Bess would be relatively docile and that there was no need to meet her before the day. But fate conspired against us yet again. Bushey Park was shrouded in thick fog when we arrived, making it impossible for work to start. The BBC weather centre told us that the fog would lessen and probably lift entirely, by lunch time. We decided, therefore, to be ready in all departments so that we could spring into action the moment visibility allowed. Costumes were donned, make-up completed. Jack looked magnificent in his Turpin outfit but seemed strangely subdued. I asked him if there was anything wrong and he muttered he had never ridden a horse in thick fog before. The producer sensibly suggested that he use the time to get to know his steed and I watched Jack, the horse and its handler, cross the road into the Park. It was at this moment that the truth began to dawn on me. Not only had Jack never ridden a horse in thick fog before, quite probably he had never straddled a horse, or if he had, it had been on a donkey on the beach in Bognor.

I ran across the road and reached Jack just as he was making his third attempt to mount Black Bess. He assured the handler that it was the costume causing the difficulty. I asked him cheerfully if all was well and he chided me weakly for asking a silly question. When eventually he got into the saddle, he posed as only an actor can and was obviously disappointed that only the handler and I could see him in all his glory – he was not used to playing to such a small audience. The handler said, 'She's all yours, Jack,' and Jack's eyes widened with what was undoubtedly terror. Summoning courage, he gave Black Bess a gentle squeeze with his heels, and, to our horror, she took off into the fog. As they disappeared, we could see Jack with his arms around the horse's neck, literally clinging on for dear life – his black cloak billowing out behind him.

We ran after them into the fog, shouting as we went. But to no avail for, when we stopped for breath, we could hear nothing. Surely Jack would be shouting for help or was he lying unconscious somewhere amongst the trees? For some ten minutes we searched and then we realised the fog was lifting. We hurried on and soon the visibility was some 100 yards. To our astonishment we saw the outline of a horse quietly grazing and then, even more astonishingly, we could see Jack sitting upright in the saddle. His hat was askew and lop-sided, his costume and cloak were covered in mud. He was sweating profusely as we approached, unnoticed.

'Are you all right, Jack?'

I think he must have been asleep for he jumped visibly and then turning his head, replied, 'Perfectly. Why shouldn't I be? I just thought I would go for a little spin.'

There was silence as the handler led Jack and Black Bess back to The Crown.

The fog lifted, allowing us to start filming mid-morning. We suggested to Jack that he should only sit astride Black Bess for the static and most dramatic shots when Turpin is actually holding up the coach, communicating with the passengers and robbing them. The handler would then dress up as Turpin for the chase shots. Jack was outraged at this suggestion but reluctantly and unselfishly agreed that it would be a magnanimous gesture for the handler to be allowed to share some of the action.

And so it all ended happily as we got everything in the can as dusk fell. I often wonder if the handler was suitably rewarded for his vital contribution – we certainly could not have filmed Dick Turpin chasing the coach with his arms around Black Bess's neck. In those days, the unions were not quite as strong and I wouldn't think the handler was an Equity member. Come to think of it, Jack may not have been either.

Ditching

'Rocked in the cradle of the Deep'

Emma Hart Willard

IT WAS SEPTEMBER 1944 when the German Army was being driven northwards in Italy but were holding back the Allied advance with their almost fanatical resistance at Monte Cassino. This was the time when I was with 254 Wing at Biferno on the Adriatic coast, a few miles south of Termoli, still in German hands. We were not involved with the enemy forces in Italy but were relatively independent – The Balkan Air Force – helping Tito and his partisans to harry the Germans as they withdrew from Greece through Yugoslavia. Our war was a very personal one and our tasks required precision and timing of a very different kind to the heavy bomber raids over Germany. We encountered relatively little opposition as we knocked down river bridges, cut railway lines, attacked German convoys as they snaked through the mountains and dropped agents behind the German lines (Randolph Churchill and Fitzroy MacLean were involved and have written of these operations) and established Tito at his headquarters on the island of Vis, a few miles off the Yugoslav coast. Had we been stationed at Foggia, the base of the Allied Air Forces in Italy, we could never have broken the rules and taken the chances we did, risks essential to the kind of operations we were faced with or the kind of warfare being conducted by the partisans.

This episode, however, is not about a daredevil operation; it should have been uneventful and completed in a few hours. We were to take off mid-morning, have lunch at Vis, complete our business and be back at base before nightfall. Our Padre was coming with us to conduct the funeral of an RAF clerk and we were delivering documents to Tito. We were flying in a Ventura, cousin of the Lockheed Hudson which did such solid work for Coastal Command in the Battle of the Atlantic The Ventura was a wide-bodied, medium bomber and had plenty of room for extra personnel. Captain Shuttleworth, CO of 25 SAAF (South African Air Force) was our pilot and we took off on a grey morning into a stiff northwest cross wind which threw up the sand along which our airstrip was laid. As soon as we were airborne and had gained sufficient height, we banked eastwards over the Adriatic.

We were in clouds within two or three minutes when quite suddenly our two engines cut; there was an eerie silence and as I was sitting on the floor I pulled myself up and looked out of a small window. We were now below the low cloud and Shuttleworth was able to turn the aircraft into the wind and maintain flying speed as we lost height. I could see a very rough sea getting closer every second and when we hit the water, I was knocked head over heels down the body of the aircraft. I scrambled to my feet, aware of blood dripping from my face. The aircraft was settling very quickly and the four of us in the body of the aircraft struggled to the exit door but were unable to open it. The body and tail of the Ventura started to lift as the weight of the nose and engines tilted the aircraft deeper into the water. I realised that, if they had not been killed or injured on impact, Shuttleworth and his co-pilot would have released the canopy over the cockpit and would have been able to get out. By now the aircraft was slowly sinking deeper into the water and we were still struggling with the door when it suddenly opened. (Shuttleworth and his co-pilot had escaped, run along the outside of the body and released our door.) As one of my colleagues clambered out ahead of me, I just had time to grab the edge of the opening and haul myself up. As I climbed out, the aircraft started its slide beneath the water, closing the door on my left leg. I was wearing flying boots and, as the aircraft disappeared beneath the waves, my leg slid out of the boot and I shot to the surface. Padre Campbell and the other member of the crew were never seen again.

I could see Shuttleworth and his co-pilot a few yards away in a dinghy which had been released automatically when the door had been opened. The seas were even higher now and as neither I nor my friend had a

Mae West, we had to struggle not only to keep afloat, but to reach the dinghy. I could see Shuttleworth and the co-pilot paddling furiously with their hands and eventually we reached them and were hauled in. No one spoke as we looked back at the white horses covering our friends but there was nothing we could do for them. The dinghy's paddles had been lost in the sea and even though we were only a few miles from our base, the wind was now westerly and we were being blown eastward, toward Yugoslavia. We had no rockets or flares to fire above the low scudding clouds and though Shuttleworth had been able to alert the Wing before we hit the water, we knew nothing could be done for an immediate rescue – there were no boats of any kind at Biferno. We wondered how many hours it would take to be blown across the Adriatic and if we made land, would we find ourselves behind enemy lines? We were all very wet of course, but not cold; I was still bleeding from a cut on my chin, but it was not deep.

After about an hour, visibility improved and the wind eased but the clouds were still too low for any chance of us being spotted from the air. Suddenly Shuttleworth said, 'Listen!' We fell silent and could distinctly hear the unmistakable throb of an engine, a boat's engine, and it was getting louder but it was coming from the North. We all knew the implication. It could be German, Italian enemy or Italian friendly. We watched and waited as our dinghy was tossed and turned by the still angry sea. The noise of the engine was getting louder, competing with the howling wind, and then, as if we had directed our saviours, we saw the bows of what first looked like a large whale but turned out to be a dilapidated fishing boat heading straight for us. We were shouting and waving as the boat hit us amidships, knocking us all into the sea. We could see men leaning over the side of the boat gesticulating wildly and shrieking loud enough into the wind to reassure us that, at the very least, they were not Germans. They turned their boat towards us and still calling upon the Almighty and demanding his assistance, they hauled us one by one into their boat – they were Italian fishermen.

Never before or since, have I experienced such hospitality. The cabin was small and warm and we were wrapped in blankets and plied with food and drink. I never knew what the drink was but it was very strong. They dressed my wound and rubbed our hair with towels. Their concern and excitement was so vocal, the noise of the storm and engine faded into the background as we tried to understand what they were saying. A map was produced and they indicated they had come from Termoli, still in German hands, but they intended to take us south to Bari, many miles behind the Allied lines. They were mystified by the letters SAAF on Shuttleworth's uniform but when they saw RAF on my uniform, they actually cheered and raised their glasses in salute. Several hours later we reached Bari and they proudly escorted us to the local carabinieri and handed us over as if we were heroes. We tried to thank them but they were so busy hugging and kissing us, they never realised how much we owed them, how much we appreciated the considerable risk they had taken in delivering their official enemies into safe hands before returning to their official allies. We walked back to the quay with them and waved as they put to sea heading north into the mist. Termoli was liberated within three weeks and I had hoped to meet up again with those brave fishermen but, on the one occasion I was able to visit Termoli, they were at sea. We arrived back at Biferno late that night to a muted welcome. It was getting dark and the waves were settling into a grey swell as I walked across the airstrip and stood on the sand looking out to sea, wondering who had taken Padre Campbell's place at the funeral on the island of Vis.

All this happened on 28th September 1944. I have a waterproof membership card of The Goldfish Club, the inscription reading 'This is to certify that PO RN Baldwyn has qualified as a member of the Goldfish Club by escaping death by the use of his emergency dinghy.' It seems as if this is the equivalent of The Caterpillar Club which celebrates those who escaped death through use of their parachutes. I received the card on my return to the UK when the war ended but have had no further contact with other Goldfish Club members.

There is a postscript to these happenings however. In the autumn of 2005, sixty-one years later, Kim and I went on a cruise to the Mediterranean on the *Queen Elizabeth II*. One of the places we visited was Dubrovnik, on the Croatian coast, almost immediately opposite Biferno on the Italian coast. I particularly wanted to go ashore at Dubrovnik because we had sent Beaufighters to put rockets into the Excelsior Hotel which, we had learnt, was the German naval officers' mess. Tragically, our CO, a Wing Commander Johnston didn't pull out in time and crashed into the rocky hillside immediately behind the hotel. The Excelsior is now a very large and opulent hotel – quite the most exclusive and expensive in the town. I tried to find someone of my age who might remember this attack and maybe show me exactly where the Beaufighter had crashed. Alas no one, either in the hotel or in the town, could help.

When we arrived home, I looked out my Goldfish Club Card – 28th September was exactly the same date and month that we had landed there from the *QE2* – it had taken me sixty-one years to progress from a dinghy to one of the largest liners in the world!

Manchester

'Lighten our darkness we beseech thee O Lord; and by thy
great mercy defend us from all the perils and dangers of this
night.'

Book of Common Prayer

I HAVE HAD A soft spot for the city of Manchester for over half a
century – even though Manchester United has never been my soccer
team. However, for some strange reason, two of my grandchildren,
Sally and James, are MU fanatics, Sally even adopting the 'red' for her
wedding dress! No, I would be as content to see Manchester City achieve
the heights that MU have scaled particularly because Kevin Keegan was
once their manager before he moved to manage my team, Fulham,
nursing the club back to the premiership after years of floundering in
the lower divisions. Thanks to Harrodian Al Fayed and his money, the
club is just surviving among the giants with their huge stadia, happy
to be at Craven Cottage-on-Thames. It has to be one of the cosiest
grounds in the country with its capacity limit at approximately 21,000,
tucked away in the park overlooking the river. When first I watched
them play, I stood in the stand on the terrace which boasted the prime
position between the pitch and the river and, come March or April, if
I was bored with the soccer or couldn't bear to watch my team losing,
I could turn round and watch the boat race instead, hoping that Oxford
were pulling away. But I have diverted and must get back to Manchester.

I have many memories of that city, by far the most poignant the
one in 1958 when I was working for Paul Hamlyn, the publisher, selling
remainder books in the basement of Lewis's department store. Our

books were piled high on a square of counters, most of them selling at 2s 6d and we sold thousands every day. It was winter and we had had a long day. After throwing the dust sheets over the books, we headed for the exits on the ground floor. It was raining and through the dank darkness, I could see a large crowd around the newsvendor on the corner. There was a strange silence as I pushed my way through the throng. I saw the headline – 'United Team in Munich Air Crash. Many Dead'.

I suppose this was the foundation of my affection for the city but there are other reasons and I feel I must relate a rather unusual experience which took place only a few weeks after the Munich tragedy. Again, we had been working in Lewis's on a special sale of books and on this occasion, Bobby Hamlyn, Paul's wife, had travelled up with me to prepare the display and help behind the counters on the first day of the January Sale. We had had a gruelling day and, having booked two rooms at the Grand Hotel, we made our way across the square, looking forward to an evening of relaxation. But a mistake had been made and there was only one room available. Obviously, I deferred to Bobby but I was able to wash and change in her room and have dinner with her before setting out to find myself a bed for the night.

It was after ten o'clock as I stepped out into the rain to hail a taxi. I can't remember exactly what I said to the driver beyond saying I wanted a bed for the night. I was very tired but not too tired to be aware I was being driven out of the city centre. I made some comment but he cheerily assured me not to worry and he would see to it that I was fixed up for the night. Soon we arrived at a somewhat dreary terraced house and, as I paid him, he winked at me and bade me a very good night. I walked up the steps and rang the bell; the door was opened by a middle-aged lady who led me into a somewhat gaudily furnished sitting room and then asked me to tell her exactly what I wanted. I shrugged and told her that as I had had a meal, all I wanted was a bed and, in the morning, some breakfast. It seemed I had said something very unusual for she stared at me for several seconds and then asked me again if I was sure that was all I wanted. I reassured her, told her that the taxi driver had recommended her establishment and that I was very tired and would like to go to bed at once.

She led me up several flights of stairs and on the way she pointed out the lavatory and the bathroom before opening a door at the end of a short landing. She simply said, 'This is your room, 12a.' We exchanged 'goodnights' and I closed the door. I was in a cubicle in which there was a bed, a chair and nothing else; there was a skylight but no window. It was very cold and the bed was scantily clad. I was so very tired, I decided I must just make the best of a very bad job. I undressed and placed my old RAF overcoat over the bedclothes and got into bed expecting to fall asleep immediately. My optimism was short-lived however, for as I tried to get warm under the bedclothes and my overcoat, I became aware of some very strange noises – thumps, groans, heavy breathing and little cries; and when I felt movement next to my bed, I switched on my shadeless lamp to examine the wall, discovering it wasn't a wall but a partition. However naive it may seem, it was only at that moment I realised I was in a brothel!

I managed a weary chuckle and thinking of Bobby in the luxurious many-starred Grand Hotel, I fell asleep. I awoke several hours later as dawn penetrated the skylight. The house was silent. Exhaustion had evidently set in. I went to the basin in the bathroom, washed, shaved, returned to my room, dressed and went downstairs just after eight a.m. There was a roaring fire in the dining room and Madame, bless her, served up a superb cooked breakfast. When I came to pay the bill, she said she hoped I would find her charge reasonable. Indeed it was – even for a cubicle; I imagine she thought I might have found it excessive as, after all, I hadn't used all her services. I hadn't seen a soul except Madame and she seemed quite sad I was leaving. It was still raining as I taxied my way back to Lewis's and I realised I had slept well and had eaten a breakfast that even the Grand could not have surpassed. But I had forgotten to ask Madame for a receipt enabling me to claim expenses. But do brothels give receipts? My claim would have been far less than Bobby's but who would have believed my story?

The Princess

'A four-legged friend, a four-legged friend, he'll never let you down.'

J Brooks

I RECORDED PRINCESS ANNE (now the Princess Royal) in 1990, reading the book she had written, *Riding Through My Life*. I suppose I was indulging my own tastes in thinking that such a book could be commercially successful on tape and I was certainly influenced by Charlotte's involvement with horses. Be that as it may (the tape sold about 6000 copies – not a bad result) when I considered the idea, I didn't really think the Princess would have either the time or inclination to spend a whole day in the studio when she packs in more engagements each year than any other member of the Royal Family. You can imagine my surprise and delight when I received a phone call from her PA within a week of my letter to Buckingham Palace, telling me she would like to do it.

At that time I was using very pleasant studios, Sanders and Gordon, just off Tottenham Court Road in Gresse Street. Security carried out their usual check on the building early in the morning and the only comment they made was that there was only one loo on our studio floor and as it was likely she would want to use it at least once during the day, it could be embarrassing for the Princess to wait outside if it was already occupied. Fortunately, there was an ordinary lock on the door as well as the usual sliding bolt which the occupant slid across to show 'Engaged'. Accordingly a sign 'Not in Use' was placed on the outside of the door and the Princess was given her own key to get in and out as she pleased. She told us this procedure was a 'first' for her!

We usually allowed five or six hours recording time for a two-hour abridgement with at least one hour's break for lunch and I always liked to take the reader out to lunch, generally walking a few hundred yards down Charlotte Street to an Italian restaurant which was always busy and reasonably informal. I realised such an arrangement would not be practical on this occasion and I phoned the PA who told me she would like mineral water and mixed fruit in the studio. I ordered her requirements accordingly, adding mixed sandwiches for myself. I had been told that apart from a security man outside the studio, she would be unaccompanied.

I waited on the steps of the building in Gresse Street for her scheduled arrival at 9.15 a.m. Several policemen were there and at 9.25 a.m. the inspector told me she had just left Buckingham Palace. Within ten minutes, her car drew up and I went down the steps to greet her and introduce myself. She apologised profusely for being late and said that she had had great difficulty in getting Peter and Zara off to school. There are no lifts in the building so we walked up to the second floor and after introducing the engineer, we went through the usual pre-recording procedures and started the day's work. I'm sure she must have been nervous for most certainly she would never have spent a whole day in a studio recording and very few people read well (including professionals). I too was nervous of course, for quite different reasons, but I soon found out that I need not have been because the Princess was fun, seemed to relax very quickly and took production very well, having patently done a lot of work on the script beforehand.

Her book is certainly entertaining, covering her introduction to horses at a very early age, her years with the Garth Pony Club near Windsor (the Garth was Charlotte's pony club), her adult competition years, including of course her membership of our Equestrian Olympic Team in 1976, and subsequently her presidency of the Riding for the Disabled organisation. We had to abridge the book to a two-hour schedule which meant we had to cut some material which would have appealed to the more knowledgeable fraternity rather than the very general public at whom, for commercial reasons, the book was aimed.

During the day, we laughed a lot and had continuous discussion, sometimes about pronunciation. I remember we debated whether the 't' at the end of 'Trait' should be sounded. The Princess thought it should be – I disagreed. It turned out we were both right – sounding the t at the end is the American way. (I gave way on this one.) I had always placed the emphasis on the first e in 'equerry') – she placed it on the second. I felt I should definitely give way on this one; she had had far more to do with equerries than I and the Oxford Dictionary's entry reads 'an officer of the British Royal household who attends members of the Royal Family'. But this time, she decided to pronounce it my way and I have a feeling I may have been wrong! She also writes about the European Championships in Kiev (1973) and the stop-off in Vienna to refuel the heavily horse-laden aircraft. She worried that with such a load, they would never get off the ground 'as they taxied down the runway'. The publishers hadn't picked up that aircraft taxi to the runway and then take off down it. She was always animated in discussions and accepted corrections graciously; she seemed completely at ease with any of the studio staff she came in contact with during the day and when we had lunch together at a low table in the studio, I noticed her eyeing my sandwiches. I offered the plate to her and to my delight and dismay, she tucked into them. We talked of children, horses, houses, the countryside and many other things. It was thoroughly enjoyable.

Charlotte, our youngest daughter, was training to be a physiotherapist at the Middlesex Hospital just round the corner from the studios. She 'happened' to call in at the end of the day and I introduced her to Princess Anne; they spent at least ten minutes discussing horses and their injuries. (Charlotte of course later started her own animal physiotherapy business and horses are by far the greatest proportion of her clients.)

The Princess left us soon after 4.30 p.m. and I was telephoned by her equerry the next day to say how much she had enjoyed herself. As I edit this piece in 2006, it is fascinating to watch Zara following in her mother's stirrups. She is undoubtedly a fine rider and could well be in our 2008 Olympic squad. Her mother and her father, Captain Mark Phillips, must be very proud of her.

Will & May

'Every man high up likes to think he has done it all himself;
and the wife smiles and lets it go at that. It's our only joke.
Every woman knows that.'

J M Barrie

WILL AND MAY HORN were my great uncle and great aunt, and in a strange way I find it hard to believe that I am not writing of fictional characters. I think of others I knew at the same time – some fifty to eighty years ago – and they still live in my memory as real people. But not Will and May. They seem of a different age and were it not for the evidence, I think I could convince myself they never existed and that I was romancing. But, my God, they did exist. The evidence is irrefutable.

They lived in Welwyn Garden City for the last decades of their lives, having originally farmed the land on which the Garden City was built. Brickwall, a gaunt Victorian house, was their first home and has only recently been demolished. It stood on the A1, halfway up the long hill leading to Old Welwyn. They sold the land before the plans for the new town had been mooted, but had they known what was to happen in future decades, they would have become millionaires. However, wealth would have made scant difference to their way of life for they were simple in their tastes and were content with the Handside Lane house in which they eventually lived. 'Bramfield' still stands, as does 111 Handside Lane, the house immediately opposite in which Jack and Mitt (Mildred) Will's brother and sister lived. They are all buried in Lemsford churchyard, opposite the imposing gates of Brocket Park.

As a small boy I was terrified of Uncle Will and, even as a young teenager, I was frightened by him – with some justification. He seemed to me to be a bully, an authoritarian with little compassion. Although I never heard any suggestion he was violent to May, he did break his young cousin Lionel Harvey's elbow at a family meal. Apparently Lionel had been told that he must eat something on his plate he didn't like and to show his displeasure he put his elbows on the table. This was, it seems an unforgivable breach of family etiquette at that time and Will, probably in his late teens, struck Lionel a considerable blow, breaking his elbow. It was set inadequately and he lived with a crooked arm until he died in old age.

Will and May were first cousins but they seemed complete opposites in character; it is hard to imagine how they came together in marriage. They were Victorians; Will in the sternest sense, May in the dutiful but determined sense. He was nearly six feet tall and boasted a large belly – hardly surprising as he loved his food, and May was a wholesome and generous cook. The one compensation for staying at Bramfield, for me, was 'the table'. I didn't speak unless spoken to but that was tolerable because it gave me more time to survey the spread, anticipate and enjoy the eating without interruption. Will sat at the head of the table and carved the joints or spooned the casseroles; May sat at the opposite end of the table, confronted by an array of vegetables which she distributed on to the held-out plates. The deliciously thick gravy was the only item to which we were allowed to help ourselves and it was only at such time that my uncle seemed to take pleasure in watching other folk enjoying themselves. He was even glad to give second helpings. But even at meal times his treatment of May was embarrassing if not cruel. She was not tall, but heavy with ample breasts and, at one roast pork lunch, May was ladling the potatoes, cabbage, carrots, onions and parsnips (all home grown) on to large plates, stretching forward to reach the far dishes, when Will, in his loud gruff voice, barked down the table, 'May, take your boosies off the table!' She eased them away as gracefully as she could, showing no emotion and returned to her duties.

Will was a magistrate and a churchwarden at Lemsford Church. I wish I had been old enough to attend court when he was on the bench. His administration of justice must often have been outrageous. I remember vividly his description of some of the characters who appeared before him. Even as a small boy, I remember thanking God that I had been born neither 'working-class' nor 'a woman' before him in court for, had I been, I would certainly have been found guilty. He drove a four-seater soft-top Bull Nose Morris Cowley and commanded the highway where ever he went. Everyone else's driving was appalling and anyone appearing before him on a motoring offence needed heaven's help.

As a churchwarden at Lemsford, he read the lesson regularly; he did not have a pleasing voice, nor did he read well. He had no need to question his ability, for he was doing his duty and, if he didn't approve of the particular passage he was obliged to read, he would alter the words and, so far as I know, the vicar never protested. He was particularly outraged by any passage or word that had anything to do with sex and I remember well when he read the gospel verses about the woman 'taken in adultery', he coughed and spluttered his way through that 'wicked' word rather than let it pass his lips. (I always wonder how he allowed himself to have sex with May but they produced Bill – and Bill looked like Will – so he must have managed it at least once.)

Uncle Will always liked my elder brother Tony who was a very responsible person and destined to be a doctor. When World War II was imminent and Tony became a doctor in the RAF, he positively glowed in Will's eyes. Meanwhile, I had left school when I was sixteen and a half years old and, after a brief flirtation with Harrods, had embarked on a theatrical career. You can imagine this did not elevate me in Will's estimation. However, when I eventually donned RAF uniform (not as air crew) at least he acknowledged my presence. Thereafter, I saw very little of him. At the end of the war I returned to the theatre and, as a result, Great Uncle Will and I never had much in common. He died in 1964, aged ninety-four years.

Yet I may have judged Uncle Will too harshly. I am writing this in 2005 and, to check some dates, I made contact with Kay Rapkins, née Harvey, who is now ninety-four years old and an expert on family history. When I told her the gist of what I had written about Uncle Will, she agreed he was a frightening person but then told me a story which showed a softer side to his character. Kay had been a very senior WAAF during the early days of the war, driving RAF top brass around London.

She was visiting Bramfield and Will lent Kay the Morris. On one occasion, as she was returning it to the garage, her foot slipped off the brake on to the accelerator and the car went straight through the garage wall into the vegetable garden. This happened during Will's sacred thirty-minute rest after lunch, and the family begged Kay not to disturb him but to wait until he awoke. Kay, however, felt she must tell him straight away and entered the sleeping lion's den, woke him and told him what had happened. To her astonishment, he completely understood and even laughed. Kay was told many years afterwards that, thereafter, Will always praised Kay as the only person he had ever known who had had the guts to face up to him!

May was one of the most extraordinary women I have ever known. I wish I had been able to spend more time with her when I was older, able to appreciate the complexities of her character. When she was her more conventional self, she was sweet and kind, refusing to countenance the possibility of a darker side to a person, always optimistic and busy with good works, seemingly content with Will's character. She knew Bernard Shaw who lived nearby in Ayot Saint Lawrence and she corresponded with Lord Salisbury. Her unconventional side was shrouded in mystery, and her strange writings, some of which I have in my possession, do little to unravel the other world in which she sometimes lived. She seemed to have psychic powers, or could it be that she was schizophrenic. She spent a lot of time cooking in her old-fashioned kitchen and would always shut the door because 'I don't want to disturb you when I am talking to my friends'. I never knew who these friends were but often I would stand in the dining room and listen to Aunty May chatting away.

I remember one extraordinary incident when my mother and I were staying at Bramfield for a few days, early in the war. Tony had qualified and was working at Hillingdon Hospital and, on that particular day, he was joining us for supper. There was a Bramfield ritual that we all assembled in the drawing room to listen to the BBC six o'clock news, during which no one was allowed to speak. Tony was expected to arrive later, between seven and eight p.m. In the middle of the news, May suddenly said, 'Oh dear, poor Tony.' Will growled, 'Quiet, woman!' After the news, my mother asked May why she had said what she did but

May just smiled and said that we didn't have to worry and that Tony was all right. When he arrived, it was evident he was upset and he told us that he had had his gold watch (which my mother had given him) stolen. He had left it in his jacket pocket which he had left hanging outside the operating theatre. He added that he was fairly certain who had taken it. May was smiling as she said, 'It was just after six p.m., wasn't it?' Tony, puzzled, nodded. May went on, 'And the young man who went to your pocket wears glasses and has ginger hair.' Will did not notice Tony's expression of astonishment and muttered, 'The woman's mad – take no notice.' Tony never recovered his watch but told us that May was right about the time of the incident and the description of the person whom he Tony thought was responsible.

Will and May's son Bill, managed a rubber plantation in Malaya and when the Japanese overran that country in 1942, he and his wife Molly (also cousins) were able to reach Singapore. He succeeded in getting Molly on to a ship bound for Australia but when Singapore fell to the Japanese, there was no further news of him or his colleagues. It was not known whether they had been killed or taken prisoner. When this news reached May, she became a different person. She carried out her household duties but was sullen, silent, but when she did speak she was usually abusive to her family and friends. My mother had always been very close to her but even she could not get near the stranger May had become. It seems that even physically her face had changed and was barely recognisable. Usually kind and smiling, her face became frighteningly harsh and even cruel. Will told people not to take any notice and that it merely confirmed what he had always thought about her mental condition.

And then, one day over a year later, news came through that Bill was alive and, as a prisoner of war, was working on the Burma Road. From that moment, May returned from wherever she had been and, so far as we know, was never aware of her 'other self' during those long months. My mother told me it was as if a switch had been clicked on and off. And even when Japan surrendered and news came through that Bill had survived and was returning home, she never spoke of her 'absence' during those long months.

She died in 1959 aged eighty-seven years. Will's brother, Jack, died in 1965 aged ninety-one years and his sister Mitt died in 1974 aged ninety-two years. Bill died in the 1970s and his wife Molly in the 1980s. As I write this piece, I find it hard to believe that there is a blood line between these characters and me. Will and May would not have made good soap opera characters, precisely because they were such real people who seemed to extend boundaries of conventional behaviour. They are, quite simply, memorable.

The Wind of Change?

'Don't look back. Something may be gaining on you.'

Satchel Paige

I MUST TELL YOU of a lighter incident when I was with the RAF's 254 Wing at Biferno. I was a junior Intelligence Officer at the time and we had RAF, South African and Greek squadrons, flying fighters and light bombers. (Later, after the Italian surrender, we also had an Italian squadron.) We had but one runway that was nothing more than an air-strip, running along the upper part of a sandy beach on the Adriatic. There were nearly always cross-winds, demanding the highest skill from pilots when taking off and landing.

It was summer time and I thought it would be fun to organise a sports day; there were so many personnel on the Wing and plenty of space for track events and if enthusiasm and enterprise were forthcoming, we might procure a real discus, hammer and pole, enabling us to add field to the track events. In the event, we were only able to stage the track programme. I suppose that part of my motivation for promoting such a sports day was that I rather fancied myself as a middle distance and cross-country runner and felt that I might attain glory by winning one of the events. Inevitably, a lot of drinking went on in the Squadrons and on the Wing, and, not being a heavy drinker myself, this seemed to me to increase my chances of gold. As for the admin staff, the cooks, fitters and transport personnel, I felt confident I could deal with any challenge from those quarters.

I sought the CO's permission, obtained it and set about fixing the date and time, operations permitting. Word got round the site long before posters went up and details were circulated. One day, I was with one of the South African squadrons when a black, or 'boy' as they were then known, approached me and then said, 'Scuse, sir, can we run?' I must point out that the SAAF squadrons always had their 'boys' with them. They were servants and had no status whatsoever. They had a separate campsite and many of them spoke only a few words of English. They were all very tall and seemed perfectly content – in those days it seemed that no one disputed white supremacy. So, there I was, confronted by this tall, barefooted black man dressed only in a pair of shorts, not knowing for a moment how to reply. He came to my rescue by adding, 'Run in the Sports Day?' He looked down at me and his huge grin exposed the finest set of teeth I have ever seen. I heard myself say, 'I don't see why not.' Still grinning, he jumped in the air saluting at the same time and shouted 'That's good, sir, thank you, sir.'

The blacks had never participated in any of the Wing's entertainment. The question had never arisen. I thought it wise, therefore, to mention what had happened to Captain Shuttleworth, the CO of 25 SAAF. He was dumbfounded and irritated that a black had even dared to approach an officer with such a request. I told him I couldn't really see what harm their participation would do but was told it was out of the question. I should add that Captain Shuttleworth was a very likeable and courageous person.

Details of the date and time of the Sports Day and of the events themselves were circulated. I was disappointed that stewarding a cross-country event was proving too complicated; the longest distance, therefore was to be the three-mile race. This then was to be 'my' race and, as I was going to be busy organising throughout the afternoon, I decided that it would be the last event of the day. The afternoon went well enough and there had been no sign of any blacks trying to compete though the actual numbers of men running was disappointingly low but the reactions of the hundreds of personnel watching was hugely enthusiastic and drunkenly noisy.

My big moment came when the three-mile race was announced. I was doubly confident of my chances when I saw the shape of the nine other entrants stroll on to the field. Earlier in the afternoon, I had noticed that some thirty or forty blacks were assembled on a mound to the side of the arena, watching the proceedings. As we gathered at the start of the race, I heard a strange kind of cry, almost a war cry, and turning round saw seven tall blacks heading towards the starting line. Leading them was 'the boy' who had approached me a few days before. There was complete silence; no one knew what to do. There were three white South Africans in the line-up and they stood rooted to the ground. Outrage was in the air and I remember shouting to the starter, 'Why don't we get cracking?' Thankfully he fired the gun and off we went before there could be a 'white' protest.

We would be running twelve laps of the very approximate quarter mile circuit and I knew exactly what my tactics would be. I would run a medium pace for the first eight or nine laps noticing who, if anybody, was still with me and then decide when to quicken for the final laps. I had learnt in my school days of the mistake so many amateur distance runners make of going off too fast at the start. I was not, therefore, unduly worried when the seven blacks catapulted off the start as if running the 100 yards. 'Idiots, they'll learn,' I thought as I ran comfortably within myself. At the halfway stage, after six laps, there were two groups and I suppose, if I could be counted as a group, you could say there were three. I was at least a quarter of a lap ahead of the 'whites' but nearing half a lap behind 'the blacks'. By the eighth lap I began to wonder when the black competitors would start to ease up a bit because, by then, they were no longer in front of me but fast approaching from behind! It was when all seven of them ran past me in a pack and I found myself focussing on the soles of their bare feet disappearing yet again, that I realised I had made a terrible mistake. By the eleventh lap, I was leading my white colleagues by half a lap but that was little compensation when all seven 'boys' lapped me for a second time.

There wasn't a 'single' winner, because all seven of the blacks, crossed the line as they had started – in a group. I was an uncomfortable eighth, well and truly hoist by my own petard. The blacks on the mound exploded with joy at the finish and the 25 Squadron 'whites', hesitated, but then applauded when they saw Shuttleworth clapping – after all, the blacks did belong to 25 SAAF. Shuttleworth bought me a drink in the bar later. 'Well organised, Baldwyn,' he said 'you must do it again some time.' Could this have been the first gentle gust of 'The Wind of Change'?

Salad Days

'There's no business like show business.'

Irving Berlin

OUR ROYAL FAMILY IS not noted for its great love of the theatre, particularly drama. However, the *Royal Variety Show* at the London Palladium was always an evening when the Monarch occupied the Royal Box and, with the advent of television, this annual event became a leading contender for the 'ratings battle' between the BBC and ITV, who were allocated the rights for transmission on alternate years. Occasionally, members of the family attended performances of musicals and plays unannounced and, of course, our present Queen and her sister Princess Margaret enjoyed participating in pantomimes at Windsor Castle.

Prince Charles played in revues at Cambridge University and he had a great affection for The Goons, particularly Spike Milligan. Prince Edward has always been involved in the theatre and even worked for Andrew Lloyd Webber in an administrative capacity for the Really Useful Company. The last member of the Royal Family who demonstrated her love for all kinds of theatre was Queen Mary who would insist on seeing all kinds of plays, particularly controversial ones.

Those were the days, of course, when the Lord Chamberlain licensed plays to be performed in public and would often ban those that he thought unsuitable for public consumption. As a result there were several small 'club' theatres which were not open to the general public and did not, therefore, need the Lord Chamberlain's licence to mount controversial productions. Once such play (early in the 1950s) *Pick Up Girl* by Elsa Shelley, opened at the New Lyndsey Theatre in Notting

Hill. It was a play about prostitution; well written and a compelling drama, it was hailed by the critics as a worthy piece of theatre and arrangements were made for it to transfer to a larger theatre in the West End when its run at the New Lyndsey finished. However, the Lord Chamberlain stepped in and banned it because he considered that prostitution was not a suitable subject to be aired before the general public.

To the astonishment of management and cast at this little theatre in Notting Hill, Queen Mary (she had been the Queen Mother since her son George VI came to the throne in 1936) booked two seats for an evening performance. She arrived unannounced and, at the end, left unannounced. Two days later, the Lord Chamberlain lifted the ban on *Pick Up Girl* and the play duly transferred to the West End and enjoyed a successful run. I would love to know what Queen Mary had said to the Lord Chamberlain.

And I remember so well going to see *Annie Get Your Gun* at the London Coliseum. This musical was the second huge American smash hit to come to London after the war – *Oklahoma* at Drury Lane being the first. I was in the upper circle waiting for the overture when the audience stirred, rose to its feet and cheered as Queen Mary, a tall, regal, majestic figure, by now in her eighties, entered the Royal Box, acknowledged the ovation with a slight movement of her head, and sat down to watch the performance. And how she enjoyed it! At the end of the performance, she too rose from her seat to applaud.

Only two or three years later, I found myself in a theatre with her grand-daughter. It was a summer evening and our American friends, Harry and Alice Behn, from Greenwich, Connecticut, were visiting this country. Harry was not only a greatly respected poet and writer of children's books but also a crusader for the rights of the few remaining Red Indians still living in the USA. He had spent a lot of time researching their history and was outraged at the way they had been treated.

Harry and Alice were anglophiles, and, though proud Americans, they deplored any Americanisation of this country. Harry in particular, sought antiquity and gloried in our history and institutions. They were both ardent monarchists and excited that we had recently crowned a young queen but sad that on this visit there were no state occasions at which they could at least have caught a glimpse of her. Peggy and I had arranged to take them to the theatre on their last evening before they returned to the States and we chose a very intimate British musical by Dorothy Reynolds and Julian Slade called *Salad Days*. With a small cast of six and only a piano for accompaniment (played by the composer) it had originated at The Bristol Old Vic and was an immediate success when it transferred to the tiny Vaudeville theatre in The Strand. Another very British musical *The Boyfriend* was still running at Wyndhams Theatre.

We ate at a small restaurant near the theatre and took our seats some ten minutes before curtain up. There are less than a dozen rows in the Vaudeville circle and we had been able to book third row centre seats. It was a full house and, as the minutes ticked by, there were only four seats empty and these were immediately in front of us in the second row. A few seconds before the house-lights were due to go down, a small group was ushered down the side aisle, stopped at the end of the second row and I heard a quiet voice say, 'Please make way for Her Majesty.' Harry was reading his programme at the time and neither heard what had been said nor noticed the four people moving to their seats immediately in front of us. As they sat down, Alice whispered to Harry, 'It's the Queen.' Harry excitedly said, 'Where?' Alice pointed, practically poking the young Elizabeth in the back of the neck. As the circle audience realised who had come in, it rose to its feet and, as Harry comprehended what was happening, he rose to his feet just as everyone else was sitting down. Alice hauled him down as the lights dimmed and the curtain went up.

To his dying day, some twenty years later, Harry never knew what *Salad Days* was about. He didn't really mind because instead, he knew a great deal about Elizabeth II and her husband, Prince Philip, particularly the backs of their heads. He wondered if any American before him had spent nearly three hours in such close proximity to a British Sovereign! I doubt it.

Salad Days, indeed.

Guildford Rep

'The plot thickens.'

George Villiers

I WAS ACTING IN weekly repertory at Guildford in the late 1940s and the theatre was really a hall in North Street, opposite the police station. The theatre was run by brothers Roger Winton and Pat Henderson. Their mother, Mrs Henderson, had charge of the box office and supervised the refreshments in a large room above the foyer.

Such companies were wonderful training grounds for actors, even though working conditions would not be tolerated by Equity today. Salaries were low, hours were long, and dressing rooms inadequate – but of course the opportunities for actors were considerable with a huge range of parts in the different plays (not to mention pantomime) demanding skills that most of us were still trying to acquire. We did our best, and sometimes our best was good. The audiences loved to see 'their' actors in different roles week after week and sometimes almost resented guest actors who were imported from time to time for special productions. Before I joined the Guildford Company, I had worked at the Playhouse, Amersham, which seated only 120 people. There, we played nightly from Tuesday to Friday with three performances on Saturday at 2.30 p.m., 6.00 p.m. and 8.30 p.m. The Amersham Company, run by Sally Latimer and Caryl Jenner, eventually worked out a system with Guildford whereby each company exchanged venues after a week, enabling the plays to run for two weeks instead of one. A play ran its first week at Guildford, transferring to Amersham for the second week – and, of course, vice versa. This arrangement made a big difference to quality of production, giving actors twice as long to learn their lines and rehearse. Sadly, both venues closed during the 1950s. The advance of television weaned the general public away from regular visits to the theatre and, by the 1960s, the repertory movement had dwindled from over 150 companies up and down the country, to a mere dozen or so. There were still a few 'summer seasons' in seaside resorts but even those faded over the years. The little Playhouse at Amersham is now auction rooms but Guildford boasts the attractive Yvonne Arnaud Theatre (I am a founder member) built by the river and visited by touring companies, often prior to, or following on from, West End runs.

But in the days I write of, it was very much a family environment. There was always tension, trauma, excitement and a lot of laughter. There were young pros, old pros – and an odd student assisting the Stage Manager and playing small parts when required. There was drama, comedy and farce off stage as well as on it, and though at times there was bitchiness, there was generally great loyalty to the company and its members. Inevitably there were those characters that delighted in playing tricks on their colleagues – usually during the performance of a play.

I remember one such occasion when we were performing a play by Patrick Hastings and his wife, called *The Blind Goddess*. The middle act was played out in a courtroom (in those days plays were usually written in three acts). I was playing the prosecuting counsel and was on my feet for most of the act. The judge was being played by a very good actor, Robbie Jarvis, but we had all learnt to be wary of Robbie on stage because he was renowned for his sometimes Machiavellian chicanery. None of us enjoyed learning lines, especially as we had less than two weeks in which to learn them. I had always been a lazy learner and, to my discredit and at my colleagues' expense, I often paraphrased – which meant I was not always giving the right cue. On this occasion, realising that barristers often have their papers in their hands as they cross-examine, I decided not to learn my second act lines at all; I would have my script in my hand as I addressed the court.

It worked perfectly. Even the producer was not aware of what I was doing and I felt confident and convincing, as a good barrister should. On Friday nights the house was usually full and this always helped the adrenalin to flow. I was in the middle of my cross examination of the young man in the witness box and had asked the question at the bottom of the page. As the answer was given, I flicked over the paper and too late I heard myself asking a question which was totally unrelated to the previous question and to the witness in the box. I looked down at my script again and realised that several pages were missing. The wretched actor being cross-examined (who happened to be a guest artiste) stared at me, totally bewildered.

I heard the judge (Robbie) saying, 'Mr Meredith, is anything the matter? If not, pray continue with your cross examination.'

I looked across at Robbie on the other side of the stage and could see a gleam of mischief in his eyes and knew at once where my missing pages lay. I replied, 'My Lord, may I have a word with you?'

Robbie tutted and muttered, 'Highly improper but yes, if you must.'

As I walked across the stage, the rest of the cast were thinking we had gone mad, but fortunately the audience was oblivious to the play within the play. I reached Robbie and, with my back to the audience whispered, 'Give me my pages back.'

Robbie replied, 'Speak up, Mr Meredith, you know very well I am a little deaf.'

'Give me my pages back,' I repeated.

'You're wasting the court's time, Mr Meredith.'

'If you don't give them to me at once, I shall walk off the stage.'

Robbie lowered his voice for the first time, 'You wouldn't dare.'

'I would and I will. You're in charge of this court.'

Because I was standing between Robbie and the audience, he was able to pass the missing pages to me with only the jury, court officials and the witness privy to the transaction and, as I walked back to continue my cross examination, the judge thundered at me, 'For heaven's sake get on with it, Mr Meredith. You've been wasting the court's time. I shall not forget this.'

'No, my Lord, neither shall I.'

I won my case as scripted in the play and in the second interval I was able to tell my colleagues what had happened and to reassure them that I had not gone completely mad. I suppose I should have been grateful to Robbie because he had taught me a lesson. Always learn your lines.

George VI

'I think the King is but a man
As I am; the violet smells to him
As it doth to me.'

William Shakespeare

GEORGE VI WAS A good man, a family man, whose only ambition was to do his duty as a Prince of the Royal Family. He served in the Royal Navy during the First World War and thereafter had a particular interest in the country's youth. As Duke of York, he found many of his public duties arduous and sometimes embarrassing, for he had a marked stammer of speech. When his brother, Edward, abdicated from the throne less than a year after their father George V had died, this shy young man was proclaimed George VI. He was totally unprepared for such unexpected responsibility to be thrust upon him and there were many who thought that his succession marked the beginning of the end for monarchy in this country.

His wife Elizabeth, was a strong consort (she died in 2003, in her 101st year) and a devoted wife and mother of her two daughters – Elizabeth, our present Queen, and Margaret. She did not hide her anger with Edward, her brother in law, for causing such a burden to fall upon her husband, but made her determination clear that the new Royal Family would set an example to the country and prove worthy of the duties which they had so suddenly inherited.

The new King and Queen very quickly earned the respect of the nation, and when war came they stayed in London, sharing the dangers of air raids and walking in the rubble among those who had lost their homes and loved ones in the blitz. The King broadcast to the nation regularly, despite his speech impediment, and, with the Queen, worked tirelessly to further the war effort. He asked Churchill and Eisenhower for permission to take part in the D-Day landings in Normandy but was obviously refused for security reasons alone. Churchill had made the same request to Eisenhower and was apparently very angry when he too was disallowed.

During the difficult economic years after the war, the King continued to work tirelessly for his country, but he was a sick man. His people were unaware of his ill health, although the photographs of him at London Airport waving goodbye to Princess Elizabeth and Prince Philip embarking on their visit to Africa and Australia, showed how ill he was. When, only a few days later, he died peacefully in his sleep at Sandringham, the nation was shocked. It was 1952 and he was still in his fifties. People of all classes had come to respect and even love him because they recognised that this quiet, courageous man had in reality worked and died for his country.

I was acting in a play at the New Lindsay Theatre in Notting Hill at the time and I remember feeling a sense of loss when I heard of his death; I wanted to pay my respects to him. His body was to be brought from Sandringham to Kings Cross by train and would lie in state in Westminster Hall for three days. He would be taken on a gun carriage from Kings Cross to Westminster. I waited in Kingsway just outside Holborn Underground station and, as the small procession passed by, there was silence. Only the seemingly muffled tread of the soldiers pulling their monarch could be heard.

The next day I queued outside Westminster Hall among thousands of silent people, anxious to say 'thank you' and 'farewell' to our King. Westminster Hall is a dramatic enough setting in its usual empty state but when a King lies in his coffin, with his crown, still and golden on the draped royal standard and four Guards officers standing, with heads bowed, hands resting on their swords pointing to the ground, lit only by four candles, the atmosphere is almost unbearably poignant. The silence is deafening, only relieved by the gentle sound of hundreds of shuffling feet as the people move slowly through the Hall.

On the day of the funeral, I took up my position on the south side of the Mall, immediately opposite Marlborough House where the old Queen Mother, now the Dowager Queen Mother, lived. For this state occasion there was a much longer procession and huge crowds lined the route. The pace was slower and the Queen and the other members of the Royal Family followed the gun carriage in sombre black Daimler limousines. As the coffin passed the spot where I was standing, I looked up at Marlborough House and there, tall and upright, standing in the casement windows, was the old Queen Mary, waving farewell to her son with a white handkerchief. She moved away from the window as the cortège moved down the Mall.

The Great Escape

'If all else fails, immortality can always be assured by a
spectacular error.'

J K Galbraith

I REMEMBER ANOTHER ADVENTURE when I was involved with
the children's television programme *Whirligig*, which I have already
written about. On this occasion I was acting in a serial with Robert
Harbin, a magician. Also in the cast were John Le Mesurer and Hattie
Jacques – in those days relatively unknown. I cannot remember the exact
plot, but I know it involved dangerous criminals from a foreign country
who planned to capture and kill a top government scientist, played by
Harbin. Being an escapologist, the plot arranged for him to be captured
almost every episode so that he would be seen frantically trying to escape
from desperate situations as each episode ended. I recall he was once
chained to a ring on the floor of a six-foot tank being filled with water
as the credits rolled. By the end of the episode, he was beneath the
water, struggling to free himself. Children had to wait until the next
afternoon to find out whether or not he survived. He always did, of
course!

For this adventure, the gang had captured Harbin yet again, and
had condemned him to die by chaining him to a railway line a few
minutes before an express train was due to pass. I was playing the
part of one of Harbin's many assistants and we were all looking
forward to a day in the country for the shooting of the action on a
disused railway line in Kent. All Harbin's assistants were being made
to stand on the embankment to witness his demise – in the hope

that we would then be persuaded to give away the secrets rather than suffer the same fate.

We shot our scenes in the morning, retiring to the village pub before returning to the scene of the crime to witness Harbin's execution. We stood behind the cameras watching the crooks marching him to the track, then chaining him, spread-eagled across the line. (Obviously the shots of the express train approaching would be taken from the film library.) There had been two or three takes up to the point of the crooks walking from the track when, to everyone's horror, a distant train whistle was heard. We saw Robert move his head, and were conscious of a weird whining sound which seemed to be coming from the track. The lines were vibrating! The cameras were not rolling of course but Harbin executed his escape procedure in record time. He was unchained and standing erect within thirty seconds, whereas on camera, he would wrestle and writhe for nearly two minutes, rolling out of the path of the express with seconds to spare.

We heard Robert say to Michael Westmore, 'For Christ's sake, I thought this was a disused line.' One of the locals standing nearby said, 'Tis. But it's still attached to the main line round the corner. You can feel the vibration for miles when an express goes by. Safe enough though. Points are all rusted up.'

There was silence all round, and then Robert Harbin was duly chained up again. In due course, the cameras rolled and shooting was completed. Travelling back to London in the coach, we chuckled over the day's events, though I don't think our magician was particularly amused. I am sure he had never before completed his escape routine so quickly.

The Sphinx (Algiers)

'The awful thing is that beauty is mysterious as well as
terrible. God and Devil are both fighting there, and the
battlefield is the heart of man.'

Fador Dostoevsky

MANY MEMORABLE MOMENTS OCCUR when least expected. I write
of sudden emotion, a spontaneous reaction to an event, of being
surprised by joy or struck by sorrow. There is a chemistry which, in
the passing of a second will bring a tear to the eye, a colour to the
cheek, warmth or a chill to the heart. Happiness and sadness spread
themselves out to embrace, they linger to unfold over a meaningful
period of time. But 'moments' are unexpected and can only happen
without introduction. They come and go unannounced but they leave
their mark, always to be remembered. And so often the backdrop is
of little importance – even mundane, highlighting the fleeting 'moment'
all the more. Let me tell you of such an occasion.

It occurred during the war, after I had been posted to North Africa,
in 1943. I was an ordinary aircraftsman at the time and we were
stationed at the Allied Headquarters in Algiers. A few weeks after
we arrived, I was commissioned Pilot Officer in Intelligence, working
for Air Commodore Woolley at the St George's Hotel – General
Eisenhower's headquarters. By far the largest contingent of personnel
was American soldiers but the Royal Navy was prominent and a
smaller number from the British Army and RAF. The 8th British Army
was pushing the Germans westward from Egypt and Libya, whilst
the largely American 1st Army pushed east from Algiers. The two

armies were to meet in Tunisia following the German surrender in North Africa.

Algiers was, of course, a French city and there were a relatively small number of Free French troops at this time. The city had always been vibrant and now, with the presence of so many military personnel from different services and countries, it was inevitable there would be tensions and clashes of opinion from the upper echelons as to how to deal with such problems. Officers from each of the services were given security and control duties outside their normal specialist role and such arrangements seemed to work surprisingly well.

One of the major problems that had to be faced was the prevalence of venereal disease, particularly amongst the American Forces. There were many brothels in the city, doing a thriving trade with servicemen far away from home. The British military were sensible enough to recognise this inevitability and decided to make all brothels 'out of bounds' except one – The Sphinx – which would be vetted by the medics and policed by officers from each of the services. Madame recognised both the wisdom and benefits from such a proposal, and co-operated fully. The medics checked all the prostitutes every week to ensure they were 'clean'. The Americans took no such action, allowing their men to visit brothels of their choice and, as a result, their VD rate rocketed.

The British Army even recognised that officers were as human as 'other ranks' vis à vis sexual activity but realised that it would be embarrassing at the very least for an officer to meet up with his NCO or 'other rank' in the queue for the Sphinx's wares. This was duly avoided by allowing other ranks access six hours during the day and officers three hours in the evening; the same prostitutes serving both!

Imagine my astonishment then when, after only a few days as an RAF Officer, I was told that once a week, accompanied by another officer from either the Navy or the Army, my duties would include a visit to the Sphinx during the day, to ensure that there was propriety and goodwill. I was extremely nervous but was calmed somewhat when I met my first duty colleague – a plump army officer – when he extended his hand and said, 'Major Alsop's the name. Makes a change, doesn't it?'

It did. I enjoyed my visits to the Sphinx and it was interesting to note the reactions of one's colleagues to what generally turned out to be a social event. It seems that there was one young army lieutenant who asked to be excused Sphinx duty on compassionate grounds. His plea was turned down; perhaps his moral fibre was being questioned! I suppose I must have had five or six duties altogether and it certainly helped to share visits with a colleague who had a sense of humour. The place was in the kasbah and, once inside the heavy rather intimidating doors, a large entrance hall lined with sofas suggested a slightly faded country house hotel. But Madam always advanced to greet her visitors with enthusiasm and there was little doubt she came from the city. Algerian, large in stature, expansive in temperament, she seemed the perfect hostess. She proudly introduced us to the girls who were not engaged at that moment, then offered us coffee. Not once during my visits was there any trouble and the girls seemed friendly and polite. Often they greeted their young clients warmly, undoubtedly having met them before, but it was Madame who injected the calm, even dignity, into the proceedings. There was a strong and quite extraordinary respect shown to her; it was not difficult to understand why as we sat and chatted about the war and the world in general.

And then one morning when I was accompanied by another army officer and we were sitting having a coffee with Madame, a young sailor came in and stood nervously inside the door. Madame got up and walked over to him. He whispered to her and they moved into another room. A minute or two elapsed and then Madame emerged, sobbing, with the young sailor immediately behind her. She walked over to the girls, spoke to them in French, and they all got up, running upstairs, some of them crying. We had not understood what Madam had said to the girls but she came back to us and apologised for showing such emotion. She then turned to the servicemen who had been sitting with the girls and said, 'I am sorry but you must go now. We are closing for the rest of the day.' The men duly got up and left; my colleague and I wondered what the hell was going on. Madame then went upstairs and over the next half hour or so, soldiers, sailors and airmen came down the stairs and left the building. Only the young sailor remained, sitting silently on the other side of the hall.

When Madame came down the stairs, she walked over to the sailor, took his hand, brought him over to us and we were introduced. She told us he had brought some terrible news – a friend of his, another sailor who often visited the Sphinx, had been killed in an accident on his ship. I can remember her saying, 'He was only a little boy – just learning.'

The young sailor left and we asked if there was anything we could do. Madame thanked us as she placed the large key in the door to let us out and we walked away through the kasbah, pondering on Madame and her girls in an empty brothel, mourning the death of one of their clients – a young boy from the Royal Navy. This had been a moment of surprise and sadness, yet one of warmth, never to be forgotten.

Wilson

'There are three classes which need sanctuary more than others – birds, wildflowers and Prime Ministers.'

Stanley Baldwin

IN 1977, YORKSHIRE TELEVISION produced a series of twelve episodes of *A Prime Minister On Prime Ministers*, written and narrated by Harold Wilson who had left Downing Street the year before, having been the longest-serving peace-time prime minister in the twentieth century. He had sat on the front benches either in government or opposition, for nearly thirty years and in 1940 had become a member of Churchill's Cabinet Secretariat – a national government had been formed when Neville Chamberlain resigned in 1940. At the age of thirty-one years, he was appointed President of the Board of Trade in Attlee's 1945 government. His sudden resignation from the premiership in 1976 astonished everyone. Rumours abounded, including suggestions that he had been involved in a serious national security crisis but they were all discounted. As his biographer Ben Pimlott writes, 'In short, the conspiracy theories that have been designed to solve what some have seen as the riddle of Wilson's early retirement, do not add up. The straightforward explanation for his departure, that he left because he had lost the desire to carry on, requires no amplification.'

When I saw Wilson's television series and subsequently read the published book later that year, I decided to try and contact him to ask him if he would consider recording extracts for the Listen for Pleasure audio book series. I had never before included a political title in the catalogue, but as I had always admired Wilson and had greatly enjoyed the series,

I went ahead and set up a meeting with him in his room overlooking the Thames at Westminster. He was, of course, still an MP.

I then wrote to him, pointing our that we would only be able to include two of the twelve prime ministers broadcast on television, since the time factor on the cassettes allowed only that number. Jigga Dunn and I subsequently went along and found him a very relaxed person to talk with and we started by discussing which two prime ministers he was going to select. In his television series, he had included the younger Pitt, Sir Robert Peel, Palmerston, Disraeli, Gladstone, Lloyd George, Stanley Baldwin, Ramsay Macdonald, Neville Chamberlain, Winston Churchill, Clement Attlee and Harold Macmillan. I had expected him to choose at least one recent Labour PM and perhaps a nineteenth-century premier. However, I was not too surprised by his first choice – Churchill – since he had worked with him in the war. I knew also that he admired him enormously, not only as a great war leader, orator, author, statesman and politician, but also as a great parliamentarian. Indeed, as Prime Minister, Wilson ended his tribute to Churchill in the House of Commons the day after his death, with the words, 'Each of us has his own memory, for in the tumultuous diapason of a world's tributes, all of us here at least know the epitaph he would have chosen for himself – 'He was a good House of Commons man.' But I was astounded by his second choice. 'It has to be Macmillan,' he said quietly. He could see my surprise and went on, 'He was the last of his kind – a diplomat and a gentleman.' It was certainly an interesting selection. Wilson, from a Yorkshire, working-class background, choosing two Tory aristocrats!

He came down to our Hayes studio for the recording and we really did have a 'fun' day. He read extremely well, questioned his own delivery and always took direction without demur. During the morning we were interrupted on one occasion by a phone call for him from his private secretary, Marcia Williams, asking him for instructions as to how she should deal with the press over his support for Jeremy Thorpe – whose name was linked to a mysterious dog shooting incident and who was to be accused of attempting to murder a homosexual model, Norman Scott. When we offered to leave the studio, he ignored our offer and berated the caller for interrupting the recording!

Wilson also turned out to be a very good mimic. He was writing about Churchill's very difficult relationship with de Gaulle during the war. French gold, owned by the Banque de France and held on 'customer's account', was in the vaults of the Bank of England. It did not belong to the French government and when de Gaulle asked for it, the bank rightly refused to release it. De Gaulle appealed to Churchill and the story has it that, in his impeccable but excruciatingly anglicised French, Churchill replied, 'Mon cher General, quand je me trouve enface de la vieille dame de Threadneedle Street, je suis fait impotent.' When Wilson reached this point, he asked if he could do his Churchill impersonation rather than just read it. I agreed, of course, and it really was an excellent impersonation. Wilson wrote that Churchill should probably have said 'impuissant' rather than 'impotent', but he wrote down the story as it had always been told. Churchill admired de Gaulle nevertheless. However, midst all the massive burdens he had to shoulder during the war, he once declared, 'The only cross I have to bear is the cross of Lorraine.'

I had asked Wilson if he would mind some of the staff joining us for a buffet lunch during the break. I think he always enjoyed having an audience and he was relaxed and happy telling jokes and stories about his political peers between puffing at his pipe and eating sandwiches.

He talked of his relationship with Churchill and how he and Aneuran Bevan had been approached by him after they had resigned from Attlee's government over the arms policy in 1951. Winston (in opposition at the time) expressed his sympathy, adding that he had been in a similar position several times. Later that evening, Brenden Bracken brought Wilson a message from Churchill, asking him to convey his sympathies and understanding to his wife because he recalled on how many occasions in his career, his actions had caused suffering to Clementine, his wife. When Wilson got home at one a.m. and conveyed this message to Mary, she burst into tears of gratitude and asked him to thank 'the old boy' for his message. The next morning, Wilson carried out his assignment and related that tears flooded down Churchill's face – apparently not a rare event. When Wilson returned home the following morning at two a.m., Mary, still awake, asked if he had passed on her message. On telling her what had occurred, Wilson recounted that once again she burst into tears and he was moved to say that whereas two days earlier he had been a Minister of the Crown, red box and all, now he was reduced to the position of a messenger between her and Winston Churchill – each of whom burst into tears on receipt of a message from the other! One is tempted to intone, 'Those were the days.'

Few dispute Wilson was a brilliant politician and he certainly had a considerable popular and affectionate following – yet he was often vilified by groups of MPs from all the parties. He was certainly an enigmatic personality but always a very private man; a family man too. He retired to his small home on the Scilly Isles and died of Alzheimer's disease in 1995. And that is where he lies. I cannot but note that his hero, Winston Churchill, also lies buried in a simple grave in the village churchyard of Bladon in Oxfordshire. Go to either churchyard and you will have to search for where they lie.

Chinnor – 30th November 2003

'Music, when soft voices die, vibrates in the memory.'

Shelley

THE 30TH NOVEMBER 2003, a Sunday, was a memorable day. Not only was it St Andrew's Day – and Chinnor Church is St Andrew's – but it was also the day on which the organ, originally installed by my grandfather, the Reverend Leonard Baldwyn, in 1908, was to be rededicated after extensive work and reconstruction had been completed.

It was due to my grandfather's energy, enthusiasm and love of music that the organ was installed and, until his retirement in 1934, he played his beloved instrument not only for services but also for his own pleasure. As a small boy I remember lying in bed on winter nights, listening to his music as it reached the rectory through the wind-blown trees. The fine oak case around the organ remains to this day and it seems that he himself paid for a major part of the project. I am told that his vision and motivation in commissioning an organ worthy of the church has left an indelible stamp on the services of the present day, different though they may be.

J J Binns was the original builder and they carried out a simple refurbishment in 1953. By 1971, the organ was in danger of becoming unplayable and it was only thanks to the church organist, John Ewens – who tragically died just before the recent rededication – that it survived and was extensively rebuilt in 1973. However, thirty years later, it became evident first to the organist, then to the choir and even the congregation, that all was not well. It seems that the one and a quarter miles of lead tubes carrying the air to the pipes were leaking profusely and various other working parts were proving increasingly unreliable.

Once more John Ewens masterminded the rebuilding of the organ. He negotiated and agreed the details with the organ builders, Foster-Waite of Newbury, and proceeded to build up an organ fund which had reached almost half of the required sum at the time of his death. To quote from notes on the history of the organ, 'The rebuilt organ is very much John's organ, just as the original vision was that of Leonard Baldwyn.'

Elsewhere I have written about the family graves and how, quite inevitably because they are situated in a corner of the churchyard no longer cared for, they have become completely overgrown – and how from time to time, Phillip and Julian have helped me to clear a path through the wilderness and then scythe, mow, saw and fork grass, branches, brambles and nettles to expose the graves to the light of day. On 15th November 2003, Jenny and Sally joined me to prepare the graves for the rededication of the organ at the end of the month. They were wonderful and we left Chinnor knowing a job had been well done. Phillip would have joined us but work commitments prevented him from doing so.

Sunday, 30th November 2003, was a beautiful day with a radiant sun in a blue sky and the weather pleasantly mild. We arrived at St Andrew's at 9.40 a.m. and the six church bells bade us welcome. Kim and I took our seats in one of the front pews on the south side of the aisle, very near to the stained glass window in memory of Gampy. Jenny, Phillip and Sally, followed by Charlotte and Michael, then arrived and sat in the pew immediately behind us. Sitting there was Gampy's grandson, two great grand-daughters, a great, great grandson and a great, great grand-daughter. Gampy and Madre would have been so pleased.

I had been asked by Mike Laing-Smith, the present Rector, to read the second lesson which, for the first Sunday in Advent, was St Paul's Epistle to the Thessalonians, Chapter 3, verses 9 to 13. In itself, not a particularly dramatic lesson to read, but it was a somewhat emotional occasion for me since the last time I had confronted the St Andrew's congregation was as a choirboy some seventy years before.

The service was a family communion, and the Archdeacon of Oxford, the Rev John Morrison, preached the sermon and re-dedicated the organ.

I took Communion – the first time for many years, and of course, the first time at Chinnor – while Kim and Charlotte came to the altar rail for a blessing. Mike Laing spoke of my grandfather and told the large congregation of the family's presence. It was a warm and uplifting service and, toward the end, children became involved – which of course, reminded me of my grandmother and her somewhat disciplined control of the Sunday School. Refreshments were served at the west end of the church and we then visited the graves. I think we were all moved but happy to have participated in this celebration and rededication. Such an occasion will, I think, forever be part of our psyches.

Kim and I returned home to Bray, had lunch, relaxed, changed into less formal clothes and returned to Chinnor for a gathering in the church at six p.m. It was, of course, dark, and memories of the rectory and its shadowy grounds came flooding back. Lamps and pipe smoke, the cellar and the conservatories, the long hall and winding staircase, Kate the cook, Elsie the maid, and 'Willum' the gardener – and so many family occasions which I have written about elsewhere.

There was a talk about the organ by Tony Foster-Waite and then a recital by Keith Hearnshaw, a talented young professional organist whose personality reminded me of Nigel Kennedy, the violinist. There was a large audience and we met people who remembered my grandfather and grandmother. There was one lady who had been christened by him and we sat with her during the recital, and in the interval exchanged notes about folk we both remembered in our childhood. She was kind enough to send us copies of photographs of these long-gone times – photographs I had never seen before.

How lucky we are to be part of such history and to be able to visit our own very personal past and make a small contribution to the memories of future generations. I was reminded of a Chinese proverb – 'To forget one's ancestors is to be a brook without a source, a tree without a root.'

Memory

'Someone said that God gave us memory so that we might
have roses in December.'

J M Barrie

I LIKE NEW YORK as much as I dislike Los Angeles and, after my first
visit with Paul Hamlyn in the early 1960s, I travelled on my own. My
visits were usually in the autumn and the sun was always shining in
cloudless skies. Sometimes it was very cold, but somehow it suited the
place.

I always tried to walk to my appointments but on this particular
occasion I was between appointments and running late, so I hailed a
cab. I told the driver my destination and settled back to watch the world
go by. I happened to glance into the driver's mirror and noticed his eyes
were fixed on me. I looked away for a few seconds and then glanced
back and, to my consternation, he was still staring at me. I wondered
how he was coping with the city traffic with his eyes so focused on
me.

As we neared my destination and he was slowing down – and after
our eyes had met several times, I noticed there was a smile on his face.
I felt uneasy and wondered if I was being taken for a ride in the American
sense of the word. I was, therefore, relieved when the taxi halted at
the address I had given. I got out of the car and asked the driver how
much I owed him. He was still looking at me and still smiling as he
said, 'Algiers. St Georges Hotel. 1943. RAF Officer.'

For a moment I was speechless for indeed I had been a newly
commissioned officer in the RAF in Algiers, working for General

Eisenhower's staff in 1943 at the St George Hotel.' 'I was a sentry at the gates and saluted you every day.' I could only reply, 'Good God,' as he rambled on, 'I was right there and I always enjoyed saluting the RAF people. Your top man was called Tedder, even smaller than Ike.' He went on to tell me that Churchill was the greatest man in the world and that the RAF had saved mankind in 1940. I tried to tell him that I had had nothing to do with the Battle of Britain and that I was not even aircrew. But to no avail. He was in full flow and as I was already several minutes late for my appointment, I had to interrupt him and ask him again how much I owed him. He refused to take a cent and despite my protests, drove off waving cheerily. It was eighteen years since I had been in Algiers.

Ada Gomm

'All the lonely people – where do they all come from?'

John Lennon

BACK TO CHINNOR AGAIN in the late twenties, early thirties. Chinnor Hill was always a great attraction to Tony, Joan and me partly because it was such fun to climb the hill one way or another and partly because of the diverse characters who lived there. Our favourite way was to climb the ninety-nine rickety wooden slats through the woods; but often we crossed the railway line just beyond Eggletons Farm, trudged through the fields, crossed the Ickneild Way and clambered up the tracks and through the bushes to the top. In the winter it often snowed and there were exciting drifts to conquer when we were delivering parish magazines.

Ada Gomm lived in a dilapidated flint stone cottage at the end of a rough lane at the top of the hill. She was ragged and her hair straggled down to her shoulders. To us she looked very like a witch and yet we were never afraid of her, even though she spoke hardly at all. I suppose it was because she sold ginger beer in stone bottles at tuppence a time and we always had our tuppences with us. She sold lemonade too – but that was in glass bottles and didn't interest us.

Ada Gomm's front door was always open, winter and summer. It led straight into a stone flagged room in which there was no furniture, only the boxes which contained the drinks. Ada sat in the doorway on a stool, scowling as if to challenge any strangers to buy her wares, which were advertised on a tin board: 'Lemonade and Ginger Beer – tuppence a bottle.' Yet, when she saw the three of us approaching, her face softened. I don't know how she survived through the winter. There was no social security in those days and not many cars on the road. Trade must have been virtually non-existent but, like London's Windmill Theatre in wartime, Ada Gomm 'never closed'.

I think she must have known we were the rector's children though we visited her often enough without the parish magazine. I doubt if she could read but she always seemed grateful for the delivery, seizing it as if it was a long-awaited present. No doubt she had other practical uses for my grandfather's lovingly prepared Church News and Notices. For us, there was always excitement when we visited her. In the summer, we would take a picnic and our mouths would water at the thought of Ada's ginger beer, and our pulses quickened when we saw Ada sitting on her stool outside the cottage. We always called her 'Ada' and I often wondered if she knew our names.

I suppose our visits must have spread over some five or six years and to us she was by far the most important person on Chinnor Hill – and there were some very important people on that stretch of the Chilterns. There was a distinguished naval commander by the name of Cobb; the Benton family who owned the cement works; bearded Professor Budd was a quite unapproachable man of renown and Miss Chance an enigmatic spinster who lived alone in a large house. Had I read about Miss Faversham at that time, my imagination would have run riot.

Soon after the war I went back to Chinnor to tend the family graves. I drove up the hill and along the lane to Ada's cottage. It was derelict. I tried to find someone who might know what became of her, but too many years had passed and there was no mention of a burial in the church records. Today her cottage is a very sophisticated dwelling with all modern conveniences and a beautiful garden. I would think it is worth considerably more than £250,000 but, for me, the memory is of wonderful ginger beer in stone bottles at tuppence a time.

Golf at Wentworth

'Golf is a good walk spoiled.'

Mark Twain

I HAVE REASON TO be grateful to EMI for many reasons but I shall write about them in other chapters no doubt. When Paul Hamlyn and Jo Lockwood (Chairman of EMI) formed the joint company of Music for Pleasure and I was put in charge, so many friendships, excitements, traumas and experiences, emanated from that union that, had I a kind of Geoffrey Archer talent, I would write a novel embracing the excitements and tragedies of the record industry. I retain many of the friendships forged in those years (1965 to 1981) and I receive a just pension from EMI (which takes into account the years from 1953 when first I joined Paul Hamlyn). However, part of my gratitude to EMI centres on one particular activity in which I was allowed to indulge after I retired from that company. Golf. Let me explain.

Many younger folk take golf so seriously, they don't appreciate the companionship, the beauty of the countryside, wildlife, the hilarity, the exercise and the variety of venues involved. Indeed, I have often thought that of all the top pro sporting circuits, golf has to be the healthiest and most stimulating, not necessarily from the point of view of the nature of the sport itself but from the multifarious aspects surrounding it. Sports such as soccer, tennis, rugby, bowls, cricket, squash, athletics, boxing, are played on pitches, courts, tracks, rings, etc. and in whichever place in the world they are played, the immediate settings are very much the same. Oh yes, golf is played on courses but every one of the thousands of golf courses around the world is different and every one has beauty and variety. It was Mark Twain who said, 'Golf is a good walk spoilt'? Maybe, but at least it is a good walk!

I must get back to my story. Wentworth is arguably the icon of golf clubs in England. It has three courses. The West Course (the Burma Road) is the championship course; the Edinburgh, or South Course, and the East Course. EMI had had a group membership there for a number of years which enabled certain staff to play on weekdays and which hosted the company's Golf Day once a year to which VIPs were invited – mainly pop star managers and top business executives. Ten holes on the East Course were played in the morning, and after lunch, eighteen holes on the Burma Road. Dinner and prize giving took place in the club house. I had played on this Golf Day on three occasions when I was still working for the company, even though my golf was amongst the lowest standard of those playing. But, of course, the golf handicap system enables players of different standards to compete without affecting the opponent's game. With sports such as tennis, snooker, squash – or indeed all team games – there is no enjoyment if there is no 'return' or 'opposition' from the adversary to enable continuous play.

When I retired from EMI in 1981, friends there allowed me to continue playing at Wentworth twice a month with any friend I chose to partner. It would cost me nothing! For interest, I have calculated the commercial value of this benefit EMI so kindly granted me – quite apart from the huge enjoyment. Only the very rich can afford to play at Wentworth and though the playing fees have altered considerably over the years, I reckon I have had at least £100,000 worth of fun in the fifteen years until 2003 when EMI pulled out of their annual group membership. But fortunately, this coincided with my ageing limbs telling me that, at eighty-one years of age, I was finding it hard to walk the eighteen holes on my favourite Edinburgh course. Another useless, but fun statistic I worked out, is that over those fifteen years, I must have walked over 2,000 miles and wielded a club over 30,000 times (I am ashamed to say!).

I had expected that in such a rich man's playground, angels might fear to tread and that there would be elitism and snobbery in the air – as indeed there so often is in provincial clubs. Far from it. Wentworth has always seemed homely and entirely welcoming. I am not renowned for sartorial discipline and because I have had skin cancer on my head, I have to wear a hat. I have never liked wearing hats but gradually I became very fond of the floppy gear which sits shapelessly on my head to do its job. I always wore this friend at Wentworth and the gentlemen in the starter huts, the grounds men, the richly equipped players, with their buggies and battery-powered trolleys, invariably extended greetings to my hat and me. Officially, I have a handicap of twenty-three which was obtained at Wexham Park in 1990 and was, therefore, thoroughly out of date (handicaps should be renewed annually). My paper certificate is creased and faded and only just manages to remain in one piece – not unlike my headgear – but Wentworth has always accepted it, even respected it. Indeed, I have never had a cross word with anyone (except myself) on the estate apart from the time when I carelessly backed into a rather large BMW in the car park as I was preparing to leave in my humble, but much loved VW Passat Estate. A rich, loud-mouthed man assaulted me verbally. I apologised and suggested he should try and match his money with some manners.

One of the special delights of the Edinburgh Course was Pino's refreshment hut after the ninth hole. There, players can rest for ten minutes, refuelling with sausage and bacon sandwiches, coffee, tea, or soft cold drinks. Pino is an Italian who loves gardening and wildlife and has turned this oasis amongst the pine trees into a charming array of colour. He has created a flower garden, a vegetable patch, a small vineyard, and has placed bird tables amongst the trees on whose branches bird houses rest. At Christmas, he builds a nativity scene in the hut, flanked by a Christmas tree. The three wise men are setting out from a sandy tee and the course ahead is sandy with dune bunkers leading to the stable and its occupants on the green. With such a delightful place to rest after nine holes, the danger to golfers is obvious. The temptation is to relax, eat and drink too much before setting out to the tenth tee.

And I remember well one autumn there was a gale that brought down several trees along the Edinburgh Course. I played there a few days afterwards and, as we walked from the fifteenth green to the sixteenth tee, we came across contractors sawing up a large oak that had been a victim of the storm. As we have a log fire at home, I am always interested in fallen trees – and have a chain saw which enables me to cut branches into lengths which will fit into my estate car. I asked one of the workmen what would happen to the wood and he told me that as outside contractors, they had to take it away and would most probably burn it. I looked at my watch. We would be finished by three p.m. I reckoned that I could be back at Wentworth by four p.m., having taken my partner home. I phoned my son in law, Michael, at Wokingham and arranged to pick him up on my way back to the Edinburgh Course (he too has a log fire). I had to study my Wentworth Estate map to find how I could get to the sixteenth green via the various roads and tracks. However, we reached our destination just after four p.m., loaded the car and sped home. Having emptied our bounty, we returned to Wentworth for a second load and as we worked, two Rangers approached in their buggy. I waved merrily to them as they passed and they waved back! Contentedly we drove away, dropping off half our catch at Wokingham before reaching the safety of home. What a marvellous day. A round of golf and winter stock of wood for two homes!

The Wentworth Estate itself consists of dozens of very large houses which sell for many millions of pounds each. Grand as they are, they seem somewhat forbidding in that each is protected like a fortress, guarded with gaunt iron railings and security gates. Many high profile people, including several of the top professional golfers, have homes on the estate (the notorious General Pinochet was sheltered and guarded there before being allowed to return to Chile). The massive clubhouse itself was refurbished a few years ago to harbour restaurants, bars, the 'pro shop' and banqueting suites. To eat, drink or purchase goods there is an expensive business as is participating in any of the other sporting facilities surrounding the clubhouse. Apart from the huge driving range, club members can enjoy swimming, tennis, archery, gymnastics, snooker, squash, table tennis, badminton and many other indoor activities. Wentworth hosts two of the major golfing tournaments – the PGA (Professional Golfers Association) English Open takes place in the spring and the World Match plays in the autumn. In the summer, the Senior European Tour play their annual championship on the Edinburgh Course and it is, of course, always exciting to see the likes of Player,

Nicklaus, Ballesteros, Jacklin and many others, tackling the holes I know so well.

The fact that Wentworth is but twenty minutes drive from my home at Bray has added to the pleasure I have had, particularly because the journey is virtually traffic-free and very beautiful – either through Windsor Great Park, or via Windsor Forest, skirting Virginia Water. Indeed, my EMI/Wentworth golf days were a joy. I have had the companionship of so many friends, sharing with them all these delights and at the same time relishing a desperate contest. My opponents of different shapes, sizes and nationalities have all been younger than I – from mid-teenage years to fifty-something-year-olds. The adventures, excitements, laughs, despair and joys we have shared are legion. I remember so well the three-minute silence at eleven a.m. on 14th September 2001 to remember the dead in the New York Twin Towers disaster, only three days before. My partner and I were waiting on the eighth tee when rockets were fired to alert all the players on the three courses. And elsewhere, I have written of the day of the eclipse when Michael Hartridge and I found ourselves on the 11th green at 11.00 a.m. on 11th August, 1999.

All this and heaven too. I don't think I could have enjoyed myself anymore had I been a very good golfer because I would never have had so much hope and expectation I might improve! And had I been a low handicapper, surely my mind would have been too focused on form to have had room for the peripheral delights of golf. Happy times indeed.

Biggs

'He found it inconvenient to be poor.'

William Cowper

WE WERE LIVING AT Buckhurst Close, Park Road, Redhill, in Surrey, towards the end of the 1950s in the central part of a very pleasant Victorian house with a reasonable-sized garden. I was working for Paul Hamlyn and still writing and broadcasting from time to time. But Tony and Jenny were at private schools which meant that there was little left out of my salary and occasional earnings. We had moved to Redhill from Bletchingley where Peggy had run a small gift and needlework shop and we lived in the sloping floors above. My mother was just down the road in Nutfield. Her cottage has now become part of the M23 motorway to Brighton and Buckhurst Close has made way for a large estate of modern houses.

But back to my little story. As there was a spare room with a small bathroom-come-toilet next door, we decided to take in a lodger in order to augment our income. We needed to smarten up the accommodation and install the minimum cooking facilities, so we searched the local papers for a decorator/handyman. We had already let the room to a Mrs Doherty and had promised her all would be ready by the end of the month. There was some urgency, therefore, but in those days there was far greater unemployment which meant that it was likely we would get the work completed in time.

There were several advertisements from which to choose and we asked for quotes from three of the decorators. They came at appointed times the next day and we chose a Mr R Biggs to do the job. He duly did it promptly and efficiently and seemed a pleasant enough character.

We move on two or three years to the early 1960s. We were on holiday in Devon at our tiny Corner Cottage in Elmscott, near Hartland. We were listening to the morning news on the radio. There had been a train robbery in Buckinghamshire and millions of pounds had been stolen. This, of course, became known as 'the Great Train Robbery' and subsequently it was dramatised into a major film. Within a few weeks the majority of the gang were arrested and for the first time, names were published in the newspapers.

I cannot remember who first spotted the name 'Ronald Biggs of Redhill' in the list, but we were, of course, astonished and felt a strange whiff of fame – or perhaps infamy – when we remembered that the driver of the train had died from injuries inflicted on him by the robbers. We followed the trial with particular interest and noted that Biggs was sentenced to a long term of imprisonment in Brixton. He later escaped from Brixton Prison and lived in Brazil for many decades before deciding to return voluntarily to serve out his sentence. This happened several years ago and he is now a very sick man living in the prison hospital.

At the time of the trial, we treated our spare room and bathroom with a degree of awe – even reverence. After all, not everyone has had one of their rooms and a bathroom decorated by a Great Train Robber. If only Mr Biggs had done our work after he had robbed the train and before he was arrested, he might have bricked up a few million in our loo. As it was, we didn't really think there would be many takers if we put up a notice outside the house 'Ronald Biggs decorated here. Admission to inspect 5/- .'

Twice Nightly in Tonypandy

'Everything is funny as long as it is happening to somebody
else.'

Will Rogers

TONYPANDY WAS A MINING town in the Rhonda Valley. Now, alas,
it is a town without pits but survives on small manufacturing businesses,
a town still with a community spirit but not with the same fierce courage
and loyalty which pervaded the Welsh valleys in those bygone days.
Maybe the place is more prosperous and physically healthier, but pride
and self-respect has diminished. However, male voice choirs and brass
bands can still be heard – and laughter too.

It must have been in 1948 that I joined Harry Hanson's Court Players
for a ten-week season at the Empire Theatre in Tonypandy and several
members of the company had digs at the Cross Keys Hotel/Pub on
the corner opposite the theatre. A splendid theatre and excellent digs
but I have no idea whether either or both have survived these sixty years
– I rather doubt it. We had a wonderful time even though the season
was twice nightly, the curtain rising at 6.00 p.m. and 8.30 p.m. each
evening. The audiences always enjoyed themselves, however good or
bad the plays or performances and whatever the plays might be – drama,
comedy or farce. Mind you, they didn't suffer fools gladly!

My first story involves a farce called *High Temperature*. Nearly all the
plays were in one set because set-changing involved extra staff being
hired and, of course, the extra cost of the stage flats themselves. But
High Temperature was a risqué farce and Harry Hanson obviously thought
that its box office appeal would justify the extra cost of dropping in

three flats for the middle scene of the play. Flats are braced to the floor and then unscrewed and lifted at the end of the scene. It was a very quick change, no more than three to five minutes was involved by the time furniture had been removed and reset. The stage hands were always miners off shift, which meant there was probably a different crew each night. Pay days were Friday and Saturday nights when all the men who had worked during the week would come in at the end of the second set change to collect their money. There was a strict rule that pay packets would only be handed out at the stage door as the men left the theatre. Most of them would go straight across the road to the Cross Keys and drink the extra money they had earned.

On this particular Friday evening however, pay packets were handed out in error after the second scene change of the first house – which meant that the crew could drink in the Cross Keys from the end of the Act 2 of the first house, until the end of Act 1 of the second house – a time span of some two hours. The inset was a bedroom scene and when the curtain rose, a young man (played by me) was found in bed with the attractive young wife of the very respectable Lord of the Manor. Within a few seconds of 'curtain up', the bedroom door opened and in came His Lordship but on this fateful evening, the curtain went up on cue and the Lord started to open the door on cue, but chaos ensued. In bed, Her Ladyship and I heard strange noises and lifted our heads from the pillows to see the three flats falling forwards onto the stage, and, therefore, of course, on to us. There was immediate uproar from the audience; uproar of delight for not only was there a jumble of flats occupying the centre of the stage, but the main permanent set of the play stood erect and proud around the chaos. The curtain was brought hurriedly down to a cacophony of cheers, whistles and laughter. What had happened was almost certainly funnier than any of the action in the play and the audience was grateful for it. We were rescued from under the debris and the few sober stage hands with the entire cast set about re-erecting the inset ensuring that this time the braces would be screwed to the floor, a small matter the inebriated stage hands had forgotten!

Five minutes later the curtain rose again. The audience cheered and clapped as the Lord of the Manor made his entrance. There was a moment's silence until the audience realised the set was not going to collapse again and pandemonium ensued. Boos, laughter, cheers filled the auditorium and, safely tucked in bed, my partner and I wondered if the stage was going to be invaded. Eventually, peace was restored and much to the audience's disappointment, the play proceeded.

News of the evening's events spread through the town and pits. As a result, there was not a seat to be had for either performance on the Saturday. At both performances, there were demonstrations of anticipation and then boos of disappointment when the bedroom door opened and the set didn't collapse. What followed was sheer anticlimax – the outrage of a husband finding Her Ladyship under the bedclothes with me and watching my speedy exit through the window clad only in a sheet.

My second memory is of an incident in Emlyn Williams's play *Night Must Fall*, which is a thriller involving a lovely old lady confined to a wheelchair. She is, in fact, the murderer and keeps the severed head of the last person she has done away with, in a hat box on top of a cupboard. The audience, of course, does not realise she is the murderer until toward the end of the play when she suddenly gets out of her chair and walks without a limp or stick to reach up for the hat box. Until that moment she had been the heroine, unable to walk or lift herself from her chair without at least two people helping her. I cannot remember the name of the actress playing the lead but she had been told again and again that when she rose from her wheelchair, she must not leave it pointing toward the audience because stages in all old theatres have a slight rake towards the footlights or proscenium arch. However, at this performance, she was either forgetful or careless because when she rose from the chair, she left it at a slight downstage angle. In normal circumstances, this was the high point of tension in the play as the audience realises she is a fraud and that she is not only perfectly healthy but a murderess as well. But on this night, as she walked upstage to take down the hat box, her wheelchair started to move eerily and very slowly across the stage, diagonally towards the footlights. The audience gasped, causing our actress to look back. She immediately turned, walked briskly down stage to rescue the wheelchair a few feet from the orchestra pit! There was applause as she pushed the chair back upstage, positioning it at the right angle, before resuming her steps to take down the hatbox.

The producer was front of house at that performance and said he had seldom witnessed such tension in a theatre as that wheelchair, unaided, moved slowly across the stage. He wished he could have kept the 'business' in for the rest of the week. Indeed, 'those were the days'.

Kerzenstuberl

'Of food and love, the first is best.'

Thomas Fuller

WITHOUT DOUBT, THE KERZENSTUBERL was my favourite restaurant in London. I say 'was' because sadly it is no more. It closed in the year 2000 because the rent being demanded was too high to sustain the kind of business it was. Its evening trade had always been constant but the luncheon clientele had fallen away because of the exodus from the area of several large multi-national companies and there had never been a large 'passing trade' to compensate for the expense lunches of business men. Indeed I was introduced to the Kerzenstuberl for a lunch meeting by an EMI business colleague and, for twenty-five years thereafter, I enjoyed eating there when visiting Manchester Square – which was only five minutes away.

St Christopher's Place lies between Wigmore Street and Oxford Street, an attractive pedestrian alley with small specialist shops on either side. The Kerzenstuberl, standing on the left as one walked from Wigmore Street, was small, seating no more than forty to fifty people. It was always cosy, and Ilse and Herbert (Rauscher) the Austrian restaurateurs, seemed to make every visitor feel he or she was the most important customer they had ever had. Ilse was the most discreet flirt I have ever come across, while Herbert, in his Tyrolean shorts, exuded masculinity in a jocular style. The menu was a la carte and hardly changed in those years I ate there, but the food was always delicious, colourful, hot and plentiful and there was a wide choice. Indeed one of the great attractions of the place was precisely because the menu was an old friend and one went to St Christopher's Place to meet up with it again. Ilse told me that from time to time she did add to the menu but never once in the restaurant's twenty-seven years did the addition retain its place for more than a few weeks.

The menus themselves were large and attractively designed, printed in German and English. At the bottom of the wine lists there was usually a small cartoon with a caption of some kind.

Wine makes the moment
Song makes the joy
Woman makes the pleasure
Man makes the ploy

or

You needn't think you have to stray
To tempt a woman. Pass her way
A little wine; then she'll begin
To want champagne, the road to sin.

and

If there's a woman you desire,
A little wine will light her fire;
Not too much, for never doubt
That too much fuel will put it out.

There was a wide range of starters, but I usually chose the Gebackene Champignons – deep-fried button mushrooms with tartare sauce. There was an equally large choice for the main course and I was usually torn between the Rollschinken mit Sauerkraut unt Knodel – Smoked Pork with Sauerkraut and dumplings, and Tafelspitz – a special cut of boiled beef with various cold sauces. I suppose I liked the Kerzenstuberl so much because it had essentially a family atmosphere and was distant from 'cordon bleu' cooking and décor. It was warm, friendly and comfortable and in the evenings as the hours rolled by, an accordion player, sitting by the bar, would play middle of the road music. Ilse would go from table to table singing to her customers and enticing them to join in. Everyone seemed relaxed and entirely comfortable, enjoying the food and informality.

I took a wide assortment of people to the Kerzenstuberl – many of them from the record industry in the early days – but later on, friends from all walks of life and of course, family. I never had a disappointing meal there and consequently always looked forward to returning. Consequently, I chose to surprise Kim on her sixtieth birthday. I had told her that I was taking her out to dinner 'somewhere' in London and as we walked in, Herbert played his part perfectly, asking me, with a solemn face, why I had not booked a table because there was no room at the inn! He moved out of the way to reveal Charlotte and Michael, Julian and Lesley, Tony and Jenny. We had a wonderful evening which developed into an hilarious sing-song, overseen by Ilse. It is sad we could not celebrate my eightieth birthday in similar style.

We visit London seldom these days. We would not look for a substitute Kerzenstuberl and, if we did, I doubt if we would find it. As the country has prospered, 'eating out' has followed the American fashion in popularity and the number of restaurants of all nationalities has multiplied, catering, not only for tourists, but also for United Kingdom citizens from all backgrounds. We have lived in Bray for thirty-five years and the village happens to host two of the most fashionable and expensive restaurants in the world – Michel Roux's Waterside Inn, and Heston Blumenthal's Fat Duck. The former, a traditional Franco-British eating place, with charm and courtesy, overlooking the River Thames; the latter, a conversion of The Ringers, an old pub in the high street, but now modern, experimental, youthful, pioneering the art deco of cooking – and hugely successful. Strangely, these two famous restaurants are on our doorstep but make us mourn Ilse and Herbert's Kerzenstuberl all the more. We have so many happy memories.

Last Journeys – Winston Churchill, Diana Princess of Wales and Mrs Gough

---

'To die will be an awfully big adventure.'

J M Barrie

IT IS INEVITABLE OF course; the older one becomes the more funerals one attends and, in my opinion, they are so often unnecessarily depressing occasions. Must crematoria be so bland? Does black have to be the dominant colour? Need the 'eulogy' or 'tribute' so often take the form of a CV of the deceased (facts and figures already well known to the family and the vast majority of those present); are large black limousines really needed to transport the family to and fro?

Maybe it is the thespian in me that longs for something more uplifting, dramatic and exciting. The circumstances of death, the age of the deceased, the background of the life that was, are obviously very relevant factors and the nature of the farewell has to be moulded to the individual occasion. Music and colour should always be part of the farewell; wealth, poverty and age should have nothing to do with it. There should be drama in death even if there was little in life. The Irish with their wakes are nearly there; the Indians with their funeral pyres in the open air and the sprinkling of flowers and perfumes surely come nearer to God than we do in western society. Most certainly with my love of bonfires, I would much prefer to be despatched in this way and, if my family really wanted to gather my ashes, they would at least know that they were really mine!

There are, of course, exceptions to the general run of funerals (top hats, whispers, piped music, plumed horses, black, competing wreaths, etc.) and such exceptions are usually celebratory and inspirational. We Brits stage manage the big state occasions better than any other country in the world – and how we enjoy them. It seems we are able to get rid some of our repressions by lavishing our emotions on the departed with a magnificent production of dignified spectacle and sombre but dramatic pageantry.

Who could ever forget Winston Churchill's funeral? The procession to St Paul's Cathedral through silent, crowd-lined streets, the service itself magnificent in its grandeur, the short journey westwards down the Thames to Waterloo Station, the bearers with the great man on their shoulders moving gently from the boat to the platform where the train waited to take him on his last journey from his beloved London, through Berkshire, to the Oxfordshire village of Bladon and its little church bordering the Blenheim Palace estate, his ancestral home. There, after a simple service, he was lowered into a grave next to his parents – graves unremarkable in themselves – jostling with those of the very ordinary country folk whom he had served so well.

Mary Soames, his daughter, wrote a moving biography of her mother Clementine and she called the chapter about Churchill's death and funeral 'Port after Stormy Seas'. The last paragraph of the chapter reads 'We were very tired when we got back to Number 28 [their Hyde Park Gate home in London] it had been a long, long day. My mother and I and Grace Hamblin had an early dinner together and, after Grace left us, we watched for a while part of the replay of the funeral on television. Then my mother got up to go to bed and I busied myself switching out the lamps. As she reached the door, she paused, and turning round, said, 'You know, Mary, it wasn't a funeral – it was a triumph.'

Another example of how well we stage state funerals was that of Diana, Princess of Wales. The coffin's journey to Westminster Abbey was pure theatre, the drama peaking when the Duke of Edinburgh, the Prince of Wales and the two young princes, William and Harry, with Diana's brother Earl Spencer, joined the cortège in The Mall and walked behind the coffin to the Abbey. These were perhaps the most poignant moments of the day, the service itself being memorable in a somewhat theatrical way with Elton John singing and playing the piano and Earl Spencer using his eulogy to score points against the Royal Family and the Establishment. However, the days before the funeral and the scenes on the journey from the Abbey to her family home at Althorp, watched by hundreds of millions of people all over the world, were unforgettable and the tension only eased as the gates closed behind the hearse as it arrived home.

When Tony, Joan and I lived at the rectory in Chinnor, a death in the village was always a personal matter to everyone. It was a relatively small community and the five-minute bell (the smallest of the six bells) was always tolled when a villager died. If we were playing in the garden we would pause for a moment, wonder who had died, and then continue with our game. Funerals were always well attended and from our tree house in the rectory woods, opposite the north side of the church, we would watch the mourners and the hearse arrive. To our young minds, there was always drama, dignity and simplicity to those occasions – a sincerity not yet threatened by commercialism.

Although we were too young to be present at the burial itself, I remember one very dramatic occasion in the early 1930s. There lived on the northern side of the village a Mrs Gough. She had a big house and was not only very rich but very large and I don't remember ever seeing her standing up. We often visited her and were always given sweets from her ample stock. I remember too her son, Chummy! He had an open MG sports car and would take us out for rides. He used to let me steer sometimes and I can't have been more than nine years old at the time. I never knew what Chummy did for a living but I know, as children, we decided he was a spy – on our side, of course.

Mrs Gough also had a large house near Barmouth in North Wales and she was staying there in midwinter when, quite suddenly, she died – I imagine she was in her early seventies. Apparently in her will, she stipulated that she be buried in Chinnor's parish church, St Andrew and consequently arrangements were made for the funeral to be at 3.30 p.m. on the Friday, to allow for the journey to be completed in daylight. North Wales was a long way away in those days – the hearse would leave Barmouth the previous day. Although there was relatively little motor traffic in the early 1930s, there were of course no motorways or even dual carriageways.

There was commotion in the rectory shortly after breakfast on that

Friday morning. Mrs Hill arrived from the Post Office to tell my grandfather that a telephone call had been received reporting that the hearse had run into a snowstorm near Chester and it was impossible to predict the time of arrival. The rectory did not have a telephone so my grandfather asked Mrs Hill to try and relay a message back to the undertaker saying that, as it grew dark soon after four p.m., it would be better for the service and burial to be postponed until the Saturday morning. Soon after lunch, Mrs Hill arrived back at the rectory with even grimmer news. The hearse was still battling with snowstorms and it was unlikely that Mrs Gough would arrive before midnight but it was essential that burial took place immediately on arrival!

My mother kept Tony, Joan and me up to date with events and, soon after it became dark, it started snowing which, of course, added drama to the proceedings. We were allowed to stay up for a while in case we could be of some use as the evening wore on. The bearers were alerted and were invited to the rectory for beer and sandwiches while awaiting Mrs Gough's arrival. My grandmother primed extra lamps and William, the gardener, borrowed storm lanterns for the bearers to light their way to the grave. No further news had been received by ten p.m. and we were despatched to bed. I can only recount what my mother told us happened that early January night.

My mother's bedroom faced directly west and she volunteered to take a 'look-out' position. The hearse would approach from the Oxford direction and as there were so few cars on the road – particularly on a snowy winter night – any headlights would cast reflection from the snow many miles away. She waited and waited, sitting in darkness at her bedroom window, relieved occasionally by Kate, the cook. There were one or two false alarms until just after 1.30 a.m. on the Saturday morning when headlight reflections were seen lighting up the sky in the direction of Kingston Blount, Crowell, and Oakley, hamlets immediately west of Chinnor on the Oxford road.

The burial posse, including my grandmother and mother, swung into action. They hurried up the tree-lined drive with lamps, lanterns and torches to welcome Mrs Gough home. The hearse pulled up outside the church and the driver and companion literally staggered out. They told my grandfather there could be no question of a church service –

however short – and that the coffin should be taken to the grave at once. When the rear door of the hearse was opened, their insistence was clearly understood. All the bearers fell back and took handkerchiefs from their pockets and held them to their faces before lifting Mrs Gough to their shoulders.

The little procession – Chummy was the only family member – wound its way by lantern light to the eastern end of the churchyard and, with my grandmother holding a lamp for my grandfather to abbreviate the sentences and prayers, Mrs Gough was laid to rest with brief, but due reverence. Snow was still falling as earth was shovelled on to the coffin and soon the churchyard was still in its whiteness once again. Goodnights were said at the rectory gates as the undertakers were taken to their lodgings, the bearers trudged to their homes, Chummy drove to his house to the north of the village and my grandparents, mother, Kate and William, walked down the drive to the warm rectory.

That eastern end of the churchyard where my grandparents, father and other relatives are buried, is now completely overgrown. My grandson Phillip and I do try and keep the Baldwyn family graves in reasonable condition by extricating them each year from the grass, weed, bramble and trees, but somewhere very near them, lies Mrs Gough. I would dearly love to find her grave and give her some light and fresh air.

Her funeral was a far cry from that of Winston Churchill or Diana, Princess of Wales, yet there was a fitting and memorable grandeur in the watch that the little band of villagers kept for Mrs Gough that night.

Snow

'The first fall of snow is not only an event but it is a magical event. You go to bed in one kind of world and wake up to find yourself in another, quite different; and if this is not enchantment, then where is it to be found?'

J B Priestley

IT DOESN'T SNOW MUCH in Devon and Cornwall, particularly along the northern Atlantic coast line. Indeed during the twenty-five years or so I had been visiting Hartland at the time of this memory, I had only witnessed the odd flurry of snow which did little to impress the fields and lanes. Biting winds and fierce gales make up a large part of the Hartland peninsula's character, but seldom snow. However, one of the delights of the place is surprise.

It was New Year's Eve and we were expecting our friends the O'Dells to dinner. Gill North (as she was then) and her fiancé Keith were with us – Gill helped us to look after Charlotte at Cannon Lodge; I imagine, therefore, that the year was 1978 or thereabouts. After lunch, Kim decided to stay at Mount Pleasant to prepare the dinner while Gill, Keith, Charlotte and I, accompanied by Lundy, our yellow Labrador and Puff, our mini Yorkie, decided to brave the bitterly cold wind, drive to Shipload and then walk round the cliff path near the Point and the lighthouse.

By the time we got back to the car, our faces were stinging, but we were warm inside and out, and when we reached the shelter of the house, smelt the dinner, downed tea and toast and lit the fire, life seemed very much worth living. We had only just passed the shortest day of the year and it was nearly dark at 4.30 p.m. I drew the curtains and settled down in front of a roaring fire.

It must have been about an hour later that I was passing the front door to go to the kitchen, when I noticed that the small glass panel was white. I remember calling out, 'How extraordinary!' thinking that a piece of paper had been blown against the panel by the wind. I opened the door and was greeted by large flakes of snow. Closing the door quickly, I drew back the curtains from the windows overlooking the valley and could hardly believe my eyes. It seemed we had been transported to a different place, rather like Dorothy in *The Wizard of Oz*. We looked out on a world that in less than one hour had been painted white. The glare on the snow from the house electricity dazzled us and we turned all the lights off to find ourselves looking out on a valley of utter enchantment. Never before had the panorama been like this. The colours, shapes, shades, contours and shadows created an entirely new world and the silence was almost overpowering. We all stood for several minutes gazing out onto the new world. Only the dogs remained unaware, asleep in front of the fire after their walk in the old world.

The curtains were closed and the lights switched on. I put on my Wellingtons and stepped out into the snow. It was less cold, but the snowflakes still floated down and the white carpet was already several inches thick. I walked down our steps and path to the lane and realised that Mount Pleasant was already cut off from the world so far as mechanical transport was concerned, and I trudged up to the drive where our cars were parked and they were only recognisable as two solid blocks of snow. I trudged back to the house, exhilarated at the prospect of isolation. We had no telephone, nor had the O'Dells, but we knew that they knew there would be no dinner party at Mount Pleasant on this New Year's Eve.

The hedgerows and banks are high in this part of Devon and very often the roads and lanes are below the level of the fields. When we awoke in the morning, the whole valley was covered with several inches of snow, but when I tried to walk up Ball Hill to the village, I found the lane completely blocked – six to eight feet deep, whilst the fields on either side had but two or three inches covering them. The wind had blown the snow into the lanes, blocking the arteries very effectively.

There was no question of moving the cars and we all donned suitable attire and shuffled, slipped and trudged our way up the hill to the village. Fore Street, the main street of the village, was already being cleared and the villagers were out in force, clearing the steps and relating their adventures of New Year's Eve and wishing Happy New Year to the world as it passed by. We went into O'Donnell's, the one shop open, purchased boxes of matches, gossiped with friends, and then slid down the hill to Mount Pleasant and spent the rest of the day indulging in winter sports – snow-balling, snow-manning, tobogganing in the paddock and sliding down the front path. As the days passed, rather like King Canute, we tried to stem the tide of thaw, but sadly the day came when we saw that those solid blocks of snow had turned back into motor cars which would carry us back inexorably into the real world.

There was another reason why those days were memorable. I was convinced I had cancer. For the previous few weeks I had noticed a swelling just above my groin, on the lower part of my stomach. It didn't hurt and I only thought about it when I was in my bath. It was getting larger and I decided to make an appointment to see my GP when we returned from Devon in the New Year. It so happened that a former employee of mine, Chris White, had retired with her husband to a village near Hartland and her Christmas card told us that she had cancer and was in the middle of treatment. I suppose it was this news that convinced me that my lump was also cancerous.

However, prior to the snow, I had already determined to visit Chris in the tiny hamlet of Philham, only two miles from Hartland. I had not told Kim of my swelling and maybe I felt a bit of a martyr carrying this burden of uncertainty over Christmas and our New Year excitements and keeping it to myself! On the second day after the snowfall and before the thaw set in, I decided to walk to Philham along the top of the drifts in the lanes. It was a memorable walk on a brilliantly sunny day and quite hard work too; the countryside donned a perspective I had never seen before, nor since, and my mood of concern both for Chris and, I suppose for myself, stirred my emotions.

I had coffee and mince pieces with Chris and her husband Bert, and though she was the usual cheerful self I remember her to have been when we were together in our record industry days, she had lost weight and her colour was ominous. Sadly she died a few months later and I attended her funeral in Stoke Church, a mile towards the sea from Hartland.

~~~~~~~~~

As for me, I kept my appointment with the doctor a week later, preparing to be brave when he would surely tell me I had cancer. He examined me for only a few seconds and then casually said, 'It's just a common or garden hernia. We'll soon have that dealt with.' For a moment I felt almost insulted. For weeks I had been secretive, building my courage, preparing to fight, when suddenly the bubble burst and anti-climax held hands with relief. I then had to summon a different kind of courage to tell Kim what had been going on for the last few weeks. Quite justifiably she was angry, but I'd probably do the same again!

I suppose the drama of the snow, the silence, footsteps falling without sound, the brilliance of the scenery, all heightened the excitement of life and the realisation of death's finality. There was a vivid awareness of contrasts.

Top of the Pops

'Words make you think a thought. Music makes you feel a feeling. A song makes you feel a thought.'

E Y Harbug

IT WAS 1980, THE year of the Queen Mother's eightieth birthday and my last year with EMI as Managing Director of Music for Pleasure. LPs, cassettes and singles were the dominant audio carriers with compact discs waiting in the wings, fighting other systems to take over the record business. Music for Pleasure was a 'budget' company selling quality LPs from the past, and making new concept recordings at a very low price. MfP's label 'Classics for Pleasure' reissued famous old recordings and, with the aid of sponsorship, was able to make new recordings with such orchestras as the London Philharmonic, The Halle and the Scottish National. Huge quantities of 'middle of the road' LPs were sold and unheard-of quantities across the classical range. The low price enabled people – particularly the young – to explore the classics for the first time and, with clever marketing, original repertoire ideas and excellent sleeve design, MfP and CfP were highly profitable labels. For obvious reasons, we were not popular with the conventional industry companies, nor, indeed with our parent company EMI Records who were jealous of our success as new boys. But they took some comfort in the fact that we were not competing with them in the 'singles' market which was, of course, dominantly 'pop' orientated. And, of course, we were very popular with the factory; with our demand for volume, the presses were never idle.

However, the strangest things happen in any business and one morning I took a phone call from Kay O'Dwyer, who was MD of EMI Music Publishing. She told me she had been sent a demo tape from St Winifred's School in Stockport, Lancashire and it was entitled 'There's No one Quite Like Grandma'. She thought it was a catchy tune and had potential for the autumn and Christmas trading period. EMI Records was not interested and she felt that our market was the right one for such a single. I pointed out that we had never issued singles, but I realised there was nothing in our brief to prevent us doing so. I respected Kay but even so I thought it highly unlikely that we would enter the cut-throat singles market, particularly with a Lancashire school choir singing a song about Grandma. However, I asked Kay to send me the tape.

It arrived the next day, Friday, and I listened to it in my Hayes office. It was catchy enough, but I certainly wasn't bowled over. It dripped sentiment and the opening line of the lyric was 'Grandma, I love you, Grandma, I do!' I took it along to my sales director, Ted Harris, handed him the tape, told him the history and asked him to listen to it. Within five minutes he was back in my office, placed 'Grandma' on my desk, laughing, and asked me what I'd like him to do with it! Later that afternoon, I played 'Grandma' again and though the melody was pleasing, I felt that Ted was probably right and decided I would ring Kay on Monday to tell her we would not be entering the singles market.

I was pottering in my greenhouse on the Saturday morning and heard myself humming a tune. For a moment I was unable to recognise what it was. Suddenly, I realised it was the 'Grandma' melody and, when this happened again on the Sunday, I decided I would listen to the tape again on Monday before telephoning Kay. I listened to it several times and something told me we should take a chance. I dared not tell Ted. Indeed I told no one that I had phoned Kay to say we would issue it. A single of this ilk wouldn't cost a fortune to record and surely to issue it would be in the spirit which had earned MfP its success and reputation in the industry. When I finally told Ted and his sales staff of our new venture, there was laughter and some bewilderment. Maybe a degree of excitement too, but some of the young Turks were undoubtedly thinking I was getting too old for the job and that a mistake of this kind was inevitable – but understandable!

The plan was to release the record in August or September, hoping to link the publicity in some way to the Queen Mother's birthday in August. I travelled up to Stockport to visit St Winifred's and meet the headmistress, Sister Aquinas, and the music mistress, Terry. I was also going to participate in the audition to pick the girl who would sing the verses leading into the chorus which would be sung by the whole choir. I found enchantment. Sister Aquinas, small in stature but oh so large in personality, vital and with a vast sense of humour, had a smile to melt the hardest heart. Terry, the music teacher, was a very attractive lady in her late thirties, blonde, and a disciplinarian, but obviously loved and respected by her pupils. The school was patently a happy one and had a considerable music pedigree, having been involved in several recordings as backing for stars and groups such as ABBA. They had never before made a recording of their own and I had an exciting day listening to the choir and choosing a quaint little girl with fuzzy hair to sing the solo lines.

Back at the ranch in Hayes, we decided to have a full colour sleeve to celebrate our entry into the singles market. We set up a session in our drawing room at Bray, borrowing a grandma from next door and collecting three or four children to sit and kneel around her as she sat in an armchair reading to them in front of a roaring fire – in mid August. Charlotte, our eight-year-old daughter, knelt on her right side, leaning on the arm of the chair.

The single was released in October and we all prayed for a miracle – which didn't seem to happen. Towards the end of the month, Grandma crept into the eighties at about the position where the vast majority of singles appear for a week, only to disappear a week later. However, early in November and much to our astonishment, Terry Wogan played 'Grandma' in his early morning show, introducing it with words something like, 'Now I just have to play you a record sung by the worthy pupils of St Winifred's School in sunny Stockport. It's called "Grandma", and I have to warn you that by the end of the song, Grandmas all over the country will be watching their parrots falling off their perches to the bottom of their cages.' The following week, sales soared, and Grandma reached the thirties. Week by week, it climbed and by the end of November, it was in the top ten.

You can imagine the excitement at St Winifreds, Sister Aquinas would phone me every day – and one morning, much to my dismay, she assured me she was doing her bit by visiting different record shops and stores every day to buy copies. I told her as gently as I could that she was not really allowed to do this because she was so much involved in the record. Such practice is of course, illegal, and I was just about to tell Terry she must stop Sister Aquinas doing this, when events overtook such worries.

We were told that with Christmas so close, it was just possible that 'Grandma' would reach the prized No 1 spot. Tentative arrangements were to be made for the choir to come down to London to appear on the BBC TV, *Top of the Pops*. And then, in the first week of December, John Lennon was tragically shot dead in New York. The Beatles were, of course, also signed to EMI and they rushed out a Lennon single which reached the top spot for the first two weeks of December – with 'Grandma', lurking at No 2. But the old lady was just biding her time and the week before Christmas, she stormed to No1! The full choir, some thirty children, came down to London and appeared on *Top of the Pops*. They stayed the night at the Forte/Trust House Hotel at Heathrow and returned to the school the next day in triumph, tired but happy.

'Grandma' retained her No 1 spot for two weeks over Christmas and in all, well over half a million copies were sold. We had, of course, agreed to give any profits to the school and as a result of this fairytale adventure, St Winifred's were able to buy a new bus – or people carrier as it is now called. I visited the school a year or two later and Sister Aquinas and Terry were still making music but when I called again several years later, the secretary told me that Sister Aquinas had retired. I hunted her down and when she opened the door, she stared and clearly didn't know me. I just said 'Grandma' to her and the old smile returned as we shared a big memory hug.

Douggie

'Fasten your safety belts, it's going to be a bumpy ride.'

Joseph L Mankiewicz

I HAVE WRITTEN ELSEWHERE of the exciting and romantic few weeks I had in Athens during the civil war at the end of 1944, only months after the Germans had pulled out and were fighting their way back through Yugoslavia being harassed by Tito's partisans and the Balkan Air force to which I belonged. My posting from Italy had come to an end and early in January I was waiting at the Athens airfield for the aircraft which was being sent from Biferno, my base in Italy, to pick me up. As I stood near a hangar, I was wondering which of the several types of aircraft that we had on 254 Wing, would be sent to fetch me. Mustangs and Beaufighters would be too small, so it would either be a Ventura, Baltimore or a Marauder. Surely they would not be insensitive enough to send a Ventura, the aircraft in which I had ditched in the Adriatic only three months before. And who would be flying the thing? Obviously we had a wide range of pilots from several nationalities on 254 Wing. There were good ones, bad ones, very serious ones and a few crazy ones. And then there was one very good, but nicely crazy one, and his name was Douggie Leadbetter.

On my way out to Athens some four to five weeks earlier, we had landed en route at Bari and I was standing near the aircraft, waiting to depart, when a light bomber belly-flopped on the runway and burst into flames. It had bombs and ammunition on board, and within a few seconds, the place became like a battlefield, with ammunition whistling overhead and in all directions. We all flung ourselves to the ground until peace broke out and we were able to go about our business. It was understandable, therefore, that having had two escapes in as many months, I was praying for an incident-free flight from Athens back to Biferno, with a nice solid pilot, flying a nice solid crate. The thought of Douggie Leadbetter with a Ventura tried to break surface but I managed to suppress it until a speck on the horizon grew into a Ventura, which, once landed, produced Douggie Leadbetter bounding down the steps. He let out a roar of delight when he saw me and gave me a bear hug. His crew of two were worryingly subdued as we walked to the nissen hut to prepare for our return flight. Douggie slapped me on the back, 'Becoming a bit of an Old Jonah, eh, Windyballs? Ditching in the drink, then trying to blow up Bari! Worry not, old boy, we will get you home safe and sound.'

As we roared down the runway, Douggie let out his signature roar before lifting his steed off the ground. I breathed a sigh of relief as we gained height, flying westward along the northern coast of the Peloponnese. Douggie smiled at me: 'Smooth as a baby's bottom, eh?' Gratefully I nodded assent and started to feel relaxed as, before long, we could see the Adriatic. I had just closed my eyes to say a prayer of thanksgiving when one of our two engines 'coughed'. It was quite a polite 'cough', but a 'cough' nevertheless. We all pretended we had not heard it and smiled cheerily at one another to show how little we cared for a minor 'cough', until the engine 'coughed' again. Douggie busied himself at the controls, seeming to make things worse as we now had a hacking cough to deal with. It turned out to be terminal as, in a few minutes, the port engine spluttered to silence and the prop to complete inaction. My three companions slowly turned their gaze on me; I shrugged my shoulders and tried to smile reassuringly. Douggie shouted, 'This bloody old machine can't maintain height on just one engine, we have a maximum of ten minutes, and I'm buggered if I am going to get wet! Find me somewhere to land – that's an order.' The navigator (I cannot remember his name) frantically unfolded an enormous map and searched. I saw him show Douggie a point on the map and it was obvious from their expressions that they were very uncertain as to the facilities there might be on whatever they had found. We banked steeply and headed south and I marvelled at Douggie's skill and courage as he maintained his outrageous optimism as we headed for some isolated spot somewhere over the rainbow. We were rapidly losing height, mountains were surrounding us and apart from the sound of the single engine, there was silence. We were getting uncomfortably near the ground when Douggie roared, 'There she blows' and ahead of us we could see what looked like a very minor road or dirt track cul-de-sac; at the end of it there was a sheer rock face stretching several hundred feet into the sky. Douggie was uncharacteristically quiet as we touched down, screeching to a halt less than fifty yards from the rock face: 'Great life,' he said, smiling.

It turned out that this air strip was a small maintenance unit for the RAF and had been used as a staging point for fighter aircraft, but had been built and used by the Luftwaffe during the German occupation and would certainly have been one of the bases from which their fighters took off to attack the Italians on Kefallinia Island (dramatised in Louis de Bernieres' *Captain Corelli's Mandolin*). We found a sergeant and a corporal in a nissen hut nearby. They told us they were billeted in a village some ten miles away which they reached using a very old army jeep. Douggie had a conference with them, the outcome of which was that the next day our friends would 'have a look' at the engine and see if there was anything they could do – they were eager to use their skills again as they had few customers. In the meantime, we had no option but to pile into the jeep and bump our way for nearly an hour to a village at the foot of the mountain.

We were dropped off at a building that used to be an inn and were given two virtually unfurnished rooms except for two beds in each. I was the only one who had luggage and a toothbrush since Douggie and his crew had not anticipated being away for the night. We were busy unpacking my belongings to decide how we could divide my toothbrush and other possessions, when something happened which even froze Douggie into complete silence. Quite distinctly, the sound of very English female voices floated up the staircase. A huge grin engulfed Douggie's face: 'God Bless you Windyballs, we're in luck – we'll leave the unpacking until later.' We crept down the stairs into the café, and we could see, leaning on the bar, two rather plump, determined-looking ladies in army uniform, with the letters SCF on their shoulders. Douggie whispered, 'Jesus, Senior Camp Followers!' We proceeded down the stairs and coughed loudly. The two ladies swung around and the larger of the two (neither was insignificant) boomed, 'Well, well, well, what have we here?' Douggie was splendid and told them exactly what they had there – and within ten minutes it seemed we had all known each other for ten years, drinking Ouzo and Ritzina and having a 'jolly' good time.

We soon found out that SCF stood for Save the Children Fund and that these brave women had been working for three months in appalling conditions trying to rescue children from the legacy of the German occupation and now the terrors of civil war. Although we were in the village for several days, we saw very little of them; they would disappear in their truck early in the morning and return late at night. Douggie would go back with the army lads each day to work on the Ventura's engine and then one evening he came back and told us that the engine was 'fixed' (fairly confident) and that we would be moving on next day; that night we celebrated and had a wonderful party with the SCF ladies and the Greek villagers.

At seven a.m. the following morning, we stood at the end of the airstrip and stared somewhat apprehensively at the rutted earth stretching before us. Fortunately the prevailing wind was westerly which meant that we were taking off into the wind, thus giving us the best chance of getting airborne before the end of the short airstrip. But we needed enough speed not only to get off the ground but also to climb above the rock face. Douggie reassured us by estimating (after scribbling in an old note book) that if they had 'fixed' the engine properly, then we had a reasonable chance of a successful take-off. I ventured to suggest that, as every yard would count, we could enlist the help of the locals and extend the runway by a few yards. 'Windyballs,' cried Douggie, practically knocking me over with a slap on my back, 'you're brilliant. Quite brilliant.' The army lads miraculously produced a dozen or so Greeks using spades and hands to extend our lifeline. We gained some ten yards and there were hearty cheers as two old tractors hauled an even older Ventura to the very end of our air strip.

Chocks were placed in front of the wheels and Douggie assembled our Greek friends to thank them for their hospitality and hard work. He explained that we were about to depart and was asking them for one more favour – to hang on to the aeroplane as he revved the engines (he wasn't sure about the brakes) and not to remove the chocks or let go until he signalled from the cockpit. There was applause and head-nodding as we climbed aboard the Ventura, waving like royalty as we disappeared inside. We watched as the Greeks took up their positions; Douggie started the engines, gave us a 'thumbs up' to indicate they sounded sweet, and then, roaring the engines, the aircraft strained in its blocks as he gave the prearranged signal to our Greek friends.

I suppose I was too young to be terrified as we hurtled toward the rock face. I remember switching my attention for a second or two from the rock face to Douggie's face; I had complete faith in this man and this time there were no histrionics. He kept the Ventura on the ground until it seemed we were bound to crash straight into the rock face. Suddenly he lifted us off the ground and we seemed to climb almost vertically. We circled our airstrip several times as our Greek friends waved furiously, almost as if they were expecting some kind of air display; I thanked God we weren't in a smaller aircraft – for Douggie would have been sorely tempted. Our journey back to Biferno was uneventful. We were all quiet and even Douggie seemed strangely subdued. Only he knew by how much we had cleared that rock face; I suspect it was only a few feet, perhaps inches.

A Dear Friend

'Friendship. It redoubleth joys, and cutteth griefs in half.'

Francis Bacon

NORMAN NEWELL WAS A very dear friend of mine and indeed of Kim and Charlotte. He was Charlotte's godfather and could not have taken his commitment more seriously. It was always fun to be in his company and he was absurdly generous; there could have been no better host nor such a rewarding guest. Yet, despite such a pedigree, and despite the happiness he spread, he was not a happy man himself.

He did not deserve the slow deterioration in health and the suffering he endured during his last years, which he spent in a private nursing home in Rustington. He had suffered two strokes and was unable to walk or enunciate clearly. He lay in his bed, lonely, and surrounded by gold discs he had been awarded and autographed photographs of the stars he had recorded. When I visited him during the last year of his life, he cried as we held hands and tried to communicate. I would talk of the wonderful times we had shared and he would try so hard to shape the sounds emanating from his mouth into words.

In 2004, Norman Newell was awarded the OBE for his services to the record industry as a producer and lyricist. He was far too ill to travel the Buckingham Palace and instead, a gathering was arranged at the nursing home, at which the Lord Lieutenant of Sussex, in all his finery, presented the award on behalf of the Queen. On that early spring day, and for the first time for many months, Norman was lifted from his bed into a wheelchair and was taken into the large reception room where the ceremony took place. A few of Norman's relatives and friends attended and he mouthed a few words of gratitude after the presentation of the award and speeches had been made. His eyes filled with tears as he gathered in the memories of friendship and fame. He was taken back to his room where he lay on his bed for another nine months until he died in the first week of December, aged eighty-four years.

Perhaps the best known of the songs he wrote were 'Portrait of My Love' and 'More' and, as a record producer for EMI, most of his work was done at the Abbey Road Studios – the stars he produced there were legion. But the record industry's rewards are notoriously transitory and friends too often become acquaintances once commercial gain has faded. Norman saddened with age because he never understood that inevitably the industry is orientated toward youth, unlike the theatre in which so often age matures the writer and artiste, and prolongs into old age fame and respect.

I cannot recall an occasion when we were with Norman which was not a happy one (until he became ill of course). Whether such times were social or commercial made no difference; whether at home here at Cannon or at Norman's home 'Monterey', in the recording studios, restaurants or at the theatre, there was always laughter, exuberance, and so much affection. He loved the glamour of show business and even had a children's musical *Once Upon A Time*, which he wrote with Roger Webb, produced at The Duke of York's Theatre in St Martin's Lane. I hope someone will write Norman's biography, it could be a hugely entertaining book, charting his ascent from humble East End childhood, into one of the world's leading record producers and lyricists.

Kim and I had so many splendid evenings with him and I shall just write of one which was typical of the special times we shared. Even when he wasn't the principal player, he seemed to be the one to make the occasion memorable. And so it was, on 26th August, 1997, Kim's fifty-eighth birthday, when to celebrate, Kim, Norman, Alan Lockie (Norman's great friend) and I went up to the London Palladium to see Topol in the revival of *Fiddler on the Roof*. Norman had produced the original cast recording for EMI with Topol many years before and they had remained friends. Accordingly, Norman let him know we were coming to the show and he insisted that we all visit him in his dressing room afterwards.

We parked the car nearby (this was long before 'zones') had a meal in an Argyll Street restaurant and then walked the few yards to the London Palladium, perhaps the most charismatic home in the world for musicals. We had all seen *Fiddler* before of course, but this occasion was special and the performance was magical. Topol welcomed the four of us and, when Norman told him it was Kim's birthday, he produced a bottle of champagne to celebrate. We spent thirty sparkling minutes with Topol before walking back to the car. I drove across Bond Street, past Claridges Hotel, through Grosvenor Square, and into Hyde Park.

It had been a good evening and we chatted away as I drove modestly westward through the park. There were lights of different colours everywhere and I pointed out the French Embassy on our left and suddenly realised I was going through red traffic lights. Fortunately, I was going slowly enough to slam on my brakes and stop the car half-way across the road coming into the Park, from Knightsbridge. Relieved that I had not hit another car, I backed level with the lights but my sigh of relief was short-lived for, parked on the grass immediately facing the road junction, I saw a police car.

When the lights turned green, I drove slowly forward and then pulled into the kerb a few yards further on from the intersection. I looked in my mirror and saw the police car move off the grass on to the road and pull up behind me. I told my passengers not to say a word and leave everything to me. Poor Norman was sitting in the front next to me while Kim and Alan sheltered in the back seat. I saw the driver of the police car get out of the vehicle and walk towards us. My mind raced to check how many drinks I had had during the evening and I felt sure I had had only one small beer in the restaurant before the show and one glass of champagne with Topol.

By the time the policeman had reached us, I had wound down my window to welcome him. He leant down, looked in the car, and asked me if I was aware that I had gone through traffic lights. I told him I was aware and had no tangible excuse, that we had been to the theatre and were discussing the events of the evening and obviously I had not been concentrating. I added that thankfully I realised my transgression in time to stop before going right over the adjoining road. The policeman said nothing, but for several seconds, looked at Kim, Alan and then

Norman, before reminding me I might have caused a serious accident. I agreed with him and said that such a mishap would have been even more unfortunate because it was my wife's birthday.

Again there was a long pause while he surveyed the four of us but eventually he fixed his gaze on Kim and said, 'Happy Birthday, ma'am' and as he straightened up, he patted me on the shoulder and said, 'And put your safety belt on, sir,' before walking back to the police car. Kim said quietly, 'You lucky bugger!' Alan laughed and Norman was speechless! As we drove home we imagined those policeman must have been waiting for bigger fish to catch but that the one who joined us for so short a while must have been a romantic. After all, I had driven through red lights, had been drinking and was not wearing my safety belt. Mind you, Kim was looking her usual attractive self, and maybe that had something to do with it...

Nevertheless, it was Norman who had arranged such an evening and had he not been with us, I am quite sure that our magical evening would not have had quite such a happy ending. Dear Norman, we miss you so much.

The Long Walk

'If at first you don't succeed, try, try, try again. Then quit.
No use being a damn fool about it.'

W C Fields

WE RETURN TO THE West Country again and I can't remember what started the idea but I know it happened in the early 1960s when Tony was still at Bradfield College and we were living at Buckhurst Close in Redhill. I was in my forties and Tony in mid-teens when together we planned what we considered the 'long walk' from Lands End to Corner Cottage in Elmscott, North Devon. We reckoned the distance was about eighty miles as the crow would have flown but as we intended to walk along the coast path involving creek and estuary diversions, undulations and forays for the occasional pub meal, the mileage would have been over a hundred miles. I can't even remember whether or not we took this into account but quite definitely our expedition was badly planned – we set off supremely confident but woefully ill-prepared. On second thoughts it was I who was arrogantly confident and ill-equipped for the long walk; Tony was young, strong, and sensible – with hardened feet and school fitness – and would, I am sure, have completed the journey with ease.

Peggy drove us to Land's End, England's south western extremity. After we had unloaded our baggage from the car, for the first time, I tried to lift my haversack onto my back and needed help to do so! When finally it was in position, I only saved myself from falling flat on my back by taking several very quick steps backwards. Tony meanwhile stood erect, admiring the view! Mind you, we were carrying our livelihood on our backs – tent, cooking utensils, food, sleeping bags, clothes, water, etc. etc. and, looking back, I don't think we had even weighed our luggage! I soon felt confidently upright and having waved goodbye to Peggy, we took our first steps eastwards towards Penzance. It was quite soon after the first hundred yards that I wondered if I was wise to be wearing comfortable walking shoes for such a journey. Tony was wearing sturdy boots which I considered too heavy and not as elegant as shoes. I said nothing to Tony as we walked at a good pace in the early afternoon sun.

We covered the eight miles to Penzance in good time and we headed for Timothy Whites to buy an assortment of plasters and first aid supplies just in case we needed them. We stood in the porch entrance of the shop to de-haversack and, as I lifted mine off my back, I fell forward against the shop window glass. I wasn't hurt and the glass didn't break but without the weight on my back, I felt as if I could float – I felt weightless. After we had bought our bits and pieces and Tony had helped load my haversack, we set off again and passing through Hyde, we bought an early supper of fish and chips before striding out along the cliff top path, inhaling the Atlantic air and marvelling at the breathtaking views.

By early evening we must have covered some eighteen miles and I knew that something peculiar was happening in my shoes. My pride insisted I say nothing to Tony but somewhere between Gwithian and Portreath, my feet told me they were not prepared to carry on much further. I kept my eyes open for a suitable tent pitching spot and found one just before eight p.m. Even Tony was tired and we lay on the ground for several minutes mulling over our progress. Casually I mentioned that perhaps I should have worn boots and, when we decided to start unpacking and erecting our tent, I tried to get up. The pain was excruciating as I put weight on my feet; I sat down again and asked Tony to take my shoes off as gently as he could.

My bare feet were not a pretty sight. They looked as though they had balloons attached to the soles, toes and heels. Tony was better placed to survey the total scene but I could twist enough to realise that something had to be done. We decided to pitch the tent and prepare for darkness before surgery. Under Tony's direction, I moved around on my hands and knees and sterilised a Timothy Whites' needle and Tony proceeded to operate. We then settled down for the night, neither of us prepared to consider the morrow.

Surprisingly, my feet were no longer hurting and I slept soundly, presumably from exhaustion. We awoke to a brilliant morning. I travelled around on my hands and knees helping to get breakfast and strike camp. As Tony bandaged my feet, I commented I didn't think I could manage the remaining eight miles on all fours. As we eased my feet into their shoes Tony said that the only alternative to walking was to bury me on the spot but we agreed that it would at least be interesting to find out what would happen when I started walking. As we were miles from any kind of help, there was no alternative so, with a little help from my son, I rose to my feet. I then took a few steps and they were very painful ones! I had momentarily forgotten I still had a haversack to carry but when Tony lifted it onto my back, I lost all sensation in my feet and, to my astonishment, when I started to walk my feet were numb.

We passed Portreath, Porthtowan and rounded St Agnes Head. Occasionally I looked down at my feet to check they were still there. I could not feel them. By mid-afternoon we had covered another fifteen/twenty miles but I knew that, as we approached Perranporth, I was nearing journey's end. The numbness had started to wear off, to be replaced by pain as we sat in a café, I dared not take my shoes off in case they were holding my feet together. Our Elmscott cottage was not on the phone so we rang George, an elderly friend who lived in the next hamlet. He very kindly got straight in his car and drove the seventy odd miles to pick us up at Perranporth. Deservedly I felt very stupid and ashamed. All our friends had given us such a hearty send-off only the day before, not expecting to see us for several days and there we were back home within forty-eight hours. I felt deflated and defeated and very sorry for Tony. He had been splendid.

The next day I was driven down to Spekes Mill Mouth to bathe my battered and hideous feet in the Atlantic. People almost queued to have a look at them and, by the end of the day, I felt quite important! The salt water worked wonders and within a few days I was well enough to enjoy the rest of the holiday. But I had learnt my lesson and when I ran the London Marathon some twenty years later, I not only trained but I was properly shod!

Fashion

'Fashion is something barbarous, for it produces innovation
without reason and imitation without benefit.'

George Santayana

THE SIXTIES WERE HEADY years for fashion and particularly for the
record industry. For me, I had already been given responsibility as the
operating director of Prints for Pleasure and overseeing the introduction
of Supraphon, the Czechoslovakian classical label, to the UK market.
When Paul Hamlyn (later Lord Hamlyn) launched Music for Pleasure
with EMI and I was made managing director, I felt very much part of
the excitement permeating that extraordinary decade. It was 1965 and
we had board meetings in the grand boardroom at EMI House in
Manchester Square and, as a very inexperienced MD, I was quite properly
nervous. However, I had two very high-powered directors reporting to
me – Tony Morris, who later ran Polydor Records, oversaw marketing
and Leslie Hill, who became MD of EMI Records and subsequently
Chief Executive of Central Television, was my finance director. They
sat on either side of me and I was able to rely on them to rescue me
from the many questions I could not answer.

Immediately opposite me sat Sir Joseph Lockwood, EMI's chairman
and Paul. They alternated in the chair for our meetings, which were
always conducted in a surprisingly informal and light-hearted fashion.
However, Paul could just reach me with his feet and would nudge or
kick me under the table, either to encourage or condemn.

Sir Joseph was a pipe smoker and would light up at the beginning
of the meeting and puff throughout, knowing full well that Paul could

not stand smoke from a pipe, being an inveterate cigar man. But they were good friends and Sir Jo had always admired the young entrepreneur who was at least twenty years his junior. I too was a pipe smoker but would never dare to take my pipe out in Paul's presence. At one meeting, Sir Jo was obviously feeling mischievous and said to me, 'Baldwyn, aren't you a pipe smoker?'

I nodded.

'Here,' he said, passing his pouch across the table, 'have a fill.'

I could feel Paul's eyes boring into me and, coward that I was, I murmured, 'I've left my pipe in the car.'

Sir Jo smiled and said, 'No you haven't, it's sticking out of your top pocket.'

'Oh,' I said pathetically, 'so it is! Thank you.' I filled the bowl and returned the pouch as the meeting continued, intending to delay ignition until after the meeting.

But Sir Jo was determined. He slid a box of matches across the table and turned his head to Paul. 'You don't mind, do you, Paul?' The eyes of the ten board members focused on me as I struck a match, sucked and billowed forth smoke. I looked at Paul, hoping for a glimmer of understanding, but his head was down – he was pretending to be engrossed in the figures. Once I was well and truly alight, Sir Jo moved us on to the next item on the agenda. Paul never referred to the incident and I made quite sure I left my pipe in the car for future meetings.

After the meeting, we had the customary sandwiches and drinks and I was standing talking with Sir Joseph. He had his head lowered and was looking at the floor when he suddenly broke the flow of the conversation and said, 'Baldwyn, do you see what I see?'

'Where?' I asked.

'Down there,' he replied, 'on the end of your legs.'

I looked down and, to my dismay, I could see I was wearing odd shoes, one suede and one brown leather. 'Oh,' I said.

'Is it a new fashion?' asked Sir Joseph.

I smiled bravely 'No, Sir Joseph. Just carelessness.'

'Thank God for that,' he replied.

These momentous events took place in the main boardroom of the country's biggest record company, with 'Nipper' looking down at us from the wall at the end of the room. Abbey Road was only a mile or two down the road and the Beatles were popping in and out of the building from time to time, passing Sinatra and Cliff Richard on the stairs. The Sex Pistols were waiting in the wings and Kate Bush was growing up. Indeed, those days were headier than I realised at the time and I wouldn't know how board meetings are conducted now. I doubt if they could be quite such fun.

The Student

'Laugh and the world laughs with you. Weep and you weep
alone.'

Ella Wheeler Wilcox

I SHALL NEVER FORGET Laura. She made me and the rest of the
cast at Guildford feel so ashamed. She was a quiet and very earnest
girl and she was besotted with the theatre, willing to do anything for
anybody to help. Seldom did a week go by without some kind of incident
involving a member of the company. Usually, the incident took place
on the stage during a performance, but sometimes in the dressing rooms,
sometimes in the town and, more rarely, in the audience. These
occurrences were usually funny and caused hilarity amongst members
of the cast, though actors seldom enjoy their own misfortunes onstage.
But, very occasionally, there was tragedy of a kind that is not recognised
at the time.

Laura was a young student working as the Assistant Stage Manager
and one of her tasks was to prompt. Prompters were very important
people in 'rep' because, of course, lines had to be learnt quickly. It was
a skilful job too. To prompt or not to prompt, that was the question.
If an actor 'dried' completely, he or she would hope to be able to stare
at the prompter in the wings, imploring help and would usually get it.
But more often than not, an actor would improvise, trying desperately
to find his way back to the actual dialogue. This would not only make
things extremely difficult for the colleagues on stage but also almost
impossible for the prompt who would not know whether to prompt
or not.

Laura was a local girl, not unattractive, intent on making the theatre her life. As this was her first week as a prompter, she had taken the trouble to ask questions about the art of prompting and obviously trusted the advice given to her by 'professionals' who probably had never prompted in their lives.

Laura preferred drama to comedy and the play *The Duke of Darkness* was very dramatic indeed. Set in the nineteenth century, it is the story of an imprisoned duke and his devoted servant Gribaud. They share a dank and gloomy cell and Gribaud (the part I was playing to Ewen Solon's Duke) was delirious and dying in his master's arms. Laura found this scene very much to her liking and during the dress rehearsal had prompted us very efficiently. The evening performance had gone well and I was in the middle of my long final farewell to my master. I was aware that I was wandering from the script but was not alarmed because Ewen didn't have to speak until I had expired and I was confident that, even if I didn't actually die on the right line, I could make it quite evident that I was dead. However, I was still improvising quite happily when Laura's confident and resonant voice echoed out on to the stage and into the hushed auditorium, 'Wrong!' I died as quickly as I could and poor Ewen was left to deliver his eulogy, choking on laughter and tears. The local critic was there and picked out Ewen's farewell to Gribaud as the highlight of the evening! (There is a large black and white photograph of this scene in my cuttings book.)

A few productions later, I was on the stage with several other actors in a comedy and we were playing to a very poor matinee house. The theatre at Guildford at that time was a converted hall and, as footlights had gone out of fashion, the actors no longer had the glare to shield them from the sea of faces in the stalls. (This was, of course, many years before the building of the Yvonne Arnaud Theatre.) I became conscious of a commotion in the audience and it was evident that the audience was paying more attention to what was going on in the fifth row, rather than on the stage. The curtain was not drawn across but we stopped the dialogue and could see that a middle-aged lady in the 5th row was standing up and taking off her clothes. The lady attendants rushed down the aisles and gently took hold of her and led her out of the theatre. I looked across to the prompt corner for a lead as to which line we should go back to in order to restart the play. Laura was not there. We waited for a few minutes for the audience to resettle and then found our own way back into the play.

There were only two large dressing rooms at Guildford, one downstairs for the ladies and one above it for the men. We would often gather in the ladies' dressing room after a performance, particularly if there had been an 'incident' to mull over. A member of the audience undressing in the fifth row was more than an 'incident' and we all rushed to the ladies' dressing room at the end of the performance. How we gossiped. Who was she? Had she got a good figure? Was she alone? The room was full of laughter and cigarette smoke and then I noticed Laura sitting alone in the corner of the room. She was crying.

I went over to her and, squatting down beside her, I took her hand.

'Are you all right, Laura? I noticed that you were not in the prompt corner.'

She spoke quietly: 'I'm sorry, I had to go.'

To try to cheer her up, I suggested that perhaps she had decided that the attendants removing the lady from the fifth row needed her help more than we did – perhaps Laura knew the lady.

'She's my mother,' Laura said.

The Eclipse

'Eclipse Friste, the rest nowhere.'

Dennis O'Kelly (Comment on an Epsom horserace 1769)

I HAD NOT PLANNED to be anywhere in particular for the few minutes covering the eclipse and when, some weeks before, I arranged a game of golf with young Michael Hartridge at Wentworth on 11th August, 1999 I had not realised it was the great day. Indeed, it was only a day or two before that it dawned on me we would be somewhere on the course during the eclipse itself.

It was a pleasant day, warm but cloudy. We had started our round at about 8.30 a.m. and after nine holes we were enjoying our sausage and onion rolls at the halfway hut on the Edinburgh Course. We then proceeded down the tenth fairway. Michael was two holes up as we walked from the tenth green to the eleventh tee. The temperature was falling and the light was fading as we donned pullovers. We were nearing the eleventh green when two deer emerged from the trees and hesitated before careering across the fairway to the shelter of the trees on the other side. It was nearly dark as our balls landed on the green and Michael sank a twenty-foot putt to win the hole, making him three up. We looked at our watches. We were on the eleventh green, at eleven a.m. on 11th August. We watched the eclipse before proceeding to the twelfth tee.

For some mysterious reason, Michael's game fell apart after that superb putt and he did not win another hole. Thereafter, I eclipsed him. (I should add that Michael is a very good golfer and a very generous young man. I can't remember exactly how many strokes he was giving me on this occasion but it was certainly in double figures.)

The Queen Mother

'The whole world is in revolt. Soon there will be only five
kings left – the King of England, the King of Spades, the
King of Clubs, The King of Hearts and the King of
Diamonds.'

King Farouk of Egypt (1948)

SHE WAS KNOWN AS the Queen Mum and it would be tempting to
allow such a cosy title to package her in a wrapped parcel tied with
pink ribbon. To do so would belittle the lady for, though she was
deservedly much loved, she was a much tougher and prejudiced character
than was realised by the public at large. It was generally known of course,
how, when her husband was suddenly catapulted to the throne, she
despised her brother-in-law Edward VIII for what she saw as almost a
crucifixion of her husband. It was her fury that was the backbone of
his reign, her determination to show the real values that were needed
to justify the country's monarchy.

With her background, it was, perhaps, inevitable that her views were
right wing – but it was surprising how right wing they were. However,
despite such leanings and despite her great love of horse racing – and,
we are told, gin – she was loved by all strata of society. She was gracious
and was a superb communicator, not with words but with presence.
She did not have to work at it, it just happened quite naturally, whether
she was with princes or paupers – and she constantly smiled.

Thus, when she died, peacefully at Windsor in her 101st year, we
all grieved. She had outlived her husband, George VI, by exactly fifty
years and had preserved the values that with her, he had insisted upon

during his reign which, of course, encompassed the Second World War. And although her daughter, Queen Elizabeth II, has also upheld these values, she has never had the ease and charm of her mother and has had to work much harder to maintain the common touch so natural to the Queen Mother. Despite her great age, her death still came as a shock to the nation. The obituaries were, of course, all ready and the media all over the world wallowed in tributes. But memories of Princess Diana's funeral still lingered and the press doubted if the general public would come out on to the streets in quite the numbers to mourn such a very old lady.

They were wrong. It was a different kind of grieving. Diana's life and death were the stuff of tragedy. The Queen Mother's life and death bore the mark of triumph. Diana was young and turbulent; the Queen Mother was old and serene. Diana was celebrity, the Queen Mother was royal. Both had the 'common touch', though the old lady bestowed it without guile as a matter of instinct and duty, asking for nothing in return. And though she was such a 'commoners' Queen, she loved pomp and ceremony and regarded tradition as an essential ingredient of British life. She had left full instructions for her lying-in-state and had detailed the order of service for her funeral. She did not need to confirm the simple ceremony at Windsor where she would be interred beside her husband, King George VI.

It had been decided that the lying-in-state would last for two days and that Westminster Hall would be open from ten a.m. to six p.m. The crowds were so great, however, that within a few hours of the doors opening, it was evident the arrangements would have to be changed. The orderly queue stretched west along the embankment, across Lambeth Bridge, and eastwards toward Westminster and Waterloo Bridges on the other side of the Thames. By the end of the first day it had been decided to keep the Hall open all night and extend the vigil to three days and three nights. Westminster Hall was only to be closed at six a.m. on the morning of the funeral.

It was Friday 5th April. Kim and I were watching the BBC's Ten o'Clock News and it was covering the lying-in-state, confirming that the queue was still stretching back to Lambeth Bridge – though it was likely to lessen through the night. We decided to jump in the car and head into London. Folly, our Labrador, would be fine – it was nearing her bedtime, and she would be happier at home than in the car. Soon after eleven p.m. we were in Parliament Square and I drove along the embankment to check the queue. It still stretched nearly to Lambeth Bridge but it was moving reasonably quickly. We were lucky to find a parking space on double yellow lines, in a cul-de-sac just off the embankment. The police were far too busy marshalling the crowds to worry about car parking and traffic wardens were off duty. We hurried to the end of the queue to find ourselves amongst all shapes, ages, sizes and colours, chatting quietly as we moved toward the Palace of Westminster. Every few yards there stood a friendly policeman facing the queue, joining in the quiet elation of this extraordinary display of respect and gratitude.

As we entered the Palace, we had to go through security checks and inevitably such a material procedure jarred but was understandable and tolerable after the horror of 11th September only six months before. Then we were shrouded in awe as we climbed the steps to the area commanding the western end of Westminster Hall. We paused for a moment before descending into the Hall to breathe in the majestic sight of this magnificent setting with its simple, yet dramatic, centrepiece of the Queen Mother's coffin draped with her personal standard and bearing her crown and her daughter's wreath of flowers with the simple message, 'In loving memory, Lilibet'. Four candles lit the catafalque guarded by four guards officers with heads bowed and hands resting on swords pointing to the ground. Thank God we had come.

We slowly descended into the body of the great Hall and now found ourselves looking up at the coffin as we moved slowly by. Despite the muffled sound of hundreds of careful feet and the occasional cough, the silence was almost unbearable. We were in the presence of death, but were acknowledging life and eternity. As we passed by, I thought of the little body lying so still, unable to respond to the outpouring of love and respect surrounding her. I looked back once more as we approached the doors at the eastern end of the Hall and raised my hand to say goodbye.

It was after one a.m. as we hurried back to find the car. We walked along the pavement on the other side of the road and we could see the queue still stretching to Lambeth Bridge. We drove home in silence, but at peace, receiving the usual Folly welcome as we opened the front door. We were in bed by 1.30 a.m. and, not surprisingly, slept well.

Church Bells

'Silence is the virtue of fools.'

Francis Bacon

THE SOUND OF CHURCH bells has always comforted me, steadied me, warmed me and maybe this is not surprising since I spent many of my childhood years in Chinnor Rectory across the road from the parish church of St Andrew – its six bells inevitably becoming part of my young life. On Sunday morning the bells were rung for thirty minutes before Matins, the eleven o'clock service to which all the family came, the Sunday School children sitting at the back of the church enduring the interminable prayers and psalms, not to mention the twenty-minute sermon. They would kneel and sit as still as they could under the eagle eye of my grandmother. Decades later, Matins would largely disappear to be replaced by the ten o'clock 'family' service which combines communion with traces of Matins – the children coming into the church later in the service.

I had a good treble voice and, in my holidays from boarding school, I sang in the choir. I regarded the bells as my alarm clock to get me to the church in time. I would often wait until the five-minute treble bell sounded, and this would give me just enough time to run up the drive, cross the road, sidle through the south door when my grandmother wasn't looking, don my cassock and surplice and join my colleagues looking as innocent and angelic as the rest of them as we processed up the aisle into the chancel. There was no choir at evensong and only the treble bell sounded for ten minutes. We could hear its crystal chime in the rectory. It was, however, the sound of the tenor bell – the heaviest in the tower – which remains the most vivid in my mind, not because of its majesty, but because it was tolled every time a villager died. It could be heard throughout the village so that, within a few minutes, five hundred or so people would have enquired and been told who, amongst them, had passed away. As a small boy I found this very dramatic and the single bell tolling reminded me of Cock Robin and the Bull who said he would pull the bell to mourn the little bird. Often, Tony, Joan and I would be playing in the rectory garden and suddenly the tenor bell would sound and we would pause for a moment and wonder for whom the bell tolled.

Those times were in the 1920s and early 1930s; it was not until 1970 when the family moved to Bray that church bells again became my immediate neighbours. Our home, Cannon Lodge, is little more than a hundred yards from St Michael's, the parish church, and it was with delight I heard the bells ringing out their welcome the day after we moved in. Thursday is practice night, from eight p.m. until nine p.m. and for thirty-five years we have treasured the sound of bells ringing for the family service at ten a.m., evensong at 6.30 p.m., for weddings, and of course, when the bells ring out for the last thirty minutes of Christmas Eve, summoning the faithful and unfaithful, to celebrate the birth of Jesus and again at 7.30 a.m. on Christmas Day morning to welcome the relatively few to Holy Communion.

It is good that more folk are having bells rung at the end of a funeral service to celebrate the life that has just ended, rather than tolling a bell beforehand in mourning. When my mother died –'Granny B' as she was fondly known – there was sadness of course, but there was also rejoicing and celebration for the eighty-nine years of her life which had brought happiness to so many people. When she was brought from the church and the bells, which she had always enjoyed so much, rang out their greeting, there was peace and contentment. Nearly twenty years later, when Charlotte and Michael were married, the same bells greeted them as they emerged from the church as man and wife. Again, a moment of pure joy. Ah yes, if ever we move from Cannon Lodge, I shall miss the messages the bells send out. But there are people, I understand, who regard their sound as intrusive. Sad people, surely?

I will touch upon my well meaning but pathetic attempt to become a campanologist later on but must record that on 26th April 1980, I was elected a member of the Oxford Diocesan Guild of Church Bell Ringers. My membership number is 15,769 and my certificate is signed by the Master, William Butler and the Secretary, Ken Darvill. Over the years, I have taken dozens of friends up the tower on a Thursday evening and they have always been welcomed with open arms by the bell ringers who have answered their questions patiently and taken them to see the bells themselves which are now in the chamber immediately above the ringers, having been moved down from the top chamber two decades ago, to protect the tower which was in danger from the weight of the bells at the top. There is considerable movement when the eight bells are ringing – hence the complex and extensive operation involved when lowering them to the second chamber.

Although the many erudite books on campanology insist it does not require great skills, I can assure you from personal experience, that to get beyond a very elementary stage, you need to be a specialist. I never enjoyed mathematics and I am pathetically suspicious of technology and when I first ventured up the tower at St Michael's and was given a warm welcome, I did not realise that with my non-technical mind, I was too old a dog to advance beyond a kind of primary school stage. I suppose it is not unlike golf. To become a Tiger Woods, one needs to start swinging a club at the age of four years. To be a proficient campanologist, one needs to start pulling the rope as soon as one's hands are big enough to grasp it and have the strength to pull it. I was in my mid-fifties and though I delighted in Thursday evenings' practice and ringing on Sundays, I soon realised I would never conquer the more advanced practices of 'change ringing'.

When one has learnt how to pull the rope (which in itself requires a degree of skill) and then ring the bell, the first and simplest order of ringing is 'rounds' which involves a regular pattern of one bell following another, starting with the treble and ending with the tenor – however many bells there might be in between. 'Rounds' nearly always start and finish a peal of bells. However, it is what goes on in between that puzzled my will and persuaded me not to venture into undiscovered country. There are two methods. The simpler is 'call

196

changes', whereby the Captain calls out the numbers of the bells when he wants to change order – he might call 'one after six' – so that instead of following the tenor, the ringer on treble would have to quicken to come in after six. One just has to listen carefully, adjusting accordingly. This method is relatively simple but unfortunately seldom used at St Michael's, Bray.

Here, and indeed in the majority of towers in the land, 'change ringing' is practised, whereby a particular pattern is decided upon before the ringing commences and then the Captain calls 'bob' to initiate the changes within that pattern. I never got beyond 'Rounds' and 'Plain Hunt' but thereafter, more complicated patters such as Plain Bob, Steadman and Grandsire were beyond me. There are, I understand, many thousands of changes which eight bells can ring and this fact alone illustrates the skill necessary to understand and react to the Captain's call. The permutations are mind-boggling.

Few people realise that whereas there are, and have been since the fourteenth century, hundreds of towers from which bells have been rung in this country, bell ringing abroad is a relative rarity. There are only eight such towers in America and the same number in Canada. Australia have some twenty-five towers and there are only a few ringing towers in European countries and Russia. The heaviest bell for actual ringing in this country is the Emmanuel Bell of Liverpool Cathedral – weighing just over four tons. There are several far heavier bells just for chiming – Great Paul at St Paul's Cathedral in London, weighing 334 hundredweight and Big Ben, weighing in at 270 hundredweight, are the heaviest examples. Britain's oldest bell is almost certainly at Caversfield in Oxfordshire, dated around 1250. Bray has a bell that is nearly 400 years old. The West Country boasts the most number of towers, though 'method' ringing first began in Eastern England and of course, in London; the West Country preferring call changes, proud of the purity of their striking.

I dared to make myself known to the bell ringers at St Nectan's Church, Hartland's beautiful church at Stoke. It has the tallest tower in Devon and the steps to the ringers' chamber are crumbling. I knew the band used the 'call change' method which was so much easier than 'change' ringing. Accordingly, I climbed the tower with surprisingly

197

confident steps and, as in every tower I ever visited, was welcomed with warmth and enthusiasm. We started with 'rounds' and I was at ease. But when the Captain called the first change, I could not understand a word he said – his North Devon dialect was so broad! I did not know whether he had called 'one after three' or 'two' or 'six' and the result was a horrible cacophony of sound for which I was entirely responsible. Despite the language difficulty, the ringers seemed eager to have me back and over the years I rang in St Nectan's Church three or four times. The church is in the most beautiful setting, less than a mile from Hartland Quay, The Warren and Broad Beach. The Atlantic gales howl up the valley and to hear the sound of the bells defying the elements is awe-inspiring. Everything seems to fade into the mists of time.

Roger and Sue were close neighbours in Bray and lived in one of the cottages opposite the Hinds Head. Sue had been born completely deaf but had learnt to speak and lip read remarkably well. I had told her about the bells and my involvement as a very inadequate ringer. She was immediately intrigued and asked me to take her to the tower one Thursday evening. It was a beautiful summer evening and we walked together through the churchyard to St Michael's. The bells were already ringing and I asked Sue if she could hear them but she smiled and told me to wait until we got to the tower. When we reached the tower, she placed both her hands on the closed heavy door and turning to me said, 'I can hear them now.' She stood there for several minutes, smiling as the vibrations relayed the music of the bells.... Tragically, only a few months later, her husband Roger was killed in a car crash returning from a rugby match. Sue was very brave and eventually moved to Anglesey to be near her relatives.

It hardly needs saying that church bells are rung primarily to summon people to worship God, but there are many other reasons why bells ring out and indeed one reason why they were silenced. In the last Great War, they fell silent, only to be rung if the country was invaded. However, I remember wonderful State occasions – jubilees, weddings – at which rejoicing was made more abundant by their sound, and, of course, state funerals when the bells are muffled, creating an extraordinarily uplifting, yet sombre, mood. There is a fascinating history of the relationship between the clergy and bell ringers and it wasn't always a happy one.

The bells were often rung to celebrate a non-spiritual occasion by ringers who had permanent barrels of beer in the belfry!

~~~~~~~~~

I have one confession to make. I was still an inadequate bell ringer when my grandchildren, Phillip and Sally were born, twenty to thirty years ago but I was able to ring them in. When later, James and Grace were born, I had not pulled a rope for many a year. However, I climbed the tower and asked if I could try again – just a few rounds! Needless to say, I was made welcome and managed, with a little help from my good friends – to ring a welcome to the new arrivals! Whether or not I shall have the strength to welcome any children that Charlotte and Michael might have, I leave in the hands of the Almighty. But I do hope so.

P.S. And now, nearly sixteen years after Grace was born, Charlotte and Michael's Harvey arrived. He was born on Monday, 18th April, 2005. I dared myself to go up the tower the following Thursday, 21st April 2005. I was welcomed in the usual way and assured my friends that I was not trying to stage a permanent 'comeback' as a bell ringer. I told them of the new arrival and asked if I could try and ring a few rounds to welcome young Harvey. They seemed delighted, and, with the Captain of the tower standing by me, I managed to ring in my youngest grandson!

Best Friends

'Near this spot are deposited the remains of one who possesses beauty without vanity, strength without insolence, courage without ferocity, and all the virtues of man without his vices.'

Lord Byron

DOGS HAVE BEEN AROUND me for as long as I can remember but the first dog I can claim as my own was in 1943 when a mongrel picked me up in Algiers during the war.

I can just remember Rover, a handsome English Collie who belonged to my grandparents at Chinnor and somewhere there is a photograph of me as a very small boy standing by his side with my arm sloping upwards and my hand resting on his back. But it was in the mid-thirties when we were living in Mecklenburgh Square that I realised I was a dog addict. We had a small brown bitch whom my mother christened 'Baggage' – 'Bags' for short. We were told she had some Shetland Sheepdog in her but there was no evidence to support this! She was a wonderfully social dog which was just as well living at Meck, a boarding house with some twenty to thirty occupants.

In time, Bags produced puppies that were called Pooh, Roo, Tigger and Piglet. Tigger was immediately adopted by Robert Henderson, a student medic at Barts who shared a room with my brother Tony and boyfriend of my sister Joan. Robert and Tigger were inseparable when Robert wasn't at the hospital and he trained Tigger to perform tricks from a very early age. The party trick which was performed many times daily was yawning on demand. All that had to be done was to tell Tigger to sit and then Robert would chant lyrically, 'What do you do when the sun goes down?' Tigger would look at his interrogator as if to say 'Oh no, not again' and then with an extremely bored expression on his face, execute a massive yawn. He never let us down.

When I arrived in Algiers, I was a leading aircraftsman. Within a few weeks I was commissioned and became Pilot Officer Baldwyn which made my encounter with Bruce even more embarrassing. I was walking near St Georges Hotel, General Eisenhower's headquarters, in my new uniform and feeling quite important, when I became conscious of a very mongrelled, mustard Labrador kind of dog walking immediately behind me. I made polite conversation with him and then suggested he went home. Deliberately I turned down side streets and climbed up steps but Bruce continued to shadow me. I was billeted in a small room of a house commandeered by the Americans and I decided that, just for a night, Bruce could share my room. He stayed with me for over a year, accompanying me to Tunisia, Naples, Caserta and Biferno. I could not bring him home at the end of the war because there were quarantine restrictions; I left him with Hans, my German batman, who had become devoted to him.

When I was demobilised after the war and went back to the theatre, we lived in Coulsdon just south of Croydon. During those years we had two dogs. First Co-Co, named I think after his colour, and then Dombey – vaguely a Dalmatian. As I was away in Repertory all day and every evening except Sundays, poor Peggy had the task of looking after them. Co-Co wasn't too troublesome and though there were sizeable gaps in the garden hedges, he didn't wander too much.

Dombey was another matter altogether. To say he was lively would be an understatement. As a small boy, I called Dalmatians 'Damnations' and I think this must have been Dombey's breed. He not only found all the holes in the hedges but made new ones. He was called Dombey because when we bought him, I was playing Captain Cuttle in an adaptation of Dickens' *Dombey and Son*. So the new member of the family was to be either Dombey or Cuttle. The family vote was unanimously Dombey. However, during Dombey's relatively short stay with us, he made two claims to fame – or perhaps notoriety would be a more suitable word.

We were presenting Shaw's *Tobias and the Angel* at Guildford and whenever Tobias appears on the stage, he always has a real live dog with him – breed not specified. I was playing the part of the Angel and volunteered Dombey for the part of Tobias' dog. To have hired a dog would have been expensive and Rep companies needed to cut costs whenever possible. My suggestion therefore was welcomed not only by the producer but by the management too. However, we had made a terrible mistake. In retrospect, I realised how stupid I had been. In the play, the dog is in awe of the angel and I was playing the part of the angel; in no way was Dombey going to be in awe of me.

At rehearsal, every time he came on stage with poor Tobias who led him tethered on a rope, he would see me standing angelically on the other side of the stage and would bound towards me with delight practically pulling Tobias' arms out of their sockets as he dragged the young actor across the stage. Our producer was a lady called Molly Hartley Milburn, and, quite justifiably, she got rather tired of Dombey overacting. The climax came at a midweek rehearsal when she had just told Toby to control the dog in a more professional way when Dombey decided he had had enough of this nagging voice from the darkened auditorium. He pulled himself free from Tobias, leapt from the stage and chased our producer up the side aisle, barking with delight, trailing the rope behind him. I, the angel, leapt from the stage just in time to see Molly disappearing through the front-of-house doors. She sent a note round to say that rehearsals would continue without the dog and that Dombey was to leave the theatre, never to return. I can't remember who got Dombey's coveted role but I know we all felt that the production lost a lot of its verve and spontaneity with his departure.

And then there was the time when Dombey disappeared for several days. We phoned the police but he had not been handed in. Eventually I phoned the Battersea Dogs Home – even though it was twenty miles away. I described him, his physical make-up, habits, personality, etc., and I was immediately told he was safe and well in Battersea, revelling in the companionship he was encountering. We drove straight up to London to collect him and he seemed reluctantly pleased to see us – undoubtedly he regarded his adventure as a well deserved holiday. It appears he had climbed into the back of a furniture van in Coulsdon and wasn't discovered until the driver reached his Clapham destination. Fortunately the driver was a dog lover and drove Dombey straight to Battersea. For domestic reasons, we gave Dombey to friends. The fact that we never heard from them again rather suggests we may have lost our friends as a result.

~~~~~~~~

And then, when we moved to Redhill, there was Paddy, a glorious little mongrel in a range of browns. She grew up with Tony and Jenny and accompanied us wherever we went. She was gentle and so very loyal; there are many photographs of her and one in particular taken in the conservatory at Buckhurst Close, with a napkin round her neck and her paws on the laid table with Jenny by her side. Paddy had puppies and Vi, my mother, chose a little white one whom she named Pippin and who proved to be a wonderful companion for many years.

Paddy loved our trips to Devon, revelling in the sand and rocks. She was small and light enough to jump from rock to rock and had no fear of the sea. This was the time when we owned Corner Cottage in Elmscott and Paddy was an essential part of our Devon lives for many years. And then one autumn, when she was in her fourteenth year and had suddenly become an old lady, I had walked her around the lanes as night was falling when she suddenly stopped walking and after a few seconds moved slowly forward. I picked her up and carried her to the cottage. We had visitors that night and lit a log fire. Paddy lay basking in the warmth and when we moved to the table for dinner, she left the hearth and moved under the table. She leant against my leg and a few minutes later, I felt her go limp and slide down my leg. I touched her and knew at once she was dead. I got a torch and a spade, wrapped Paddy in one of my old cardigans and, with Jenny, carried her down to the orchard where I dug her grave under an apple tree. We laid her in it, gently covered her with the good Devon earth and returned to our visitors. When I sold Corner Cottage to the O'Dells in the late sixties, they kept the little grave marked with stones.

Max was a West Highland Terrier, the first dog we had owned with a pukka pedigree. It was not a happy family time and I think this must have rubbed off on Max. He was a gorgeous little puppy with very sharp teeth. I had never experienced a terrier before but Max demonstrated his character when he was only a few weeks old by snarling and baring his teeth when I tried to retrieve a bone he had taken into the carpeted drawing room. He was very much my dog and insisted on sitting on my lap when I was driving the car. He enjoyed Devon and moved with us from Crawley to Richmond but when Peggy and I separated and I moved away, Max went and stayed with Lorna, my second cousin in Ashburton in Devon and had a wonderful time. When subsequently, Kim and I moved to Bray, Max came home to prove himself a wonderful guard dog.

Shortly after we moved into the village, we were visited by Charles Birney, the head of the local Conservative Party Association. Virtually everyone living in Bray was a Tory (and still is) and Charles was calling to welcome us to the village and to enlist us in the local Tory ranks. Gently and tactfully I was explaining that we were not, and would never be Tories, when Max rushed out from the hall and seized Charles' trouser leg in his teeth. Charles quietly said, 'Nor, it seems, would your dog.' From that day on, Charles was our friend.

Two years later Charlotte was born and Max was not amused. One day, after Charlotte had started to crawl, I walked into the drawing room to see Charlotte moving on all fours towards Max who was sitting in the well of my desk against the wall. As the little girl approached, Max, who was trapped, growled and bared his teeth. I picked Charlotte up and we knew then that we could not risk keeping him. He had been diagnosed with heart trouble the year before and the vet told us he would not make old bones. We decided it would be fairest to have him put to sleep. He was only six years old but he had had a good and eventful life. We went down to the West Country and stayed in a large hotel in Bude, bidding him farewell in a veterinary clinic the next morning. He was a tremendous personality but a real terrier. I loved him and felt flattered that he seemed to be very possessive of me. Yet, I don't think he felt the warmth of companionship and he certainly wasn't a lap dog! But no dog I have owned had greater personality.

With Lundy and Puff, for the first time we had two dogs in the household. Lundy, the yellow Labrador and Puff, the Mini-Yorkie – and what good companions they were. Lundy came from Cornwall – only just – two miles over the border from north Devon – and Puff came from West London. Some would say this reflected their personalities, Lundy being warm and affectionate, never wandering and loving the countryside, participating in all family activities and revelling in water, particularly the sea. I could not swim out to sea without him in pursuit and when he reached me, he would try and paw me with excitement, oblivious to the damage he could do (and occasionally did) to my skin with his flailing paws. Puff could not have been more different; independent, arrogant, demanding and alert to all that was going on. In some ways he reminded me of a cat except that he scorned laps and only tolerated cosiness with Lundy. But even then it was only the physical need for warmth. He was closer to Kim than me and I have always had a sense of guilt over my feelings for Puff – he was the only dog I have ever owned and never bonded with – even though, like Max, he always insisted on sitting on my lap when I was driving. Perhaps terriers always feel they should be in the driving seat.

Puff was an inveterate escape artist and would go missing for hours. A door or window had only to be open for a few seconds and Puff would be gone to explore the streets, gardens and bitches of Bray. How he survived for so long without being run over, we shall never know. On one occasion, he knocked himself out by running into a gatepost and was revived by a liberal dose of brandy. He was not a country dog and loathed the sea but sometimes I would carry him a little way out, point him in the direction of the shore and place him gently in the water. He would swim furiously ashore, emerging rat-like, shaking, running and rolling, eventually submitting to a towel. In his wanderings around Bray, he must have fathered many a pup and I am sure he knew of his excellent pedigree and thought it entirely appropriate to live in the Royal Borough of Windsor & Maidenhead.

Lundy, on the other hand, wouldn't have been at all interested in his excellent pedigree. He was humble in all he did, relishing the simple pleasures of life and accepting old age gracefully. And then, one summer's day, in his thirteenth year, when Charlotte was having a party in the garden with her young friends, he had a stroke and though he could still walk, he could only move in a circle. Lundy, of course, loved his food, and when, that evening, he was entirely disinterested in his dinner,

I knew he was ready to leave us. He was not in pain, so we decided to wait until the morning and pray for a miracle. But his condition did not change. I was leaving for an Open University Summer School that morning and I knew that Lundy had to take his leave before my departure. Accordingly Kim, Charlotte and I took him to the vet where he was put to sleep. Kim and Charlotte had to endure Cannon Lodge that night without him and I sat in a starkly furnished university room in Hampstead, writing a poem about Lundy late into the night. The poem is somewhere in my 'Scribble' file. Dear Lundy, oh so dear, you really did give us all such love, such pleasure.

Puff was as ebullient as ever. Age did not slow him down but a year later when in his fourteenth year, he took off on one of his adventures, he did not come back. He had been run over on the main road in the village and though he was killed instantly he had been taken to the vet. We went at once and saw little Puff, lying uncharacteristically still, and seemingly unmarked. I suppose Puff was loveable in a strange way and I think he missed Lundy during that last year. I am quite sure that Lundy looked up to Puff for his energy, independence and assurance.

Within a few days of Puff's death, Kim and Charlotte were pining for a puppy but felt guilty about replacing him so quickly. I needed no encouragement and when Kim's sister Elizabeth, told us there were King Charles Cavaliers for sale at a Chalfont St Giles kennels, they drove over to investigate. It was no surprise to me when they returned with a very sweet eight-week-old bitch whom we immediately christened Posy. We took her out onto the lawn and put her down gently and noticed that when she walked one of her front paws was uneven – it appeared to be bent. We immediately drove back to the kennels and were told that the paw would probably straighten in time! However, they agreed to take her back. We were then told that the rest of the litter had been sold and was being shipped to France. We saw the litter scrambling around the bottom of what looked like a witch's cauldron. I insisted that as we had been sold a 'pup' and as they had agreed there was something wrong with Posy, if they didn't let us choose a replacement from the litter, I would get in touch with the Kennel Club. They relented and we chose one of Posy's sisters and called her Rosie.

We convinced ourselves that Rosie needed a companion and as it was nearly two years since dear old Lundy had gone, we toyed with the idea of getting another yellow Labrador. We contacted Mrs Beckett in Devon from whom we had bought Lundy some fifteen years before and she told us that her yellow bitch Libbie, was 'expecting' in August and that, if she produced a yellow bitch, we could have her. We were having our last holiday in Mount Pleasant when the pups were born in Welcombe. There were seven and the only bitches were black and they were all sold. However, later in the day, Mrs Beckett sent a message that Libbie had gone back into hospital because she felt sure there was still another pup to come! She was right. During the night another bitch was born – and she was yellow. We named her Cider that very day, partly because of Laurie Lee's book *Cider with Rosie* and partly because Libbie had kept our puppy 'inside 'er inside' far longer than the rest of the litter.

In early October, I drove down to Mount Pleasant for the last time. My sadness at saying goodbye to the house was mitigated by the excitement of collecting Cider. I took with me a large cardboard box which I placed in the well of the front passenger seat and the puppy was deposited gently in the box for the three-hour journey back to Bray. She slept nearly all the way and her introduction to Rosie was touching to behold. She was still smaller than Rosie (though only for a very few weeks) and they seemed to become close friends at first sight, playing and sleeping together in a large open basket which they shared for many years to come. Even in the coldest weather they slept in the enclosed verandah outside and in the mornings when I went downstairs to get our breakfasts, they were always snuggled up together. There is a memorable photograph of Rosie lying on top of Cider – both of them fast asleep.

The times of adventure and happiness we had with these two dogs are legion. They were both enthusiasts for life in their own very different ways, Cider loving everyone regardless of status or attitude, Rosie far more particular when bestowing her patronage. Cider encouraged people to lie on the floor so that she could straddle them, challenging them to try and get up. Rosie would curl up in the corner behind the television set observing whatever was going on. For some strange reason, she became very much my dog, following me everywhere and lying at the front door if I went out until my return. When we packed our suitcases to go away, we would invariably find her lying on top of the clothes in the open suitcase and if I had been away for several days, she would literally cry on my shoulder when I returned. We used to tease Cider and call her stupid but she wasn't stupid at all. She was very honest and open and had no guile compared to Rosie who could be very devious – but sweetly so if that is possible!

We took them with us almost everywhere we went – the West Country, Scotland. Wales, the North, East Anglia, the Midlands and even London. They stayed in many hotels and everyone loved them. They enjoyed good health and, apart from having hysterectomies when they were older, their visits to the vet were far and few between. Rosie didn't mind going to the vet at all but Cider would tremble even before we got out of the car! They loved the garden of course and one of Cider's joys was hedgehog hunting In the summertime when I would let her out before bedtime; I would wait for the sound of barking and panting and grunting before rushing out with a torch to find Cider trotting round the garden like a dressage horse, head held high with an enormous hedgehog in her mouth! She would defy me for a while before laying it down on the grass and not once did she harm a hedgehog. She had managed to pick it up by digging a trench around the animal so that it was in effect on a small island. She was then able to get her mouth under the hedgehog and lever it into her mouth. She obviously found the excitement of the hunt outweighed the discomfort of the prickles. Rosie was not interested in such vulgar sport but would sometimes pick up the fleas which Cider had collected.

They were with us in Devon to welcome the Millennium but thereafter they both seemed to age rapidly. They were both in their thirteenth year – a good age for both breeds – and we knew the time would soon come to say goodbye. I went into hospital in May for a hip replacement, and, unknown to me, Rosie became very ill. She was not in pain and Kim and Charlotte decided not to have her put down in my absence. Charlotte even brought them to the hospital and parked outside my window so that I could look down and see them in the car boot. I returned home in the middle of May and Rosie gave me her usual emotional welcome, Cider her boisterous greeting. Rosie seemed reasonably well for a week or two, eating well, enjoying walks and trotting to her usual place behind the television where she always thought (mistakenly) she couldn't be seen!

On the last day of May at around ten p.m., she got up and left the room and I assumed she wanted to go into the garden. I found her squatting by the verandah door but when I opened it for her, she couldn't move, I picked her up and she weed in my arms. Her little tongue lolled out of her mouth and I knew the time had come to let her go. She was still conscious as I held her in my arms while Kim phoned to arrange for us to take her to the duty vet. We phoned Charlotte and Mikey and they sweetly said they would meet us at the vets. Kim drove and I cuddled Rosie. She was warm and comfortable and her eyes opened now and then as if seeking reassurance. We all bade her goodbye, feeling desolate but thankful for all the joy she had brought us. We stayed with her till she was gone and then returned home with heavy hearts.

Cider missed her greatly; they had spent over twelve years together but, with the excitement of the arrival of Charlotte and Mikey's Scrumpy, she took on a new lease of life. She had had this choking cough for several months but it didn't seem to affect her quality of life. It got worse, however, and the vet was not sure what was causing it and it seemed the only way of finding out would be to operate – a major operation. We deliberated and agonised; she was nearly thirteen years old – a good age for a Labrador – and to expose her to such trauma with the uncertainty of the outcome, seemed a selfish option so near the end of her natural life. The cough got worse week by week and so, on the 9th August 2000, less than three months after she had lost Rosie, the vet came to Cannon and put her to sleep. She was in her own home and she had a peaceful end. Sweet Cider, like Rosie, had given us so much and we know only too well that grief is inevitably the price we all pay for love but, my God, it is worth it.

I had had Cider and Rosie with me day by day for nearly thirteen years and, within the space of three months, they had both gone. The place was empty and there was no corner of the house or garden in which I could escape that emptiness. Kim was still working during the daytime but she too missed them sorely – especially when she walked through the front door at the end of a long day's work. Again there is a poem in my jottings file which sums up my feelings at that time.

Kim had always said she wouldn't want another Labrador, not because she didn't adore Lundy and Cider, but because, as puppies and youngsters, they can be destructive. However, in the summer a few weeks before Cider was put to sleep, Charlotte and Mikey had decided to find a Labrador puppy for themselves and we went with them to choose from a litter of puppies only two or three weeks old. I saw Kim cuddling a black puppy and she seemed to make broody noises! She even inquired whether the pup was already sold (it was), and then I heard her asking that we be notified if by any chance the sale fell through.

I knew then that there was a chance that, when the time came, our Labrador lives might continue and in September only a few weeks after Cider's death, we made inquiries through the 'Labrador Lifeline Trust' – a wonderful rescue organisation – about acquiring a young bitch. We decided that, after Lundy and Cider, we would consider a colour change and that if the right 'black' became available, she would be welcomed with open arms. We were very lucky in that, within only a week or two of our contact with Labrador Lifeline, we were offered a seven-month old black bitch. We were told she came from a country family with children; that the mother who worked had had her hours extended so that the dog was being left alone far too long. Without debate, we said we would take her.

The great day came and Kim had taken time off to welcome the new arrival on delivery. We were both unashamedly excited and, when she jumped out of the car, we could see that Molly was a very fine specimen. Her temperament too seemed perfect – she returned every bit of fuss we made of her and rushed around the garden with contented enthusiasm. Because Tony had had a black 'flattie' in Belgium called Molly, we had decided to call our new family member 'Folly' and from the moment of her arrival over seven years ago, she has been a total joy and worthy successor to all the dogs I have written about. We have not had one disturbed night and, touch wood, she has never had a serious health problem. She is a very loving dog and when out walking, meeting other humans and dogs, she will always greet the human first, and only after she has enjoyed a chat will she take an interest in the dog.

One of her greatest joys is her relationship with Scrumpy – Charlotte and Mikey's dog – the bitch they chose that day in the summer. In fact, Folly is a few weeks older than Scrumpy, and though they are the greatest of friends and swap board and lodging at each other's houses whenever circumstances dictate, they are as opposite in temperament as in colour. Scrumpy is yellow and a complete extrovert. She is absurdly intelligent, mercurial in behaviour and is only still when exhausted. She is a 'licky' dog and though she enjoys cuddling on the bed with Charlotte and Mikey – and now Harvey – her greetings are definite but transitory. Her speed is phenomenal and her energy inexhaustible. She travels with Charlotte, visiting stables and kennels and is entirely obedient, seldom on a lead. She is devoted to Charlotte and Mikey and has a touching relationship with Harvey. She is a very loyal dog.

Charlotte and Mikey gave me a superb pastel portrait of Folly and Scrumpy by Mary Browning for my eightieth birthday in 2001 and it certainly conveys the different temperaments. Folly, relaxed as usual lying with her front paws crossed; Scrumpy sitting behind, alert, ready for action. They both had another close Labrador friend – Shakespeare. He was Jenny's dog – or Phillip's – and was also black. He was very affectionate and used to have wonderful games with Folly when we visited Twyford. Sadly, Shakespeare died in the autumn of 2005 when he and Jenny were staying here at Cannon Lodge with Folly. He had had a good life and was much loved.

Folly is eight years old on 9th March 2008, when I will be in my eighty-seventh year. I sometimes think she is all the dogs I have ever had, rolled into one to celebrate the richness of my dog life. But such romance is of course nonsense – however hard I try, I cannot find a trace of Puff or Max in Folly's make-up! There is every chance she will outlive me. I hope so. I would find it hard to say goodbye to such a loving friend yet again.

Murder in Liverpool Cathedral

'Acting is a masochistic form of exhibitionism. It is not quite
the occupation of an adult.'

Laurence Olivier

I WONDER WHAT COURSE my life would have taken had I not seen
the advertisement in the *Daily Telegraph* on that hot July day in 1953,
as a result of which I became entwined with Paul Hamlyn and his
extraordinary enterprises which gave my family and me relative security.
I was faring well enough in the theatre, having been in work almost
continuously since leaving the RAF in 1945, not only in weekly and
fortnightly rep but touring and appearing in the West End at the Arts
Theatre and The Shaftsbury (then known as The Princes). The old
Shaftsbury Theatre received a direct hit in the blitz and was totally
destroyed. I had also acted in plays at two London 'Club' theatres, The
New Lindsey in Notting Hill Gate and the tiny Torch Theatre, just off
the Strand. I had been in several radio plays for the BBC and acted in
children's television plays at Lime Grove Studios, some of which I wrote.

But I was tired and it was a hot summer's day when I chanced upon
the advertisement for a young man, with car, to sell children's books
and annuals from September until Christmas, so why not apply? A regular
income and no lines to learn were enough to tempt me to take a short
break from the theatre; the rest is history as that short break of four
months extended into forty-five years, although, for the first few years,
Paul allowed me to broadcast for the BBC and I was able to continue
writing radio plays; I also read my own short stories on the eleven a.m.
BBC's *Morning Story* programme. After a year or two with Paul, I was

brought in from selling books to management positions which led to running companies selling art reproductions, LPs and cassettes, stationery and, finally, audio books. Thus I was lured away from the theatre.

I loved the theatre and I knew I had a good voice but I shall never know how good or bad an actor I was. Often I tremble at my audacity in playing some of the roles in the hundreds of plays in which I appeared when I was a relatively immature young man. It didn't occur to me at the time, however, because I suppose youth conveniently shields one from the realities of life and confidence is so often blissfully high. Nevertheless, over the decades, I have hankered after that magical life of insecurity and every time I go to the theatre, my feelings of excitement are weighed with guilt at having succumbed to the temptations of security. It's not difficult to manufacture justification for the 'betrayal' of my profession. I had a family to keep, children to educate and besides, I would still have time to write and my new work was heavily involved with the arts. So surely there was no conflict? And yet...conscience hovered and has never gone away.

No wonder then, when some thirty-five years after my last stage appearance (at the Theatre Royal, Brighton, in the Edinburgh Festival production of *Pygmalion* with Margaret Lockwood and Alan Webb), I was asked to play one of the priests in T S Eliot's *Murder in the Cathedral*, with the Liverpool Playhouse Company, I almost literally jumped at the chance. This was in 1990 and the play was to be staged in the Anglican Cathedral, vast and modern with a magnificent interior. The acoustics are appalling and it was remarkable that so much of this great but difficult play was absorbed by the capacity audiences. It was not a good production and none of the performances was distinguished but its setting made the evenings memorable. A platform stage had been erected below the chancel at the head of the centre aisle and there was, therefore, no interference with the sight line. We rehearsed for a fortnight and played for a week at the beginning of December.

Liverpool is not a city I knew well; indeed, I had visited it only twice in my life – once during the war when I was stationed at RAF Valley on the Isle of Anglesey and then some fifteen years later, when working for Paul and we had a sale of remainder books in Lewis's departmental store (not to be confused with John Lewis and its partners). After thirty five years, I had, therefore, no leads as to where to stay for my three weeks but I was determined to book into theatrical digs and with ever helpful Equity (the profession's trade union) I booked into a doctor's house which, I was told, was not far from Goodison Park, Everton's ground. I drove up to Liverpool the day before rehearsals started, taking my golf clubs with me as I felt sure I would need to relax at times – I was right. I anticipated being nervous, not only because it was so many years since I had acted on the stage but also because T S Eliot's lines were notoriously difficult to learn. They often have a disjointed sequence which means that the actors do not get much help from each other. Not only that. I was never renowned for line accuracy in my repertory days so many decades before and I was adept at paraphrasing, which was very unfair to my fellow artistes. I remember appearing in Eliot's play The Cocktail Party at Amersham and Guildford and the lines were by far the most difficult the cast had ever had to learn. I regarded my golf clubs, therefore, as an essential diversion.

Arriving at my digs, I learnt that not only was my landlady a doctor but so too was her husband and they had several very young and delightfully active children. The house was large and extremely scruffy, however, and my small room was on the top floor with only a skylight for a window. There was a bed, a chair, a small chest of drawers and not enough bedclothes! I had the use of the kitchen as the financial arrangement was simply to rent the room. I suppose I should have complained but it was such an endearing family, so interested in the theatre, that I had neither the heart nor the courage to show discontent. Besides, I had asked for theatrical digs, and I had got them. It seems that nothing had changed in nearly forty years.

We gathered in the Green Room of the Playhouse Theatre to be introduced to each other and to be given the timetable for costume fittings and rehearsals. We had a snack lunch and were told that all rehearsals would take place in the cathedral itself. Talking with members of the cast, my guilt neurosis returned and I worried that by indulging in this escapade, I was taking the bread from some other elderly actor desperately needing employment. Very few equity members make a living and most of those who do depend on 'voice-overs' for TV or radio advertisements. It was evident that not one of the cast had regular theatre work of any kind and there was I, well off, without financial worries of any kind, indulging in my love of the theatre. But there was too much warmth and excitement to allow guilt to simmer for long and after lunch we drove to the cathedral, our home for the next three weeks. I remember arriving there and feeling great relief that there was ample free parking space; had we been rehearsing and playing in the city centre, the proceeds from our minimum equity wages would have been severely diminished!

Under the cathedral there is a rabbit warren of wide corridors and spacious rooms and, in one of these, we rehearsed. Activity in the cathedral was quite astonishing, there was always something going on apart from the daily services. There was a large and fascinating shop which sold books, cards, souvenirs and gifts and, next to it, a delightful canteen restaurant where we ate lunch during rehearsal weeks. David Shepherd was Bishop of Liverpool at the time, a remarkable man and a wonderful pastor who had captained England at cricket in the 1960s. His views were liberal and had Margaret Thatcher not been Prime Minister at the time, it was thought he might have become Archbishop of Canterbury. He was a close friend of the Roman Catholic Archbishop of Liverpool, Derek Warlock and together they worked tirelessly for poor and underprivileged Liverpudlians. Their co-operation was an example of what can be achieved when the numinous combines with the secular.

Beckett of course, dominates the play although there were no 'star' artistes in the company. There were some good character performances and great camaraderie amongst the cast. Gossip and bitchiness about the theatre in general was ever present, with whispers during rehearsal and bolder, verbal destruction in the canteen. It seemed as if it was only yesterday I was learning lines and rehearsing in rep. I wondered if relationships in other professions had remained so static over the decades. But there was change in other ways. I was somewhat embarrassed on the first night to find on my make-up table, cards and small gifts from all the other members of the cast wishing me well. This was certainly not the custom in the 'forties and 'fifties, and I hurried round thanking my colleagues and making excuses by reminding them how long it was since I had acted professionally. There was the same first-night tension of course as we dressed in the different rooms of the clergy, and I think we were all conscious of a spiritual element around us that would not have been evident in a theatre or studio. Religious belief had nothing to do with it.

There was considerable publicity for the production, not least because there was a horse in the cast. I cannot remember the name but he was a magnificent animal. Not only did he have to climb the many steps into the west door of the cathedral each night (and descend them again after his performance) but, during the play itself, he was ridden up the centre aisle, flanked by the audience, bearing one of the knights who had come to murder the Archbishop. Having delivered his charge to the scene of the crime, he was then led back to the west end of the cathedral. He behaved well during rehearsal but of course there were not hundreds of people on either side of him as he walked on up the aisle. Tension was considerable therefore on the first night but he seemed totally relaxed about the whole occasion, not a trace of first-night nerves. Indeed, he didn't put a hoof wrong during the whole week and, had I been a critic, I would have commended him for giving one of the better performances. Certainly the horse was great publicity and added colour and excitement to the knight's dramatic entrance to the cathedral. (I have never heard evidence that any of the knights entered Canterbury Cathedral on horseback. Surely they would have made their entrance as inconspicuously as possible. However, our horse added to the drama and did not seem to quarrel with Eliot's vision of the play.)

Liberties or perhaps re-arrangements had been taken by the director with the dialogue sequence, in that the long introductory declaration by the chorus had been foreshortened and some of the lines given to the three supporting priests. I was the most senior of those priests and my first appearance was highly dramatic. I stood centre in front of the high alter, flanked by choirboys on either side. As the lighting was entirely focussed on the chorus and around the platform at the eastern end of the chancel, we were in complete darkness while the chorus were wailing their foreboding about Beckett's return to Canterbury. Out of the gloom, spots and floodlights were thrown on to me and the choirboys at the top of the steps as I spoke my line, 'Destiny waits in the hand of God, shaping the still unshapen.'

The angelic-looking choirboys and I had struck up a close but strange friendship; I suppose, in view of the not inconsiderable difference in our ages, they tended not to take me too seriously especially as I was playing the part of a priest. Foolishly I had told them I had difficulty in learning lines and even though I only had that one line at the high altar before moving down the chancel to the stage, they would always try and confuse me by mixing up the words just before the lights came up for me to thunder my statement down the huge cathedral. Having survived that moment, I then had to walk down the altar steps, down the chancel, down the chancel steps and then up the wooden steps on to the stage platform. It was not until the dress rehearsal that I realised I would have to negotiate these manoeuvres without my glasses. I asked my choirboy friends for help if I needed it. They assured me they had always wanted to catch a falling priest, but thankfully I never had to test their assurance.

I was always moved by the lines I had to speak towards the end of the play just after the knights had left, having murdered Beckett. I knelt centre stage, looking down the centre aisle at the departing knights as they sheathed their blood-stained swords: 'Go, weak sad men, lost erring souls, homeless in heaven and earth.' There was such dreadful despair in those words and it seemed to echo so much of current life and, in that one line the production had achieved its purpose despite its artistic short-comings. The moment seemed even more poignant precisely because we were not in Canterbury but in Liverpool in a modern cathedral, magnificent and vibrant.

I realised what a short but extraordinary chapter I had just lived through. There had been so many outside instances bordering on the main theme. We had been given the Sunday off before the final dress rehearsal on the Monday midday of the opening night having had the first dress rehearsal on the Saturday. It had been a chill week and my digs were so cold I decided to get away from Liverpool for twenty four hours. Edinburgh was only three hours away so I decided to get up at six a.m. on Sunday and drive up there to spend the day with our very dear friends, the Frames, leaving early Monday morning for the drive back to Liverpool. In retrospect, it seems it was a high-risk venture – there were no understudies in the company and had I had an accident or breakdown my two fellow priests would have had to share my lines between them. All went well, however, and I had a great day in Edinburgh and was able to go over and over my lines in the six hours driving. (This still did not stop me 'drying' on the Friday night; one of my colleague priests rescued me, however, and not even other members of the cast were aware of my memory lapse.)

There was another drama being played out on the world stage at the same time as we were playing out the murder of the Archbishop. Margaret Thatcher's demise was imminent and I remember sitting in one of the Canon's rooms in the cathedral watching her coming down the steps of our Paris embassy after the first ballot on her leadership, declaring she would fight on. In the same room, a few days later, having watched Mrs Thatcher leaving Downing Street in tears, I watched Michael Heseltine conceding defeat to John Major. It seems that Mrs Thatcher believed she was stabbed in the back by her own grandees but there is no doubt that Beckett was stabbed to death by the king's knights. I doubt, however, that T S Eliot would have been inspired to write a play *Murder in 10 Downing Street* (Agatha Christie maybe).

My memories of those three weeks are legion. In the evening we enjoyed excellent meals at the Everyman Theatre canteen just a few hundred yards down the road; several times I looked in at the Philharmonic Hall where the Royal Liverpool Philharmonic was recording Dvorak's New World, with Vernon Handley conducting for Classics for Pleasure, the label I had started when I was managing director of Music for Pleasure a decade before. I played golf at two courses and, on both occasions, was joined by Liverpudlians who insisted on looking after me at the nineteenth hole – and one of those kind gentlemen drove me around Liverpool to show me the sights. Hearing that I had worked for EMI (the Beatles record company), he pulled up outside John Lennon's family home. Those folk had reason to be proud of their city.

Our daughter, Charlotte, came to the last performance, and afterwards we all gathered in a large room in the Crypt over refreshments, exchanging farewells. David Shepherd graced us with his presence and I know we were all deeply grateful for the experience we had had. Charlotte and I left the cathedral just after midnight, arriving in Bray some three and a half hours later. It was three weeks since I had left home and, as I turned the key in our front door, I felt I had experienced some kind of a time warp.

Atlantic Coast

'Break, break, break
On thy cold grey stones, O sea!
And I would that I could utter
The thoughts that arise in me.'

Alfred Lord Tennyson

I KNOW OF NO more dramatic coastline than the few miles between Clovelly in North Devon and Morwenstow in North Cornwall. To call it rugged would be a massive understatement, as massive as the frightening but magnificent rock, slate and earthen cliffs which change shape year by year, battered mercilessly by the sea and wind. I remember standing in awe at the top of the Spekes Mill waterfalls having walked down that beautiful valley for the first time. A gale was blowing and I could barely stand as I stood looking down on the angry sea pounding the rocks and hurling pebbles high onto the beach. Not a soul was in sight and even the cries of the gulls were drowned by the howl of the wind and the ocean's roar.

Few people realise there is no land between Hartland Point and North America: 'Where on Hartland's tempest furrowed shore, Breaks the long swell from farthest Labrador.' No wonder this coast was a graveyard for shipping until technology rescued mariners from death and disaster as they rounded Hartland Point to the relative safety of the Bristol Channel. Wreckers lured ships onto the rocks with false signals, killing surviving members of the crew before plundering the ship's cargo. The coast is littered with the rusted remains of such wrecks and others cruelly driven ashore by the merciless elements. Morwenstow's famous pastor in the nineteenth century, Robert Hawker, anguished over the wrecks and resulting deaths of the sailors along this coastline and Piers Brendon's book *Hawker of Morwenstow* vividly outlines the effect these events had, not only on Hawker, but his parishioners too. The chapter 'Shipwrecks' encapsulates this drama with the lines: 'From Padstow Point to Lundy Light, Is a watery grave by day or night.'

Paradoxically, the delights and charm of this coast are as great as its awesome authority. On a warm summer's day with a gentle breeze, there can be few more idyllic havens in the whole wide world than the inlets and crannies embracing snatches of sand and exclusive pools amongst the rocks. The beach at Spekes has always been very special to us. The avenues of sand between the strata of rock vary from year to year, their width being dictated by the winter tides and storms. Yet there is always enough sand for belly surfing and pools in the sand for children's fun. At the foot of the path winding down from the cliff top is a small natural swimming pool fashioned by the considerable rocks. At high tide, one can dive into the water quite safely; at low tide there is no pool.

Spekes is never crowded, even in high summer. It is over a mile down the road via a pitted track and though it is possible to drive down to the cliff top, not many folk repeat the journey after collecting bramble scratches, mud and cowpat on their vehicle's glossy surface. I have had many cars over the past half century and all have been ritually baptised with Spekes mud. There are many other beaches of course and each has its own magical individuality – Shipload, Berry, the Quay, Mouth Mill and some four miles to the south, Welcombe Mouth. Often with more sand than Spekes, Welcombe attracts more visitors not only because its track from the road is much shorter but there is a gentler descent from the cliff top to the beach. But in the winter months there is the same solitude, and, high above the bay, Ronald Duncan, the poet and playwright, built a small wooden hut in which he gained inspiration to work.

Over the years, our dogs have loved these beaches; some braving the breakers, others showing their courage in the shallow rock pools. Paddy, Max and Rosie were small but still dared to paddle in spent waves. Puff, the smallest of all, wouldn't go near the water and I would carry him into the sea only a few feet from dry land and place him in the water facing the shore. He swam ferociously for a few seconds, tiny waves catapulting him to the beach and when his little paws touched the sand, he would shake, sprint around the beach looking very like a drowned rat. Lundy, Cider, Shakespeare, Scrumpy and Folly, all Labradors of course, would swim defiantly through whatever sea was being thrown at them and then, in their own alarming time, turn and swim back to the shallows on the beach.

And then one day in the mid-fifties I was looking at the ordinance survey map wondering what lay between Spekes and Welcombe Mouth, not by road but along the coast itself. There were no similar tracks to the cliff-top paths along the three to four mile stretch between the two bays. The road connecting the two places winds its way through farm, hamlet and wild countryside, at times only a few yards from the cliff top. Elmscott, Milford, South Hole grace the signposts along the road but along the shore there are no signposts for Spekes Mill Mouth, Longpeak, Mansley Cliff, Sandhill Cliff. Nabor Point, Gull Rock, Embury Beach, Knaps Longpeak and Knap Head. There is a glorious coastal path between Spekes and Welcombe but the distance between the two as the crow flies (the seagull is more wayward and seaward) would be considerably shorter than the distance along the shore. Farmers were uncertain as to whether it was possible to walk along the shore but thought it possible if the tides were judged aright. I reckoned it would take from three to four hours and if we started three hours before low tide, we would have six hours to play with. If we found there were promontories which never surrendered to the tide and there was no way over or through, then we would have to turn back or spend the night on a rock or cliff slope. The expedition was obviously only something a grockle would undertake but I was determined to do it. It was a challenge and surely along the way we would find lots of jetsam. I was too much of a coward to go alone or even alone with Paddy, our dog at the time. As I have said, Paddy was small and with her short legs would be able to spring from rock to rock and would be light enough to lift or carry if needs be. Tony and Jenny, then about nine and eleven years old, surely would join me.

Too many years have passed for me to remember the exact details of that first of many adventures along the Spekes – Welcombe coast. Peggy dropped us at Spekes and met us as Welcombe some four hours later where we wallowed in a rough sea, relieved and happy. We'd had little idea of what to expect because we knew no one who had been there before but I remember well the magic of those hours, the excitement of discovery, the caves, the untrodden valleys of sand, the shapes of the rocks, the shrieks from the gulls at the presence of strangers, the roar of the sea, the crumbling cliffs, the seaweed and paradoxically, the feeling of solitude. And we did collect jetsam –'oggy' balls as we called them. These were the fishermen's glass floats, green and amber, bound with cord. As the years went by, these were replaced by plastic floats – not collectors' pieces!

The physical aspects of the journey were fascinating. One moment we were stretching and jumping from one rock to another, then walking across strata of rock often covered with slippery seaweed, striding across bays of pebble and sand and at one point wriggling through a twenty-foot tunnel several feet up on a rock – the only way to get from one bay to another. As we had anticipated, little Paddy had no difficulty – we only had to pick her up on three or four occasions. We took a picnic with us —sandwiches, boiled eggs, crisps, milk chocolate and ginger beer. Verily we were in heaven on earth.

After that first adventure, the challenge was always there when we visited Hartland and I've had many other companions including Philip, Julian and James. And over all those decades, I never met another soul en route except on one occasion when I rounded a large rock and came face to face with a bearded, near naked, man sitting on a boulder at a cave entrance. I said hello but he didn't respond and, staring out to sea, seemed oblivious to my presence. I have written an unfinished play for television around this character – unfinished because I could never think of the right ending. Had he still been there in subsequent years, I might have asked him to tell me his story. Was he a sailor, the sole survivor of one of the wrecks that litter the coast? To quote Kingsley's *Westward Ho*, 'To landward, all richness, softness and peace; to seaward, a waste and howling wilderness of rock and roller, barren to the fisherman, and hopeless to the shipwrecked mariner.' As he sat motionless, his eyes set seaward, was he remembering his old friends who perished amongst the rocks on that treacherous but magnificent coast? Or was he escaping from the land? He might have provided an ending for my play.

I write this in my eighty-first year and would dearly love to make the journey once more. The distance would not be a difficulty, rather the contortions one needs to execute in covering the terrain in the limited time the tide allows and I'd have to find someone willing to come with me – at my pace. It must be at least a decade since last I made the trip. I must do it again soon.

(In the early sixties, I wrote a fifteen-minute short story for the BBC called 'Celebration' and I read it myself on the Morning Story programme. It takes place on the cliff top and beach at Spekes where the journey to Welcombe starts. I have the script somewhere and I think it reflects my love for that wonderful place.)

Bette Davies

'You cannot dream yourself into a character. You must forge one out of yourself.'

A Proverb

IT WAS A BALMY summer Saturday afternoon and Kim and I were thinking about getting ready to go over to Crowthorne to Norman Newell's house, Monterey. Two or three times a year we would play cards together with Alan, alternating the venue, for a very small-time gambling evening. We would usually start playing at about six p.m. and then break for delicious sandwiches and wine after an hour or two's play, before settling down to raising the stakes until midnight. We dressed informally, took the dogs with us and always laughed a lot.

At about four o'clock, the telephone rang. It was Norman to say there was a very slight change in the evening's arrangements. There would be dinner instead of sandwiches and could we come an hour later, still dressing informally though perhaps marginally less informally than usual. Ah yes, there was one other change of plan. It was improbable we would play cards.

I assured Norman we would naturally do as he asked since any evening at Monterey was a special occasion. Nevertheless I was intrigued to know what had caused such drastic alterations after years of routine. 'I have an old friend from America coming. She only phoned a few minutes ago and asked if she could stay the night. She's on her way down now.'

'Anybody I know?' I dared to ask.

'Well, I expect you know her, Richard but I don't think you've ever met her.'

'For God's sake, Norman, who is it?'

'Bette Davies.'

It is irrelevant whether or not one thinks of Bette Davies as a 'great' actress for she was certainly one of the great Hollywood stars, something of an icon, and a very formidable character. It was understandable, therefore, that Kim and I should feel not only somewhat excited at the prospect of meeting her but also a little nervous. Getting rid of Errol Flynn in *Elizabeth and Essex* in the 'thirties, battling with blindness in *Dark Victory* in the 'forties and asking 'Whatever Happened to Baby Jane' with Joan Crawford in the 'sixties were but a few of the memorable hours I had spent bewitched by this very distinguished actress.

I am a romantic and I felt I wanted to thank her for the pleasure she had given me over the last few decades. Accordingly, I went into our garden and picked a rose. Norman always had a roaring fire, summer and winter, and when we walked into his large, elegant sitting room, we could see Bette Davies sitting very upright on the long sofa in front of the fire. We were introduced and after a short flurry of small talk, I proffered the rose, quietly saying it was a small token for the delights she had given me. She simply said, 'Oh, thank you,' and tucked it in her cleavage.

Not many minutes later when I was talking to Alan away from the fire, I noticed Miss Davies was still on the sofa and still alone. I was about to join her when she lowered her head and appeared to be looking down at the rose. I imagine it must have been irritating her for she snatched it from her cleavage and threw it into the fire! My heart wasn't broken but I felt a strange sadness. However, it was a splendid evening, and due court was played to the Hollywood star.

Over coffee, knowing how much they hated one another, I deliberately mentioned Joan Crawford and we got exactly the reaction and performance we expected for the next half an hour. Towards the end of the evening, we sat around the table talking through coffee, smoke and cheese debris and Bette Davies looked tired and old. She watched Kim and Alan as they started to clear the table, turned to Norman and asked where the vacuum cleaner was kept. She fetched it from the cupboard and proceeded to hoover the dining room. When she had finished, she put it away and as she walked back to the sofa in front of the fire, said, 'I've always had to sing for my supper.'

We sat for an hour talking show business and its relationship with the record industry. Norman had recorded Bette Davies in 1976 singing middle-of-the-road songs as well as she could, but the LP didn't sell and I hoped Norman wasn't planning another record. We said our goodbyes at midnight – she was still sitting in front of the fire but she was no longer the centre of attention. When we reached the door, I turned to wave her goodbye but she had forgotten us already. She looked old and tired and oh so lonely. She was a Hollywood star but she was also a human being.

Open University

A teacher affects eternity; he can never tell where his
influence stops.

Henry Brooks Adams

IT WAS A CASUAL conversation with Tony, my son, in the mid-eighties
that pointed me in the direction of Milton Keynes. I don't remember
what we were discussing but whatever the context was, led him to
remark, 'Do you realise, Dad, that you are the first Baldwyn for four
generations, not to have been awarded a degree?' He wasn't censoring
me – it was just a matter of interest. I had never even thought about it
but he was right of course. Tony graduated in Law at Brunel. My brother
Tony, in Medicine at Bart's Hospital, London; my father graduated in
English at Pembroke College, Oxford and my grandfather in Theology
at Exeter College, Oxford.

As I have written elsewhere, I left school when I was sixteen, having
scraped my School Certificate at the second attempt. I had a brief
flirtation with the retail trade and then trod the boards until joining
the RAF. On discharge at the end of the war, I went straight back to
the theatre; it had certainly never occurred to me that I wasn't properly
educated and should consider doing something about it.

I pondered on Tony's remark, and, to my astonishment, found myself
relishing the idea of further education and wondered how one could
set about it at the age of sixty-four years. I had heard of the Open
University and knew that Harold Wilson, when he was Prime Minister,
had been largely responsible for its creation and that its courses involved
studying at home supported by radio and television programmes. I

imagined, however, that being in my mid-sixties would preclude me from being considered. I was wrong.

Although at this time I had ceased working full-time for Paul Hamlyn at Octopus Books, I was still a consultant to EMI, advising them on their spoken word cassette label Listen for Pleasure and directing many of the titles in the studio. I reckoned therefore, I would have time to study, and accordingly contacted the OU Head Office at Milton Keynes. I was sent details of the courses and was assured that the university was open to all ages, sizes, shapes and colours. Indeed, its cosmopolitan make-up and its range of maturity were pillars of its success.

As I poured over the literature and course details, I grew more and more excited. I was sitting at my grandfather's desk – the desk on which he wrote his sermons as a curate in Weston-Super-Mare, and Rector of Chinnor during the first three and a half decades of the twentieth century – and I felt he was looking over my shoulder, smiling approval and thinking 'about time too'.

The courses covered a wide range of subjects and when I spotted 'Arts Foundation Course 'A101' my heart skipped a beat; I read that music, psychology, history, architecture and English were the ingredients for the course's recipe and I knew then that I had found what I was looking for. I filled in the forms and waited with almost childish anticipation; and so it was I recommenced my education in 1986 and obtained my degree in 1991, the year I reached three score years and ten. I can truly say the experience was exhilarating, terrifying, humbling and oh so rewarding. The OU taught me the true meaning of education. G M Trevelyan died a few years before its inception and in 1942 wrote, 'Education has produced a vast population, able to read but unable to distinguish what is worth reading, an easy prey to sensations and cheap appeals.' He would, however, have applauded the OU revolution for it teaches one to teach oneself. I wonder what such cynics as Osbert Sitwell and Tallulah Bankhead would have thought of such a radical approach. The former's entry in Who's Who included 'Education: during the holidays from Eton' and the latter is reported to have said, 'I read Shakespeare and the Bible and I can shoot dice – that's what I call a liberal education.' They might well have snorted, but I think maybe they would then have applauded.

From April to September, students would submit essays to their tutor on designated subjects. These would then be marked and sent back with comments. There would be six TMAs (Tutor Marked Assignments) and every month one would wait with baited breath to read the title of the task ahead and then with even greater apprehension await the package returning one's essay with the tutor's scribbled comments and marks. These would make up fifty per cent of the total to be awarded for that year. Each month students would attend a tutorial at the local college and it was on these occasions one would meet and get to know one's fellow students.

This was one of the great joys of the OU experience. We were all gathered together for a few hours every month, on a Saturday morning, to share a common cause for the same end. The social intercourse was remarkable and the friendships and respect that emanated from those gatherings were manifold. I attended Bulmershe College, a child of Reading University, and my tolerant tutor was Barbara Vowles who seemed to listen as she lectured and comprehend the ambitions and uncertainties of the folk before her. There was only one student older than me, a widow with no car, and I was able to fetch and carry her to and from the tutorials, but most of all I recall the young mothers – some of them with two or three babies and young children – who would pin up pages from their course work books on kitchen and bathroom walls so that they could study while they prepared and disposed of meals and bathed the children. Meanwhile, I would return to my comfortable study and sit at my antique desk in a comfortable chair. No wonder I felt twinges of guilt and from time to time needed reassurance that I wasn't taking the place of someone more deserving than I.

And in those far-off days, there were summer schools in the middle years of the course and we all looked forward to the week away at a university campus. There was a wide choice from which to select and what excitement there was and how well the vast majority of students mixed the business of study with pleasure. The lectures and classes were varied and as we were all new to campus life there were no hierarchical divisions. It was indeed, a very open society; so many students were discovering they were not so stupid either academically or socially as they had thought, and in many cases the experience was quite evidently changing lives.

I went to three summer schools – Westfield College, Hampstead (part of London University), Sussex University and York University, and I have vivid memories of all three. I could not have chosen three more contrasting locations. Westfield College was, of course, the nearest to my home but because it was one of the many colleges which make up London University, the campus was smaller and less like so many modern universities where all the facilities are in one location.

It was at Westfield College that I was fortunate enough to have as one of the lecturers Arthur Marwick, a brilliant teacher, witty, eloquent and innovative. His lectures were always eagerly awaited and there was never an empty seat. I didn't realise at the time of course, how distinguished he was. He had become the first Professor of History at the OU, he had won the Gold Medal as the outstanding History graduate of his year at Edinburgh University and went on to Balliol College, Oxford. He then had a distinguished career as one of the leading social historians of twentieth-century Britain, writing several books which became essential reading for academics. He listed his interests as 'wine, women and football' and it seems these were indeed his main interests outside his work. I spent many hours with him at the bar and he always called me 'Zebidee' presumably because I was probably his oldest student. I found him to be a very kind person and was sorry to read of his recent death. His obituary in *The Times* started aptly, 'Arthur Marwick was one of the most productive, flamboyant and combative historians of his generation.'

Sussex University stands a few miles inland to the east of Brighton, with a delightful campus. The weather was glorious and we were able to lie out on the grass between lectures and on the long summer evenings. One of my abiding memories was of a psychology lecture after which we were divided into four teams to discuss it and each team appointed a spokesperson who would stand up in front of the whole class and deliver a précis of the team's deliberations. In that psychology class there was one middle-aged student who had become notorious for asking too many questions and then answering them himself at considerable length. He happened to be in my group, and once we had started deliberating as to who should speak for us, he assumed he would be chosen; however, we had in our group a very small elderly lady who was very shy and had asked no questions during the lecture. I proposed that she should speak for us but in a very quiet, determined voice, she demurred. The rest of the group backed my proposal and we eventually persuaded her to represent us. We were the last of the four teams to submit our opinions and in the five minutes allowed, she held the whole class spellbound. I noticed the lecturer gazing at her with a slightly astonished but delighted expression on his face, for what she said was succinct and eloquent. When she sat down we all applauded and our group congratulated and thanked her for her contribution. I caught up with her as she walked across the campus and asked her if she had read psychology before, she smiled and replied quietly, 'No, but I suppose it runs in the family, Sigmund Freud was my uncle.'

My last summer school was at York, one of the first new post-war universities which opened its doors to students in 1963. The campus was well planned with ample rural background to the modern halls of residents and study facilities. I was thrilled to find that Arthur Marwick was one of the lecturers and on the first evening in the bar, I approached him somewhat nervously and was about to ask him if he remembered me, when he put an arm round me and said, 'Ah Zebidee, let me buy you a drink.' It was two years since we had last met.

I enjoyed the week at York enormously. One memory persists above all, partly because Arthur Marwick was involved and partly because the climax to the incident enabled me to deliver a punch line which any thespian would relish. There was an evening lecture by a visiting professor from Liverpool University and the subject was centred on the Balkans and the German occupation of Greece and Yugoslavia. The lecture was in the university's central hall and every seat was taken. I have written elsewhere of my membership of the Balkan air force and our involvement with Tito's Yugoslavia and I therefore made certain I had a good seat in the front row of the gallery.

Arthur Marwick was in the chair to introduce the speaker who lectured well, with humour. He then asked for questions and these came readily and were evidence of the quality of his lecture. There was, however, one relatively unimportant statement about the date on which Tito had set up his headquarters on the island of Vis and as I had been directly involved, I knew the date that was given was wrong. I suppose

I wanted to show off by demonstrating the knowledge of the facts; I was nervous, nevertheless, and it was not until the flow of questions was slowing and Marwick was asking if there was any more, that I summoned up the courage, got to my feet, and queried the date. The lecturer referred to his notes and confirmed the date he had given. I persisted. The lecturer then open a large book, found the reference and politely told me he was right. I still persisted. Marwick sprang from his chair and shouted, 'Zebidee, what makes you so sure you are right?'

'Because I was there.' Everyone in the hall turned and looked at me and I am ashamed to say I thoroughly enjoyed that moment. Marwick simply muttered, 'Oh God,' then, 'Sit down, Zebidee, we'll continue this debate in the bar.'

And then each autumn we faced the dreaded exam which made up the other fifty per cent of the marks for the year. I was transported back some fifty years to my School Certificate trials at Malvern. Now we were gathered in the Great Hall at Reading University, sitting in silence, thinking and writing, only disturbed by the chiming clock and the ominous footsteps of the invigilators pacing between the rows and then kindly warning us when the time was nearly up. Each year I was convinced that I had done badly and each year I was pleasantly surprised. The final year's exam was of course the most agonising and when I heard that I had become a Bachelor of Arts, I really thought there must be some mistake.

The graduation ceremony was held at Southampton University. Kim and Jenny drove down with me to witness my 'coronation'. Hundreds of students went on stage to be given their degree by the Chancellor. The actress Jill Balcon, wife of the former Poet Laureate Cecil Day Lewis and mother of Daniel Day Lewis, the actor, was the guest speaker and sat on stage beside the Chancellor as he handed the certificates to the students. When my name was called, and I had collected my degree, as I passed Jill Balcon – an actress I greatly admired – I took her hand and kissed it, much to her astonishment and Kim and Jenny's embarrassment.

There is a postscript to these happenings. A year or two after I was given my degree, the OU revised its marking system and in 1994 a letter arrived in my post box telling me that as a result I had become a BA

(Hons)! Dean Inge said, 'The aim of education is the knowledge not of facts, but of values,' and perhaps in my relatively long life, I have, without realising it, acquired more of that knowledge. Without doubt, my experience with the Open University and listening to Arthur Marwick and his like, echo John Buchan's words, 'To live for a time close to great minds, is the greatest kind of education.'

There were those who were cynical about the OU and not only referred to it as a 'glorified correspondence course' but as 'yet another Harold Wilson gimmick'. Yet as Ben Pimlott writes in his biography of Wilson, 'it was also a brilliantly original and highly ambitious institution which took the ideals of social equality and equality of opportunity more seriously than any other part of the British education system.' By the 1980s the Open University was awarding more degrees than Oxford and Cambridge combined. By the 1990s it was planning a student total of more than 100,000 and as I write this between two and three million students have graduated from the OU. Harold Wilson had every right to be proud of his achievement and Pimlott tells us 'it was the one for which – above almost anything else in his career – he most wished to be remembered'. Robin, his elder son became an OU lecturer and Giles, his younger son, took a degree there.

I shall always be grateful to those who have nurtured the Open University since its inception some forty years ago. The dedication of the staff is remarkable; it embraces the vision of encouraging education aspiration for all.

How to Become a Professional Actor

'Being young is not having any money; being young is not minding having any money.'

Katherine Whitehorn

WE WERE LIVING IN Mecklenburgh Square when I left my job at Harrods early in 1938; Tony, my elder brother was a medical student at Barts. Hospital, and Joan, my sister was at King's College Hospital training to be a masseuse (now physiotherapist). Tony was four years older than I and much more responsible. He was popular with his peers of both sexes and was proficient at any sport he practised. Perhaps his greatest love was sailing – I remember holidays in Cawsand, Plymouth Sound when he would take a small dinghy out in any kind of weather. I remember too sailing with him on the lake in Regents Park though it was usually Joan, my sister who crewed for him. He had a passion for flying too and in 1937 went on a student exchange visit to Nazi Germany for a course in gliding under the auspices of the Luftwaffe. He came back enormously impressed not only by the hospitality but by the infrastructure and efficiency of the country. I realise now that, though he was a fun person and very adventurous, he was mature for his age and had grown rapidly into adulthood as a result of being the senior male in the family – he was only four years old when our father died.

Tony had been delighted when I got my job at Harrods. He felt that, after my early departure from Malvern, discipline at the most prestigious departmental store in the world would help to lay foundations for any career I might eventually choose. It would also enable me to contribute financially for my board and lodging at Meck. Though my mother was making a great success with 23 and 24 Mecklenburgh Square as lodgings for medical students and a variety of other folk, she was only just keeping afloat financially and I was occupying a bed which could be bringing in an income. Tony therefore, regarded my departure from Harrods as irresponsible, particularly because I hadn't the slightest idea what I was going to do next. He was right of course and we had a furious argument in front of my mother. I pushed him away and he tripped over the pouffe, fell backwards, cutting his head on the fender. I was full of remorse and told Tony that if I hadn't got a job by the time my Harrods savings had run out then I would admit that I had been wrong.

Early in my teens I had thought I would make a good clergyman presumably because of the years I had spent as a child at Chinnor Rectory. There was no question of a 'calling', however, and it would not have been on the short list, had there been one. However, two of the lodgers at Meck were at RADA (The Royal Academy of Dramatic Art) in Gower Street and having appeared in a few plays at Prep and Public School and been exposed daily to the bright lights of Shaftesbury Avenue as I cycled to and from Harrods, I decided to be an actor! Again, there was no question of a 'calling' – I needed to earn some money and it seemed to me that the theatre could offer me not only a salary but glamour too. I bought the weekly journal *The Stage* and read the advertisements which pointed me in the direction of one or two auditions. My offerings must have been embarrassingly awful and I even tried to get into RADA. The height of my naivety, innocence, immaturity or sheer conceit was when I went to the Comedy Theatre to audition for a revue called *New Faces*. (It was in this production that Judy Campbell sang 'A Nightingale Sang in Berkeley Square' making her a star.) I owned a ukulele on which I could only play a few bars and planned to sing a popular song of the moment 'I Can't Give You Anything But Love, Baby'. Happily for everyone, I was stopped even before I reached the refrain! It still hadn't occurred to me that I might have no talent. Undaunted, I got hold of a list of theatrical agents from Spotlight and decided to visit them in alphabetical order. In those days, so long before the advent of television, voice-overs, etc, there were only two or three dozen agents – now there are several hundred. Spotlight consisted of one slim volume, most entries carrying photographs of the artistes. When I last used Spotlight for choosing readers for audio books (in the 1990s) there were four fat volumes for actors, four for actresses and a separate volume for child artistes !

I set about my project knocking on doors of the very few A to C agents. There was but one D entry and that was Denton and Warner whose offices were in Cambridge Circus opposite the Palace Theatre where quite recently I had taken my mother to see Jack Buchanan in *This'll Make You Whistle*. I went up to the third floor in a very old creaking lift and found a somewhat battered door with a faded 'Denton and Warner' on it. I knocked and waited but there was no answer. I knocked again. I spent a minute or two summoning up courage to enter when a distant croaky woman's voice shouted, 'Who is it?' I pushed open the door and found myself in a passage way thick with cigarette smoke as 'Who is it?' was repeated, followed by a few seconds of desperate coughing. I really wasn't sure what to answer – Richard Baldwyn wouldn't mean anything – so I stammered, 'I don't think you'd know me.' Back came the voice, 'You'd better come in then and I'll tell you whether I know you or not.'

Through the haze I groped my way into a small shabby office largely filled by a desk littered with papers and files surrounding a huge ashtray piled high with cigarette ends. I was mesmerised by the lady sitting behind the desk. She was small, ample and crowned with vivid reddy orange hair hanging untidily over a rather frightening face. She stared at me, expecting me to open the dialogue, when the telephone on her desk rang. She proceeded to talk to someone called Barry but I didn't listen to the detail of the conversation because I was so intrigued by the posters and photographs on the wall, the programmes on the floor and chairs and the quite literally choking atmosphere. I hadn't been asked to sit down presumably because the chairs were fully occupied by paper of one kind or another and it was only when she had finished with Barry that she looked at me through her thick glasses and said 'Well?'

I was speechless!

She leaned forward: 'What do you want?'

'A job.'

'Doing what ?'

'Acting'

'What have you done before ?'

'Several months at Harrods'

'Father Christmas?'

'Men's Ready to Wear.'

'Can you act?'

'Of course.'

'Where were you trained?'

'I wasn't.'

She stared at me for a very long time, stubbed out a cigarette and lit another one. I thought I detected a glimmer of a smile.

'When can you start?'

'Start what?'

'A job. You said you wanted one.'

'Er, well. Any time really. Tomorrow. The next day. Next week?'

'This afternoon?'

Her eyes only left my face when she dialled a number on the phone. I could hear it ringing above my heartbeat and then she spoke down the phone: 'Barry O'Brien, please. Tell him it's Miriam Warner.' She was still staring at me when I heard a man's voice on the other end of the line. She interrupted him: 'Barry, I think I've got just the person you want...nice little boy called Richard Baldwyn...yes, he can start straight away...that won't be a difficulty...25/-d a week, 27/6d when he's playing...all right I'll send him right over.'

She put the phone down and started scribbling on a piece of paper and as she did so, she chatted on.

'Ten-week summer season on the pier at Eastbourne. The sea end. Clarkson Rose has his "Twinkle" summer revue this end. Barry's a good manager and John Morley is a good producer. You'll be Assistant Stage Manager playing parts when required. Go to the Saville Theatre just down the road and you'll find them rehearsing in the circle bar. You'll have to find digs quickly. Open on Monday. Final run-through Saturday. Be there by Friday. Here.'

She handed me the scrap of paper she'd been writing on.

'Good luck, darling. Anything you want to know?'

'Er, no…well, yes. Don't you want my address?'

'Write to me. I'll send you a letter of agreement.'

'Thank you, Miss Warner.'

'Miriam.'

'Thank you very much indeed…er…Miriam.'

'Off you go. You'll be late.'

I turned on my heel and almost staggered down the passage. I was in a state of shock and desperately needed fresh air. I couldn't wait for the lift to crank up and I ran down the cold bare stairs into the sunlight of Cambridge Circus. The Saville Theatre was only a hundred yards down Shaftesbury Avenue (a cinema now occupies the site) and as I walked, I read and reread Miriam's scribbled note to Barry O'Brien. It simply noted the terms of my employment. When I reached the theatre I must have floated into the foyer and up the stairs to the circle bar and it was there I started my professional career as an actor. Miriam had told no one – not even Barry O'Brien – that this seventeen-year-old had never had any training or contact with the professional theatre before. Everybody assumed I knew what to do. I started to act therefore, the moment I set foot in that Saville Theatre bar. I said very little but heard a lot and, by the end of the afternoon, my feet started to touch the ground.

I cycled home in triumph and the family could not believe my luck. Indeed it was luck. Tony was delighted but, looking back, surely he must have wondered how I could have become a professional actor in one afternoon when he was just starting his fifth year of training to become a doctor.

This all happened on a Tuesday. I left for Eastbourne on the Thursday and found wonderful digs with Mrs Doherty at 25/- a week, inclusive of all meals. I played small parts in most of the plays during the ten week season which meant that I had 2/6d pocket money! Riches! The first play was called *All the King's Horses* and Dame Irene Vanbrugh was the guest artiste. At the last rehearsal, the girl playing the part of the maid fell ill. The part was changed to a butler and of course, I played it. I had one line – 'Dinner is served, your Ladyship.' Halcyon days indeed!

This'll Make You Whistle

'Youth is vivid rather than happy, but memory always
remembers the happy things.'

Bernard Lovell

I WAS JUST SEVENTEEN years old and I felt very grown up when I
took my mother to the theatre for the first time. It wasn't any old theatre
– it was the Palace Theatre in Shaftesbury Avenue, London. I had left
school when I was sixteen years old, I was working in my first job at Harrods
earning 'real money'. We lived at 23 Mecklenburg Square in Bloomsbury
where my mother ran a very extraordinary family boarding house, mainly
for medical students. My brother Tony was studying at Barts and my sister
Joan was at King's, training to be a Masseuse (now physiotherapist).

Every morning I cycled from home through Bloomsbury down
Shaftesbury Avenue, Piccadilly, Knightsbridge, on my way to Harrods,
and every morning I would dream of theatre land as I passed the Saville,
the Palace, The Shaftesbury (now a fire station after having been
destroyed in the Blitz; the present Shaftesbury Theatre at that time was
called The Princes), the Queens, the Apollo, Lyric and the Globe. As a
bonus, I passed the Criterion as I banked round Piccadilly Circus.

I knew my mother was a fan of Jack Buchanan and the musical *This'll
Make You Whistle* was enjoying a long run at the Palace Theatre. He
and Elsie Randolph were the stars and their names lit up the front of
the theatre in Cambridge Circus. Quite definitely, I would book for this
show with my own money. One evening on my way home, I got off
my bicycle, leant it against the front of the theatre and, for the first
time in my life, I walked into the foyer of a London theatre to book

seats. I felt so grown-up that I booked a box (I confess it was a top box) and then pedalled furiously home to tell my mother what I had done. She was as excited as I was.

I wore my best suit and my mother looked splendid in a long black dress. We went by taxi and the commissionaire opened its door when we arrived. I was a little disappointed that the staircase up to the top boxes was not carpeted as the stairs to the lower boxes were. But no matter, we had a wonderful evening and the theatre was packed. We were able to gaze down on the audience in the intervals, remembering a review we had been taken to a year or two earlier at the same theatre – C B Cochran's *Streamline* with Florence Desmond. She was certainly the star of the show, but there was an enchanting number in it, sung by an actress named Nora Howard. Dressed as a society nanny, she walked on to the stage pushing a very large and elegant-looking pram, singing a simple song. It was a magical number and brought the house down night after night; I have always remembered the chorus lyrics –

Other people's babies,
That's my life,
Mother to thousands,
And nobody's wife.

I have seen many great shows at the Palace Theatre since those 1930 days, including *King's Rhapsody,* the last of Ivor Novello's musicals and the one during which he had a heart attack and died quite suddenly. (The show went on with Jack Buchanan bravely taking over the lead after only three nights closure.) *Jesus Christ Superstar, The Entertainer* with Laurence Olivier – and many more. But none could have produced the enjoyment of that evening when I escorted my mother to the top box of that lovely old theatre.

After the curtain calls, we stood and lingered in our box watching the audience leave the auditorium. We ambled down the stairs into the foyer and studied the photographs, theatre bills and posters. Outside, it was a clear winter's night and we decided to walk home up Shaftesbury Avenue, past the British Museum, round Russell Square and down Guildford Street. We were two very contented people.

Christmas

'And girls in slacks remember Dad
And oafish louts remember Mum,
And sleepless children's hearts are glad,
And Christmas morning's bells say "Come" '

John Betjeman

I SUPPOSE CHRISTMAS IS a very special time for most Westerners but for many different reasons. Certainly it has become a very commercial festival but, underlying that, I like to think many folk do have loving thoughts even though they are not practising Christians. Certainly thousands upon thousands, who seldom enter a church during the year, attend Midnight Service on Christmas Eve and whatever else, they are enriched by so doing and they are sharing a celebration with millions of people throughout the world. As I have written elsewhere, I am still busy searching for the secret of faith. I doubt if I shall ever find it, but I know that the continuity of search is very important.

As a small boy I was very lucky to spend most of my Christmases at Chinnor Rectory where I was not only part of a large family but St Andrew's, just up the drive and across the road, was an adjunct to the rectory, my home at that time. Therefore, quite apart from the excitement of decorations, wrapping presents, pretending to help Kate and Elsie in the kitchen, keeping secrets, being allowed to listen to the occasional programme on the crystal set, the music and walks in the snow (I'm sure it snowed more at Christmas in those days), it seemed there were as many preparations at the church. We would take over greenery from the rectory to wrap around the pillars, there would be choir practice when we dusted off the carols and my grandfather would smile happily as he played his beloved organ. The bells would peel and the villagers attended to the graves of their loved ones with berried holly. And on one of the evenings prior to Christmas Day, the grown-up members of the choir would come to the Rectory and sing carols in the large conservatory between the front door and the hall. Mulled wine and mince pies were handed round and for half an hour I was in wonderland.

I suppose I have carried those memories, and felt the same wonder, right through my life, wherever I have been. Most certainly the few Christmases at Mecklenburgh Square were magical and, at the time, my brother Tony was a medical student at Barts. We always visited the hospital on Christmas Day and the festivities amongst the patients, doctors, nurses and general staff were quite extraordinary. I was away for three Christmases during the war in Algeria, Italy and Greece. Though the settings were totally different, the Christmas spirit pervaded. In Algiers, we shared a lot of activities with the Americans (though not the food!). General Eisenhower was C–in–C and perhaps his forte was ensuring that all the different nationalities were well looked after. (The French were part of the Command too.) In Italy, I was on a Wing at a place called Biferno on the Adriatic coast. Our runway stretched along the beach – our camp consisted of Nissen Huts and tents. We had to rely on our own resources for our celebrations and entertainments and most probably this was why the Italian Christmas was the most memorable – not because so much drink was consumed but because there was companionship, worship and laughter. The Christmas in Athens was the most dramatic because we were in the middle of a civil war, and half the city was in the hands of ELAS, the Communist revolutionaries. It was the only time during the war when I had to carry a gun at all times. It was particularly dangerous to go out at night as snipers, who knew the city much better than we did, would infiltrate the Allied lines. Nevertheless, it was still very much Christmas and Churchill visited us instead of Father Christmas.

I have been very fortunate with my Christmases and I hope I have to some degree passed on the addiction which has stayed with me. And then of course, after the war, marriage and children – Tony and Jenny;

Christmas became even more meaningful. Those late 1940 years were difficult for the country but children did not suffer – indeed, although there was strict rationing all through the war and for many years afterwards, children had never been so healthy and indeed have never been so healthy since that time. And, of course, families relied on their own entertainment and festivities, listening to the radio and occasionally going to the cinema. Television for the very general public was still many years away.

Our Christmases at Coulsdon were in this context and we always shared them with Stephen and Amy Knight who lived just up Warwick Road. I was in repertory during those early years of family and was in pantomime at Amersham and Guildford. This must have been hard on Peggy and I suppose I didn't realise at the time the strains upon her. But I was earning a living and this enabled us to have traditional and happy times. As Tony and Jenny grew up, we celebrated the festivities at Blechingley where I produced my first nativity play with Jenny playing an angelic angel. Then on to Buckhurst Close in Redhill, with Granny B in her sweet little cottage at Nutfield – now no more. The M23 to Brighton sweeps past the site within a yard of Granny's fence! Then as Tony and Jenny progressed from teenagers to adults, there was Pound Hill near Crawley and, subsequently, Richmond. Through all these times, Christmas was an anchor as indeed it should be and I am eternally grateful to everyone who contributed happiness to those eventful and sometimes difficult times.

And then, of course, in my fiftieth year, which, as I write this, was nearly thirty-two years ago, I married Kim and we moved to Bray where we still live. Charlotte arrived and yet another dimension was added to Christmas for, though we experienced all the joys of parenthood at such a time, we had the added delight of watching our children of considerably varying ages – Tony, Jenny, Susan and Julian, not to mention Granny B who lived three minutes away – revelling in the 'family' festivities returning to days gone by.

I suppose the setting of Cannon Lodge and the house itself is exceptional. Not in a grandiose way but in homely terms. It is a cosy place and, though in the centre of the village and very private, it has always been a hive of activity not only for family but for friends as well.

There have always been animals – originally Max, a Westie. Then with Lundy and Puff, a yellow Lab and a mini Yorkie, a cat, Trushka, a handsome Birman. Cider, another yellow Lab and little Rosie, a King Charles Cavalier, lived with us for thirteen wonderful years and managed to see the new millennium in before setting out for that undiscovered country. Then, of course, Folly our present black Labrador. I mention our four-legged friends again because they have all contributed so much to our Christmases, participating not only in the general excitement of music, colour and food, but in the opening of presents from under the tree, not restricted by the name on the label.

Surely the delights of home, with the church and its bells only two gardens away, can never be surpassed at Christmas time. And of course Christmas 2002, only two days before Charlotte and Mikey were married in St Michael's, was quite magical. The family – including little Lizzie, my great niece and her Dad, Michael, from Oregon – and so many friends crowding the house with happiness and glorious activity, all revelling in the festivities and anticipation of the joys to come.

However much commercialism has taken over, there is still more goodwill than at any other time of the year – and that can only be good. Let us hang on to that, whatever the cynics might say.

Nigel Tetley – A Voyage Too Far

'Everything can be found at sea, according to the spirit of your quest.'

Joseph Conrad

IT WAS TOWARDS THE end of June 1968 and I was flying back from the south of France with other Hamlyn directors; we had been Paul's guests in his Cap Ferrat house, dividing business and pleasure in a wonderful setting. We were flying Air France in a Caravelle and I remember that passengers board and exit the aircraft at the tail end. As we approached the runway at London Airport late on a Sunday night the wheels were lowered and it seemed we were just about to land when there was full throttle and the aircraft gained height rapidly. After a few minutes circuit, it seemed we were coming in to land again when exactly the same thing happened and we soared back into the night sky once more. A French male steward appeared and, with a relaxed smile on his face, announced, 'Ladies and Gentlemen, we apologise for the delay in touch-down, but we have a little problem with our landing gear. However, I am sure you will agree it is better to land a little late than never to land at all.' Two crew members in white overalls then appeared, took up a portion of the carpet from the centre aisle and disappeared through a trap door into the bowels of the aircraft.

Recalling the adventures I had had in aircraft during the war, I felt rather more than apprehension as I listened to clanging noises coming from below. I had been reading *The Sunday Times* and, hoping I did it with nonchalance, I plunged back into an article which I had just started reading before we had made our first landing approach. It was about the Golden Globe Race which *The Sunday Times* was sponsoring and it involved sailors circumnavigating the globe, sailing single-handed without stopping. The entrants could start any time between 1st June 1968 and 31st October 1968 and there would be two prizes; the Golden Globe would be awarded to the yachtsman who completed the first circumnavigation and £5,000 would be given for the fastest time. The voyage had to be undertaken without any outside physical assistance and no food, water, equipment or fuel could be taken on board after the start. Already three young British sailors – John Ridgway, Chay Blyth, and Robin Knox-Johnston had started the race and two Frenchmen and another Briton was due to start in August.

The sub-heading to the article 'Around the World in Eighty Symphonies' caught my eye just as we were starting on our third circuit before another attempt to land. The story was about Nigel Tetley, a naval commander who hoped to enter the race in his trimaran *Victress* on which he and his wife Eve lived. They loved classical music and had a stereo system aboard. Tetley had been unable to get sponsorship and when he mentioned this to a reporter, it was suggested he try and involve a record company – hence the sub-title of the article.

My stomach was churning as we made our third approach and I swore to myself that if we landed safely, the Hamlyn company Music for Pleasure, of which I was managing director, would offer Tetley sponsorship.

I heaved a huge sigh of relief as we touched down without incident and as we left the aircraft we were told that there had been an electrical fault which caused the light in the cockpit, which confirmed the locking of the undercarriage, when lowered, had failed, and therefore the pilot was not sure whether the wheels would collapse on landing. My first action on that Monday morning was to contact Terry Bartram, our PR manager, and tell him to try and organise sponsorship.

Terry worked with speed and efficiency. Our sponsorship was to include supplying Nigel with dozens of classical cassettes for him to play during the long lonely months of the voyage. The letters 'MfP' were to adorn the top of the mainsail and 'Music for Pleasure' would feature in bold letters on the side of the boat. I travelled down to Plymouth and went aboard *Victress* as she was being fitted out by Nigel and Eve, ready for the September departure. He was a quiet, poetry-loving man, and, even though he was a naval officer, I found it hard to imagine Nigel enduring four to seven months of gruelling hardship, danger and loneliness. He and Eve went about their business quietly and methodically – they were a very likeable couple.

Meanwhile there were two other boats to sail. An Italian, Alex Carozzo, and Donald Crowhurst, sailing a trimaran not unlike Tetley's. While these three were all starting in September and October, weeks and months after the other entrants, in theory there was still a chance that one of the trimarans could win both the Golden Globe and the £5,000 because they were so much faster than the monohulls. Nigel Tetley left Plymouth the first week in September, Carozzo later that month, and Crowhurst toward the end of October.

The one thing all these men had in common was courage and what they were attempting to do bears little resemblance to modern single-handed yacht racers, whose safety net through high-tech advances is hugely wider and vastly more efficient, enabling them to have virtually permanent contact with the outside world. The men who set sail in 1968 were in small, unsophisticated boats and their only means of communication was through their own radio transmitters. They were exposed to horrific conditions and experienced loneliness only tempered by their struggles to survive; each one of them had a different reason for accepting such a challenge and only one of them succeeded in completing the course. That was Robin Knox-Johnston after ten months at sea in a rather heavy old-fashioned boat called *Suhaili*; because he was the only entrant to finish, he won both the Golden Globe and the £5,000. During one period of his voyage, he had not been heard from or seen for nearly three months and there were considerable fears for his safety.

When Nigel Tetley set off, we had a large map pinned to a blackboard in the foyer of Hamlyn House in Feltham and Terry Bartram kept us all up to date with the progress of *Victress*. It was steady but unexciting progress. Nigel reported that he was eating well and thoroughly enjoying listening to his music. He encountered gale force winds in December, but more often than not he was experiencing light winds and became somewhat depressed as did the sponsors of the race, *The Sunday Times*, by his relatively slow progress. He thought seriously of heading for

Capetown and retiring. However, he met with rougher weather in the Indian Ocean though he was still able to enjoy a traditional Christmas lunch, having survived a Force 9 gale only two days before. He opened his presents and listened to the MfP recording of 'Christmas Carols from Guildford Cathedral'. Perhaps his relatively eventless voyage during the last months of 1968 was fate's way of preparing him for what was to come as he entered the Southern Ocean south of Australia.

He encountered seas he had never experienced before and was astounded that *Victress* didn't break up. We hired an aeroplane to take pictures of him near Hobart but were unable to find him. He still had nearly 5,000 miles of the Southern Ocean to cross before rounding Cape Horn in March. He had some terrifying experiences during those weeks between New Zealand and Cape Horn and had again considered pulling out of the race. But the winds subsided and he continued sailing east to become the first multi-hull to round Cape Horn.

Nigel was astonished to hear that his friend Moitessier had dropped out of the race and he already knew that Blyth, Ridgway, Fougeron, King and Carozzo had been forced to quit. Though *Victress* was in poor shape, Tetley realised that he was now in the running for one or both of the prizes. Only he, Crowhurst and Knox-Johnston were still in the race and the latter had not been heard of since 21st November 1968. It was on 6th April 1969 that a tanker passed close to *Suhaili* and Knox-Johnston was able to get a message via Lloyds that he was heading up the Atlantic, fit and well – his boat tired and rusty – but barring mishaps, likely to win the Golden Globe.

Tetley was relieved to hear that Knox-Johnston was safe and though this meant that he was unlikely to win the Golden Globe, he could still win the £5,000; if he nursed *Victress* safely home, his voyage would still be several weeks faster than that of Knox-Johnston. Only Crowhurst could snatch that prize from him and Tetley was looking over his shoulder, knowing that he was being caught. *Victress* needed tender loving care but Nigel knew that if he was to win what, in those days was a very large sum of money, he could not afford to handle her gently; he must sail her to the limit and risk everything. He was still some 5,000 miles and six weeks from Plymouth but, with fair weather and good fortune, *Victress* might hold together.

Early in May, he entered the North Atlantic and in the third week reached the Azores. On 20th May 1969, the winds strengthened and Tetley, worrying about his boat, reefed the sails. Later that night the wind rose to a Force 9 gale and he lowered the sails to ride the storm. He turned in to catch some sleep, his only comfort being that he had crossed the line he had taken on his outward journey. He had circumnavigated the globe, the first man to do so in a trimaran.

He was woken just after mid-night by noises he had never heard before. *Victress* was breaking up and water was pouring into the cabin. He just had time to send a May Day message, pull the life raft on deck, then into the water, where it automatically inflated, grab his log book, radio transmitter, camera, sextant and some warmer clothes – throw them into the raft, climb into it, cut the line that was holding him to his sinking boat, and drift clear.

His May Day call had been picked up and a US Airforce Hercules from the Azores found him in the late morning and he was taken aboard an Italian tanker later that afternoon. *Victress*, his boat and his home, was gone but he was safe and had come agonisingly close to fulfilling his dream. He had been compelled to ask so much of *Victress* and wondered if he would have reached Plymouth had Crowhurst not appeared so suddenly and pursued him so relentlessly.

Donald Crowhurst was not one of his close friends but Nigel felt admiration for a sailor who had achieved so much. In fact, Crowhurst had achieved little but ignominy. He had not sailed round the world, but had abandoned his voyage in the Atlantic on his way south and had then sailed and sheltered off the South American coast, maintaining radio silence for weeks on end, occasionally sending out false messages as to where he was. He planned to re-appear in April and race for home; he knew that only he, Tetley and Knox-Johnston were still in the race and realised he could not beat Knox-Johnston to Plymouth but had every chance of catching Tetley.

Crowhurst's sudden re-appearance after no contact between the Cape of Good Hope and Cape Horn and subsequent claims of the mileage he was covering day by day were already raising queries in the UK sailing fraternity. Sir Francis Chichester was one of those insisting that the details of Crowhurst's messages and position statements, particularly those before leaving the South Atlantic and entering the Southern Ocean, be thoroughly examined. Chichester wanted to know why he never gave exact positions between Good Hope and The Horn.

As he re-entered the race Crowhurst realised that his deceit would be hard to cover up once he returned to Plymouth and the turmoil in his mind increased as he gained on Tetley during May. But when he heard of Tetley's sinking on 23rd May, his mood changed; his transmitter failed and it seems from his log book and writings during the weeks that followed that as a result of what he had done and the deception he had practised, he had neither the moral courage nor conscience to complete the hoax. Throughout June he drifted navigationally and mentally, writing thousands of words of what seem to be nonsense.

His boat, *Teignmouth Electron* was found drifting by a Royal Mail vessel *Picardy* on 10th July 1969. The boat was in a filthy state and the cabin was a scene of squalor, log books were found and the life-raft was still in place. The weather had been calm for weeks and it seemed unlikely that Crowhurst had accidentally fallen overboard. His deception, mental instability and apparent suicide were front-page news in all the national papers.

Nigel Tetley meanwhile had returned to England and to Eve. *The Sunday Times* awarded him £1,000 consolation prize which he immediately put toward building a new trimaran. His aim was to sail around the world again and break the record for the fastest circumnavigation. We (MfP) held a reception for him and presented him with an oil painting of *Victress*. It was a great occasion graced by the presence of Sir Francis Chichester and Robin Knox-Johnston; Eve was there too, of course.

The Tetleys' home lay at the bottom of the Atlantic and as soon as the new boat *Miss Vicky* was finished, launched and sea trials completed, they moored her on the River Stour at Sandwich and made her their home, as *Victress* had been before. Nigel was trying to rebuild his life but had no money to equip Miss *Vicky* for a new round-the-world challenge. He had shown no bitterness about the circumstances which almost certainly led to the sinking of *Victress*, nevertheless, he had driven himself so hard perhaps it never occurred to him that life could never be as it was when he set out on *Victress* nearly four years before. Sadly, a challenge in *Miss Vicky* was never to be. He wrote a book *Trimaran Solo* about his voyage and it mirrored the kind of man he was – modest, decent and always generous to his fellow competitors, but it told little of what he was enduring within himself. When published, the book did not sell well and it seems he felt it harder to face the trials and tribulations of life on land than to battle with the storms and great waves of the cruel sea. His friends say he had appeared relaxed and his usual pleasant self when he was last seen alive on 2nd February 1972; there seemed to be no problems other than his search for funds and a sponsor. On 5th February 1972, Nigel was found hanging from a tree in woods near Dover.

His death did not make headline news and I did not hear of it for several months. I wished I had not read that article in *The Sunday Times* on that June night in 1968 when coming in to land at Heathrow – perhaps Nigel and Eve would have still been living on *Victress* in the West Country, enjoying his retirement from the Royal Navy. (He was only forty-four years old when he resigned his commission in the Royal Navy to set sail that September.)

But no, that circumnavigation was his destiny. His courage and sensitivity were self-evident not only in the achievement itself, but in the music he listened to, the words he wrote in his log book, and the books he read. He even wrote 'silly' lyrics to some of the lighter music and occasionally he wrote poetry. To conclude, I quote from his log book.

'I now put on Vaughan Williams's *Sinfonia Antarctica*. Fired by the magnificent music and verse, I switched on the second tape recorder to interject some impromptu lines:

Rose up the leviathan from the deep:
Plunging around the ocean bed,
Up to the surface floating, spume flying...!

Rain, rain, falls down sheet upon sheet,
From the window trickles one after the other
Endless drops flowing together, flowing towards the sea.

Can you hear the yacht creaking?
Swaying, swinging?
No wind outside – not a breath.
We sit, just waiting.

Yesterday there was too much wind:
It blew, it blew and it blew.
All sail down, I rode out the gale.

When the morning came, I did not feel like hoisting sail.
I was afraid until the sea had subsided;
Then we crept forward,
All day at slow pace, the wind moderating,
And now no wind; but rain.

Can you hear the yacht creaking?
The yacht is happy;
It is in its element;
But am I?
Maybe; but maybe not.
I cannot tell.
It is so strange: everything is strange.
After a time one has to make up one's life again,
That is the acid test.

Peace, peace through resting,
Peace through quiet,
Can it be peace that way?
No! Peace through fighting, Yes,
Fighting always;
That can only bring peace.

Change…all is change,
And ever shall be. Amen.

I am reminded of the words in Psalm 107, from the Holy Bible

> They that go down to the sea in ships:
> And occupy their business in great waters;
> These men see the works of the Lord
> And his wonders in the deep.

Gwen Watford

'Finish, good lady, the bright day is done,
And we are for the dark.'

Shakespeare

GWEN NEVER BECAME 'A star' but she was not only a very good actress – she was a lovely person. She was a gentle soul with a soft, endearing voice and I cannot imagine she had an enemy in the whole wide world. She was greatly respected and graced the theatre and television with many critically acclaimed performances; yet her name is not widely recognised by the general public.

I first met her more than fifty years ago when we were both resident artistes in Doris Yorke's Repertory Company at Croydon's Grand Theatre – now sadly demolished. It was weekly 'rep' and we therefore acted many times together, playing a variety of parts. I directed some of the productions but whether I was acting or producing, it was always fun working with Gwen.

There is a curious chemistry in many artistes' personalities, which makes them highly vulnerable to fits of near giggles on stage; It was surprising, therefore, that Gwen, a quiet, rather shy person, was liable to 'corpse' at the slightest provocation and some of my happiest – and sometimes embarrassing – memories in weekly rep, were either corpsing with Gwen or watching her struggling for composure with another actor. I didn't act with Gwen again after those Croydon days and so I never knew whether her penchant for corpsing was confined to weekly Rep. Film and television work is, of course, seldom 'live' and so lacks the tension of theatre performance, surely one of the ingredients of spontaneous loss of control. In this modern age, television companies sometimes arrange to 'produce' mistakes deliberately, enabling the out-takes to be sold for the compilation programmes featuring the ever popular 'things that go wrong'. But oh no, it wasn't like that with Gwen. I remember well she always felt ashamed and apologised profusely when such incidents happened, particularly because, more often than not, they occurred in the more 'serious' plays. Mind you, such lapses were nearly always professionally covered up and the audience seldom knew anything untoward had happened.

For many years after Croydon, I had little contact with Gwen. We exchanged Christmas cards and occasionally spoke on the telephone. But when I launched the spoken word cassette label 'Listen for Pleasure' in 1977, I asked her if she would like to read for us. She jumped at the chance and subsequently read several books, including *The Secret Garden*, *What Katy Did* (and the subsequent Katy books) and a poetry anthology, with Richard Pascoe. She read quite beautifully and her preparation before coming to the studio was – unlike so many 'star' readings, researched in great detail. She was always a delight to direct, and I can say that of all the many distinguished actresses I have worked with in this series, she, Juliet Stevenson, Jan Francis and Wendy Craig were by far the most proficient.

I love poetry and I have always enjoyed directing it. We had re-issued several of the classic Shakespeare recordings, and compilations, which included such artistes as Peggy Ashcroft, John Gielgud, Richard Burton, Alec Guiness, Derek Jacobi, Michael Redgrave, Peter Ustinov, Robert Donat, Michael Horden, Dorothy Tutin, Prunella Scales and Flora Robson. I directed some of the best loved Shakespeare speeches and sonnets, performed exquisitely by Juliet Stevenson and Simon Russell Beale; a compilation of favourite poetry read by Peter Butterworth and Tim Pigott-Smith; Hannah Gordon and Bill Patterson reading Robert Burns' poems; war poetry read by Tony Britton and Rufus Sewell; John and Hayley Mills reading A A Milne's *When We were Very Young* and *Now We are Six* – a catholic spread which proved popular.

Amongst these series, there were so many beautiful poems about death and dying, I felt that a cassette of such verse would find a market and be a comfort not only to those who mourned, but also to the dying.

I telephoned Gwen to ask her opinion and she was immediately enthusiastic. She offered to join me in research and to let me have her suggestions. Over the next few months we kept in constant touch and agreed we should use four readers – and, needless to say, I insisted that Gwen be one of those readers. She agreed on one condition – that I would also read. The joy of working with Gwen, again as an actor, persuaded me not to resist! We contracted Tim Pigott-Smith and Helena Bonham Carter to be the other two readers. Over the next few months, the compilation was completed and I telephoned Gwen to firm up recording dates for later that autumn. My plan was to release the cassette the month before Easter in the New Year.

When I spoke to her again to suggest an actual date for her half-day recording, she said it was an ideal date because 'it will be a day or two before my chemotherapy session'. I was nonplussed and may be said, 'But Gwen...' before she went on, 'Yes, Richard, I've got cancer and I'm not worth knowing for a few days after the chemotherapy.' I asked her if she wanted to withdraw from the recording, but she laughed and was emphatic she was looking forward to the half-day in the studio. I had no means of knowing how critical her cancer was, but felt that if she was so eager to record, then maybe she was going to be all right. Nevertheless, I would have preferred the content of the poems we were about to record to be about life, rather than death.

We were using the Sanders & Gordon Studios, just off Tottenham Court Road – a friendly, modern building – but with no lift and our studio was on the 1st Floor. Gwen arrived with her husband, Richard Bebb, and they came slowly up the stairs. I had not met her for over twenty-five years, though I had of course seen her on television. She looked frail, but not as ill as I had feared. We had coffee and then settled down to a relaxed recording and, as the morning wore on, Gwen became more and more animated. At the end of the morning, she was glowing and when she left, she kissed me and said, 'Oh Richard, it's been a wonderful few hours. Thank you. Do you know, I think this is the start of my fight back.'

Alas, it was not to be. We were staying with friends in Devon, early in the New Year, when news came through on the television that Gwen had died. I was strangely shocked. We had not been in touch since the recording a few weeks before and I suppose I had assumed that no news was good news. It seems that the recording was the last work she did. One of the poems she read was 'Remember Me' by Christina Rossetti.

> Remember me when I am gone away,
> Gone far away into the silent land;
> When you can no more hold me by the hand,
> Nor I half turn to go yet turning stay.
> Remember me when no more day by day
> You tell me of our future that you planned;
> Only remember me: You understand
> It will be late to counsel then or pray.
> Yet if you should forget me for a while
> And afterwards remember, do not grieve:
> For if the darkness and corruption leave
> A vestige of the thoughts that once I had,
> Better by far you should forget and smile
> Than that you should remember and be sad.

Gwen read it beautifully and I decided to call the complete cassette 'Remember Me' and dedicate the anthology to her. She was such a special person.

Sonny Days

'Where in this wide world can man find nobility without
pride, friendship without envy, or beauty without vanity.'

*Ronald Duncan (*In Praise of Horses*)*

THERE WERE SO MANY joys in our Hartland lives it is hard to grade
them in terms of delight. Perhaps I could categorise them between
summer and winter, or even land and sea, but certainly the yearly carnival
which always takes place on the second Saturday in August is one of
the highlights. A week before, the village flower show is held on the
recreation ground and the glorious smells in the marquees displaying
the flowers and vegetables will forever be one of my most redolent
memories. The days that follow are filled with activity; concerts, the
crowning of the carnival queen, competitions, the decoration of the
streets and houses – not to mention rehearsals by the village brass band
for their most important exposure of the year – leading the carnival
procession round the narrow streets, spreading the music and drumming
the beat for the multitude behind. Yet in truth, the band was not the
leader, for ahead of them all was a lone horse and rider, the pathfinder
for the pageantry behind.

Charlotte had always loved horses and had ridden friends' ponies
from a very early age, both at home in Berkshire and at Mount Pleasant
in Hartland. She had her first pony, Hugo, a small 12hh Welsh Mountain
pony, when she was ten years old and she joined the Garth Pony Club
– the local branch in Berkshire – to which Prince Charles and Princess
Anne had belonged when they were young. It wasn't surprising therefore,
that though Charlotte looked forward to all the excitements of the

Hartland Carnival, the high point for her was the beautiful liver chestnut horse, with its lovely young rider, a lady dressed immaculately in full riding gear. Despite the cheers of the crowds, the laughter, the very loud music from the band, the coins being thrown into buckets in aid of charity, the roar of the tractor engines pulling the floats (the front of the processions always caught up with the rear as it circled the village), the horse and rider always remained calm, the rider smiling and the horse nodding his head in recognition of the applause as they went by. For two or three years, Charlotte gazed at this lovely animal with a white flash down his forehead and a white sock above his right hind fetlock, thinking to herself 'if only'. She loved Hugo very much, but already he was too small for her.

Then one autumn day when we were in the garden at Mount Pleasant, enjoying the half-term break, we heard the clip-clop of hooves coming down the steep, narrow, lane bordering our property. Charlotte was the first to realise it was the carnival horse and rushed down the path to the gate, accosting the rider with a very hearty 'hello'. We knew at once that she was also the carnival lady, though she wore casual clothes, with no helmet or cap. This was all happening some twenty-five years ago, long before it was considered irresponsible if not illegal, to ride without protection for the head. We all gathered round – including Lundy, Puff and Trushka (yellow Labrador, Mini Yorkie and Birman cat) – and were introduced to horse and rider, Sonny and Debbie. They lived at Beckland Farm, two miles up the road.

Within days, we visited the farm and Charlotte was allowed to ride Sonny along the tracks and fields. We met Paul, Debbie's husband, and went inside their tiny cottage next to the main farmhouse. Charlotte told Debbie all about Hugo and was shown photographs of Sonny and Debbie competing at events in Devon and Cornwall. Thereafter, so far as Charlotte was concerned, our Devon visits were Sonny orientated until one day Debbie mentioned that, though she loved Sonny dearly, at 14.2hh he was too small for her and she would be looking for another horse. Within days it was agreed that when Debbie found her new horse, she would give us first refusal to buy Sonny. Charlotte lived in dreamland and counted the days to the time Sonny would be hers. We had no horsebox for Hugo and we knew that as Charlotte would be competing far more often in events and travelling far greater distances, we would need to buy one. So the next few weeks were busier than ever, not only negotiating with Debbie but also searching for the right horsebox and finding a buyer for Hugo.

And eventually the great day came when we were ready to collect Sonny from Beckland Farm. Charlotte and I drove down to Hartland towing our new horsebox. We slept at the farm, planning to leave before dawn the next morning with our precious cargo. I tried to show confidence in my ability to complete the 240-mile journey through Devon lanes and on the M5 and M4 motorways. Sonny of course, was used to shorter journeys with Debbie, competing in events in North Devon and Cornwall but he had never been asked to endure five or six hours cooped up in his box. We knew that Sonny, unlike Hugo, was always easy to box, so when at six o'clock in the morning, having had a farm breakfast, we led Sonny across the yard and into the box, our adrenalin ran freely and we embarked in high spirits on our drive to Berkshire.

Neither the A361 from the M5 to Barnstaple, nor the new A39 from Barnstaple to beyond Bideford, had been built in those days, and the very twisty and hilly B3227 from Barnstaple to Taunton via such beautiful places as South Moulton, Bampton, Wiveliscombe and Milverton, was not the route to take with a loaded horsebox and a modestly powered car. Accordingly, we went south on the A39 through Kilkhampton, then east through Holsworthy, cutting down to Okehampton on to the A30 – which was not the dual carriageway road it is today. Once we had joined the M5, we knew that barring a breakdown, our journey would be relatively smooth thereafter. We stopped at a new service station between junctions 25 and 26 and, though we didn't unload Sonny, we checked his hay and water and gave him plenty of tender, loving care before embarking on the last three hours to home and stable. He was to travel many miles through many counties during the next three years, competing and going to and from Devon on holiday.

I like to think that the pleasure we had from Sonny was mutual for he became so much part of the family. He was so affectionate and full of life and he and Charlotte bonded from the first day we brought him to Bray. He was a keen competitor and, like his mistress, enjoyed and was better at the freedom of cross-country than the more regimented show jumping and discipline of dressage. Together they picked up many rosettes in the home counties and on our visits to Devon and Cornwall. But more important than the trophies was the fun, comradeship, panic, industry and excitement that Charlotte, Kim and I had in preparation and participation – grooming and mucking out, journeying and eating, cursing and laughing, cheering and despairing, and finally, collapsing exhausted at the end of a long day.

At this time, Charlotte was still at the Brigidine School in Windsor and during term time I had the task, pleasure and excitement of exercising Sonny on weekdays. I had never ridden seriously before and, looking back, I marvel at the nerve – indeed courage – I had in taking on such a task. We have no immediate open countryside round Bray since we are bounded by the river, Maidenhead and the M4 motorway. To reach open country, Sonny and I had to negotiate miles of busy main roads, having crossed a motorway bridge but Sonny had a marvellous temperament and knew perfectly well that I needed looking after – and he always did just that. On one occasion, I had walked him across the motorway bridge path across the Thames to get to Dorney Common where we could have a good canter (I never dared to gallop). We were in full flight across the common when something spooked Sonny and he swerved violently to the right. I went straight on and landed relatively unharmed on the turf. Most horses would have streaked away, enjoying their freedom having shed their load. But Sonny pulled up within a few yards and trotted back to me as if to say, 'Sorry, but it wasn't really my fault.'

Sonny is now nearly thirty years old and lives quietly in a field near Wokingham. Charlotte has always kept in touch with his owner and it is a warm feeling to know he is there, well looked after and cared for. Memories are forever and though Sonny didn't make Badminton, we feel sure it was only his size that prevented it! His heart was certainly big enough. As it is, we remember Home Park, Tweesledown, Windsor Great Park, Bellingdon – and dozens of other locations, including of course, Devon and Cornwall, where Sonny and Charlotte, in their dark green colours, were not only seen, but usually heard as well!

Sea King

'Adventures are for the adventurous.'

A Proverb

I REMEMBER WRITING SOME time ago that I would dearly love to tackle the walk / scramble / climb between Spekes and Welcombe Mouth, which with companions of all ages and sizes I had completed so many times over the last forty-five years, just once more in my lifetime. I think I must have been seventy years old when last I did it without too much difficulty, taking three and a half to four hours, which, with a six-hour tide limit, allowed plenty of time for any unforeseen difficulties. In 2003 I so nearly achieved my wish and this is the story of what happened.

We were down in Devon, staying at Beckland Farm; it was Easter weekend and Charlotte, Michael and Scrumpy were with us. Michael had often told me how much he wanted to join this exclusive club of adventurers and so, for the moment forgetting that I was now eighty-one years old, I suggested we check the tides and, if they were right on the Easter Saturday, we would venture forth. Young Mark, Debbie and Paul Symons' eighteen-year-old son at the farm, said he would like to join us and the three of us set out. With two such strong and fit young men I felt entirely confident there would be no problems. However, I hadn't anticipated the changes in the coastline over the ten years since last I had covered the ground nor had I realised how much I had slowed down. I was soon to find out at my companions' expense. The gullies we had previously been able to walk through were now half-filled with huge rocks – which had to be climbed over. The sandy or pebble beaches had virtually disappeared and were now covered with small rocks and the caves had become little more than indentations in the cliff face.

Charlotte dropped us off at the top of Spekes soon after ten a.m. and, because we had no intention of hurrying unduly, we suggested that she meet us at Welcombe Mouth around three p.m. There was a high wind, it was sunny but cold – ideal weather for our adventure. Very soon after we reached the actual beach and started stretching from rock to rock, I realised how much my balance had deteriorated. The high wind didn't help of course, and I had to proceed with care. By the time we reached the scanty remains of the Green Ranger (just below Elmscott where we had the cottage in the 1950s and 1960s), I had fallen several times but only suffered very minor cuts and bruises. It must have been about this time that I had my first doubts about beating the tides, even though there was still an hour to pass before low tide. I did not voice my doubts until some two hours later when it became patently obvious that we wouldn't reach our three p.m. deadline with Charlotte at Welcombe. My young companions had mobile phones with them and they were able to climb onto a promontory to get a signal, phoning the farm to reassure them that we were safe and well and asking them to let Charlotte know we would be late.

By four p.m. we were edging along rock faces above the water and I was being gently guided by my two young friends, accomplishing feats of daring I had never tackled before and very soon afterwards, I realised we could get no further. The sea was pounding a point just ahead of us and would soon cover promontories behind us. Michael and Mark tried to climb around, but found the rock face far too sheer. Because I had been so slow, the tide had beaten us and there was nothing we could do about it; we were in no danger because even at high tide at this time of the year, we could scramble to safety on rocks above the tide line but this would mean of course, spending the night out and waiting for the tide to go out. It was getting even colder and we had finished our drinks and had only one Mars bar between us.

To save face I was determined to spend the night out and wait for the tide. I asked Michael and Mark to try and contact the farm to let the family know what we had decided. Off they went, and I lay down on the rocky beach, tired after six hours of scrambling and climbing and wet from spray and wading through pools. They arrived back having made contact and then, rather hesitantly, informed me they had asked Kim and Debbie to notify the coastguards. It seems that on their way back to me, neither wanted to be the one to tell me what they had done. But they need not have worried because, by this time, feeling cold and very tired, I had no difficulty in swallowing my pride. It was now getting even colder and dusk was approaching. We settled down to wait watching the waves getting closer and closer. The cliffs above us looked formidable to say the least, and very crumbly. I was relieved there was no question of trying to climb them ourselves and although the coastguards would have equipment to tackle such a rescue operation, I did not relish the thought of an ascent by that route.

The light was fading fast when, some forty-five minutes later, we heard the noise of an engine and around the promontory to the south of us appeared a yellow Sea King helicopter. We waved energetically and the aircraft moved slowly toward us. We were in a very small inlet, having scrambled around a large rock as the tide came in, but there was no way the helicopter could reach us where we stood. It came into the small bay on the other side of the rock and seemed to be landing though I thought this highly unlikely in view of the rake and rock strewn state of the beach. We could see the rotary blades perilously near to the cliffs and suddenly it soared up again and went out to sea.

Unknown to us, an RAF Sergeant had been winched down and he suddenly appeared at the top of the rock shouting to us we had to get back over the rock and into the bay where the helicopter could winch us to safety. Our side of the rock was reasonably slanted, enabling me to climb to the top, but there was a twenty-foot drop on the other side – and I was not an experienced rock-face climber! Michael and Mark clambered up beside me, helping me to the top and then lowered me down holding my hands until I was just able to reach the sergeant's upward stretched arms with my feet. He then gently lowered me on to the pebbles. Michael and Mark followed and the sergeant, who introduced himself as 'Beano', seemed very concerned because he saw patches of blood on my trousers. I was able to reassure him as the helicopter edged in towards us, whipping up the spray as the winch was lowered. Michael and Mark were strapped face to face and were hauled up first, obviously thoroughly enjoying themselves.

A slightly more substantial contraption was then lowered (embarrassingly called 'a cradle') and Beano strapped me in so I could hold on to my glasses with one hand, and my old golfing hat with the other. Within seconds we were all together again and then it was up, up and away to the cliff top somewhere near Embury Beacon. We climbed out of the helicopter to find the coastguards waiting for us and in their midst Charlotte and Debbie. Debbie was roaring with laughter while Charlotte, having waited at Welcombe for several hours, without news of her new husband and ancient father, was relieved and rather more subdued.

We were then driven back to Welcombe Mouth, our original destination where Kim, several more Hartland friends and coastguards were waiting. We got back to the farm soon after eight p.m. feeling humble and thankful. I had thanked the Squadron Leader pilot as I left the helicopter and I only hope he could hear me above the roar of the engine. Obviously we thanked the coastguards too, but they and the aircrew assured us they had been glad to be called out as they had been sitting on their backsides since starting duty on Good Friday morning. I wrote to them when I got back to Bray. These are all brave men who risk their lives to help others in need and the coastguards are volunteers who give up their spare time or leave their day-time jobs to carry out this rescue service.

I certainly felt guilty for having caused so much concern and trouble, although I don't think I acted irresponsibly. I miscalculated and of course without me, Michael and Mark would have easily reached Welcombe without the help of a helicopter! They were both splendid and I never once felt anxiety about the outcome. But poor Kim suffered and I could do nothing to allay her fears, not to mention Charlotte's ordeal. Beckland Farm has always been warm and homely, but never had a hot bath seemed so seductive nor a bed so secure and cosy as on that Easter Saturday night.

Eleanor Farjeon

'Were there but a few hearts and intellects like hers, this
earth would already become the hope for Heaven.'

John Stuart Mill

ELEANOR IS BEST KNOWN for her wonderfully imaginative children's
books and her poetry but she also wrote plays which were set to music
and it was because I was cast in one of these – *The Silver Curlew* – that
I came to know and love her. 'Nellie', as she was known by her family
and close friends, was born in 1881 and lived nearly all her life in North
London.

She never went to school and, in what was perhaps her best known
book *A Nursery in the Nineties* she tells us that the only world she knew
for sixteen years was her nursery. She was miserably self-conscious at
parties or in the company of strangers. She was devoted to her brothers
– Harry, Joe and Bertie – and it was in her nursery that she read and
wrote stories with them, creating the rituals and games that dominated
their lives.

With the composer Clifton Parker and his wife, the choreographer
and dancer Yoma Sasburgh, Eleanor wrote *The Glass Slipper* which was
first performed at the Liverpool Playhouse and the following year
brought into the Arts Theatre in London. Two years later *The Silver
Curlew* was written and again first presented at the Liverpool Playhouse.
The following year it was presented at the Arts Theatre and I was cast
to play Charlie Loon in the London production. Charlie Loon was a
difficult part to cast because it not only involved acting but also dancing
and singing and it seems that whoever played the part in Liverpool was

not convincing in all three of these areas. I cannot remember how I got the part. I was not a particularly good ballroom dancer and most certainly had never had ambitions to dance on stage. Nor had I anticipated singing on stage! However, the director, John Fernald, cast me as Charlie Loon and the company was to meet for the first time in rehearsal rooms adjacent to the Arts Theatre. We were to be measured for costumes and given rehearsal schedules.

I arrived early and went up the stark staircase to the second floor and into a large barren room, lined with old wooden chairs. Sitting on the far side of the room was a small elderly woman, with thick lens glasses. She was scruffily dressed and clutched a large paper shopping bag on her lap. As I sat down on the opposite side of the room, she said, 'You must be Charlie Loon.' I asked her how she knew and she smiled and said, 'You couldn't be anyone else.' Our brief conversation ended as other members of the company came in. When John Fernald arrived, he started by introducing us to one another and then, it seemed as an afterthought, he said, 'Oh yes, and this is Eleanor Farjeon.' To my astonishment, he indicated the little old lady with the thick glasses. Still clutching her shopping bag, she stood up and, beaming with delight, said, 'Hello, everyone.'

She was a lovely person and over the years, I visited her in her Hampstead Perrins Walk cottage and we often spoke on the telephone. She wrote wonderful letters and her handwriting was as bad as her typing but in a strange way this made the content even more precious. The cottage was at the bottom of Perrins Walk with one large room downstairs and a small kitchen; a huge room upstairs was her workroom, sitting room and bedroom. It was quite the most inviting, chaotic, homely, original room I have ever been in. There were books and papers at all levels from the floor to the ceiling and her many cats curled up in the few available corners. Eleanor was always very hospitable but, usually on a one-to-one basis; she loved to talk but was an even better listener. When I left her, I always felt a much better person than when I arrived. The only time Eleanor was less hospitable was during the two weeks of Wimbledon. She would ask all her friends not to contact her during that time. She would hire a television set (in those days black and white of course) and become a recluse, watching every match from start to finish. She would not write a word for fourteen days and, at the close of play on the last day, she would switch off, get rid of the TV set as quickly as possible and then set about telephoning all her friends!

Words were magic to Eleanor and joy and delight flowed both from her pen and her mouth. She would seize on a place name and write haunting words about it; I remember she had been down to the West Country and passed through the village Zeal Monachorum. (There are two more Zeals in Somerset.) She was so excited by the name, she immediately wrote down:

Zeal Monachorum, High Cockelorum,
Behind 'em, below 'em, beside 'em, before 'em,
Snip snap snorum, riddle me dee,
Zeal Monachorum, so let it be.

Slight but so atmospheric! But of all the pieces she wrote, her poem 'Mrs. Malone' is my favourite. It is so very much Eleanor. Certainly not the greatest piece she wrote but the most endearing. It was published by Michael Joseph in the 1950s and beautifully illustrated by David Knight. Since then it has appeared in many anthologies and has been broadcast many times.

Mrs. Malone
Lived hard by a wood,
All on her lonesome
As nobody should.
With her crust on a plate
And her pot on the coal
And none but herself
To converse with, poor soul.
In a shawl and a hood
She got sticks out-o'-door,
On a bit of old sacking
She slept on the floor;
And nobody, nobody

Asked how she fared
Or knew how she managed,
For nobody cared.
Why make a pother
About an old crone?
What for should they bother
With Mrs. Malone?

One Monday in winter
With snow on the ground
So thick that a footstep
Fell without sound,
She heard a faint frostbitten
Peck on the pane
And went to the window
To listen again.
There sat a cock-sparrow,
Bedraggled and weak,
With half open eyelids
And ice on its beak.
She threw up the sash
And she took the bird in,
And mumbled and fumbled it
Under her chin.
'Ye're all of a smother,
Ye're fair overblown!
I've room fer another,'
Said Mrs. Malone.

Come Tuesday, while eating
Her dry morning slice
With sparrow a-picking
(Ain't company nice!')
She heard on her doorstep
A curious scratch,
And there was a cat

With its claw on the latch.
It was hungry and thirsty
And thin as a lath,
As it mewed and it mowed
On the slippery path.
She threw the door open
And warmed up some pap,
And huddled and cuddled it
In her old lap.
'There, there, little brother,
Ye poor skin-an'-bone,
There's room for another,'
Said Mrs. Malone.

Come Wednesday, while all of them
Crouched on the mat
With a crumb for the sparrow,
A sip for the cat,
There was wailing and whining
Outside in the wood,
And there sat a vixen
With six of her brood.
She was haggard and ragged
And worn to a shred
And her half-dozen babies
Were only half fed,
But Mrs. Malone, crying,
'My! Ain't they sweet!'
Happed them and lapped them
And gave them to eat.
'You warm yerself, mother
Ye're cold as a stone!
There's room fer another,'
Said Mrs. Malone.

Come Thursday a donkey
Stepped in off the road
With sores on his withers
From bearing a load.
Come Friday when icicles
Pierced the white air
Down from the mountainside
Lumbered a bear.
For each she had something,
If little, to give –
'Lord knows, the poor critters
Must all of 'em live'.
She gave them her sacking
Her hood and her shawl,
Her loaf and her teapot –
She gave them her all.
'What with one thing and t'other
Me fambily's grown,
And there's room for another,'
Said Mrs. Malone.

Come Saturday evening
When time was to sup
Mrs. Malone
Had forgot to sit up.
The cat said *meeow,*
And the sparrow said *peep*
The vixen *she's sleeping,*
The bear, *let her sleep.*
On the back of the donkey
They bore her away,
Through trees and up mountains
Beyond night and day,
Till come Sunday morning
They brought her in state
Through the last cloudbank

As far as the Gate.
'Who is it,' asked Peter,
You have with you there?'
And donkey and sparrow,
Cat, vixen and bear
Exclaimed, 'Do you tell us
Up here she's unknown?
It's our mother, God bless us!
It's Mrs. Malone
Whose havings were few
And whose holding was small
And whose heart was so big
It had room for us all.'
Then Mrs. Malone
Of a sudden awoke,
She rubbed her two eyeballs
And anxiously spoke:
'Where am I to goodness,
And what do I see?
My dears, let's turn back,
This ain't no place for me!'
But Peter said 'Mother,
Go in to the Throne.
There's room for another
One, Mrs. Malone.'

How can one not be enchanted with this poem? How can one not marvel at 'One Monday in winter with snow on the ground so thick that a footstep fell without sound' and 'she took the bird in and mumbled and fumbled it under her chin' or when she had taken the cat in, she 'huddled and cuddled it in her old lap'? The poor vixen with her half dozen babies was 'haggard and ragged and worn to a shred' and Mrs Malone took them all in and holding the babies 'happed them and lapped them'.

Enchantment indeed.

Eleanor was Jewish, of course, but not a practising Jew. Imagine my astonishment therefore when a few years after the 'Curlew' she telephoned me in joyous mood 'Oh Dick, I must tell you my news – I've become a Roman Catholic.' (She always called me by my family name 'Dick' – my stage name was 'Richard'.) I must have expressed polite surprise and she then went on to explain that by chance she had met the young Roman Catholic priest and she had immediately fallen in love with him! Though he was some forty years younger she felt that the least she could do for him in return for his kindness and comfort he had extended to her in her old age and recent illness, was to convert to Catholicism! She added, 'It can't do anyone any harm and he is so excited'!

When she died aged eighty-four, she left a letter for Denys Blakelock (King Nollikins in *The Silver Curlew*) attaching to it a five-pound note, asking him to assemble as many of the Curlew cast as he could and take them to her Hampstead pub after the funeral and have a drink on her. This we did and there was no sadness, only gladness! She was buried in Highgate Cemetery, only a few graves away from Karl Marx. It seems she had reserved her plot decades before and, though she must have known she would become Marx's near neighbour, it obviously didn't bother her because she had no interest in politics whatsoever. However, I feel sure Marx would have been flattered to have Eleanor sharing the same postcode.

The most important thing in Eleanor's life was 'family'. She adored her father and mother, Ben and Margaret (Jefferson) and the bond between her and brothers Harry, Joe and Bertie sealed an extraordinary love. In *A Nursery in the Nineties* she writes, 'I can write of my brothers' deaths without sadness and think of the past without longing. I would not relive any of it if I could. It is enough to have lived it once and carry its ineffaceable memories to my own end, looking forward not backward.'

Dearest Eleanor, a very special person. I was in my early forties when she died. I realise now that I would have appreciated her even more had I known her in my later decades.

Golf in California

'Sure, deck your lower limbs in pants;
Yours are the limbs, my sweeting.
You look divine as you advance –
Have you seen yourself retreating?'

Ogden Nash

I'M NOT AT ALL good at the game of golf but I do enjoy it. I've risen well above 'the hacker' stage and achieved the status of a 23 handicapper some twenty years ago – but, as I was never a private club member, I don't play in competitions and therefore my handicap officially remains the same as it was when I first got it and my certificate, though still accepted, is very fragile.

I didn't start playing regularly until I was over sixty years of age and had time to play during the week when courses are more likely to be free of over-zealous addicts and one can enjoy the ever-changing countryside and the company of friends. Gentle etiquette and a sense of humour are essential ingredients for an enjoyable game of golf and though I have witnessed 'golf rage', it wasn't dangerous and could be laughed at without risk to one's person. I love the game for many reasons and I am told I am very competitive.

In the late 1980s we were staying with our friends the Formans, in Los Angeles. I had known Len Forman for many years during our publishing days and we once played golf together on a municipal course when he was visiting the UK. I had never contemplated playing in the United States, a country which to me held visions of the Ryder Cup and beautifully manicured courses such as Augusta. Tiger Woods had never been heard of but names such as Tom Watson, Curtis Strange, Cory Pavin, Jack Nicklaus, Payne Stewart, and Tom Kite crowded my mind and I assumed one had to be very rich and a very good golfer to play golf in America.

Imagine my terror therefore, when Len casually told me that he had arranged a game of golf for the next day. I pretended I would love to play but had not brought my clubs with me. 'No problem,' replied Len, 'I've borrowed some for you from a friend.' I countered with my trump card. 'I'm left-handed.' He had remembered this, however, and on our way to the course, we diverted to a large house and picked up what appeared to be a brand new set of left handed clubs in a livid red bag.

It was only when we were nearing the course that Len mentioned for the first time we were meeting up with two of his friends at the club. They were both judges and Jewish like Len. He assured me I would love Al and Bernie. I was feeling sick with embarrassment as we neared our destination and I peered forward, expecting to see a grand entrance, Wentworth style. Instead, we turned into what seemed to be a rather tatty leisure park with shops, cafes, music and shapeless men and women wandering aimlessly about, eating and drinking. We met Al and Bernie at a pre-arranged ice cream vendor but they didn't look anything like judges to me. I wasn't expecting them to be wearing wigs, of course, but I had assumed that they would be carrying with them an air of dignity and polite authority. Al and Bernie were both small, fat, men – and they really shouldn't have been wearing shorts. Try as I might, I just couldn't imagine them in court.

I was the only one without a battery-propelled trolley and as we made our way through milling crowds to the first tee, I was still trying to think of a way of escape, but my companions' friendliness and enthusiasm for all things English made me feel ashamed and I realised the only way I could honourably withdraw would be to drop dead! But worse was to come. We were standing in a queue waiting to tee off at the first hole, when Bernie said, 'What's the wager today, Len?' They asked me what I thought and I didn't tell them I had never played for money in my life. Instead I smiled weakly and said I'd go along with anything they suggested. They suggested eight dollars a hole – each of us to put in two dollars a hole. I am no mathematician, but I carried through the quickest calculation of my life and realised I could quite easily lose thirty-six dollars. I had ten dollars in my pocket.

I was shaking as I teed off and my ball didn't go very far. Thereafter, even for me, I played terrible golf. The course was dull and ill-kempt, etiquette was non-existent and attire was near to fancy dress and would not have been allowed even on a holiday camp 'pitch and putt' in the UK! However, this did not excuse my standard of play and by the ninth hole, I was bankrupt. I had lost six dollars more than I possessed.

But, as so often in life, fate intervened. We had played thirteen holes – and I was even further in debt – when Bernie looked at his watch and said, 'Gee fellers, I got ta call it a day. I'm in court in forty-five minutes.' 'Me too,' enjoined dear Al, 'I certainly can't play eighteen.' 'Wagers off then,' Len declared stoutly. I protested of course, but to no avail, thank God. They insisted we had had a great game and I really think they meant it. We shook hands and parted the best of friends. Len and I played on, and I started winning holes. It was magic. I felt light-hearted and carefree as we got into the car. I tried hard to picture Al and Bernie sitting in judgement and wished desperately that the accused, whatever they had or had not done, could have seen them in their shorts and outrageous shirts. At least they would have known that their judges were human.

Prague – The Long Winter

'You may break, you may shatter the vase if you will,
But the scent of roses will hang around it still.'

Thomas Moore

AS I WRITE THIS, it is hard to realise that Prague, the capital city of the Czechoslovakia in the decades before the 1980s – drab, sinister and firmly in Communist hands behind the Iron Curtain – is the same Prague, capital city of the present-day Czech Republic, prosperous, fashionable and one of the most popular tourist cities in Europe. What these two Pragues have in common, however, is some of the most beautiful architecture on the continent, the love of music and the theatre (particularly 'mime') and, last but by no means least, the love of freedom by the vast majority of the people.

Paul Hamlyn started printing books in Czechoslovakia in the 1950s having discovered that by so doing, he would be able to publish books at a considerably lower price than any competitors in the UK because printing and binding costs were so much lower in that country. As business prospered, questions were asked in the House of Commons – 'Could nothing be done to stop this young adventurer from giving work to the citizens of a Communist country?' Nothing could be done of course and within a few years, those same UK publishers who had been asking questions were lining up to gain entry to other printing sources behind the Iron Curtain.

The state publishing company in Czechoslovakia was called Artia. The organisation was entirely responsible for all publishing and printing. Paul's courtship was, therefore, welcomed with hugely open arms. Artia was also responsible for the Czech record industry which was heavily weighted towards classical music under the label 'Supraphon'. Paul had eyed the record industry in the UK for some time, realising that the cost factor in pressing LPs in Czechoslovakia would be as advantageous as in printing books; he therefore decided to import Supraphon LPs and compete with the traditional UK Classical labels by marketing the records at a far lower price. The Czech Philharmonic Orchestra was, and still is, one of the most respected in the world and the recordings of the works of major composers were sought all over the world, particularly those of their own composers, Dvorak, Suk, Janacek, Smetena, and Fibich. It was because Paul placed me in charge of the Supraphon adventure that I came to visit Prague

My first visit to Prague was in the early 1960s when the Communists were still very much in control. However, there were glimmerings of disquiet over Russian Communist dominance and the Eastern Bloc of European countries were at least showing signs of de-Stalinisation. In 1960 the Czechs even dared to demolish the enormous statue of Stalin in the centre of Prague. Many years were to pass, however, before the very short Prague Spring of 1968, the Velvet Revolution of 1986 and the fall of the Berlin Wall. A new era of international politics was ushered in when the Soviet Union's empire in Eastern Europe disintegrated peacefully and the Cold War came to an end; meanwhile, Gorbachav, Dubcek and Harvel were names waiting in the wings.

As I walked from the aircraft on that first visit I remember thinking that Prague airport reminded me of UK aerodromes before the war; it could have been Croydon where Neville Chamberlain landed after his 1938 visit to Hitler, waving the letter telling us there was to be 'Peace in our time'. There was one main runway and a very depressing terminal building surrounded by huts of varying sizes, next to a few hangars. The drive into the city was just as depressing. Everything was grey and as we approached the city's outskirts, it seemed that all the buildings were neglected and the streets in dire need of repair. Cars and lorries were old and dirty and the few people in the streets, drab and unsmiling.

The next morning I visited the Artia offices with Paul. The building was cold, the floors were not carpeted, and the furniture and fittings were utilitarian in the extreme, reminding me of the immediate post-war years in the UK. As we walked up the stone staircase to the first floor, I saw a large framed painting of Lenin on the wall, facing us, and was astounded when Paul remarked in a loud voice, 'Why don't you change your decorations, get rid of that old thing and replace it with something less sinister.' The half dozen or so Czechs said nothing but they were all smiling. We entered the offices where I was introduced to a number of staff. Once we were within those four walls the mood changed, and I felt I could relax. I was amongst friends – the warmth was palpable.

So far as I can remember, there were only two top-class hotels in Prague at that time – The Alcron and The Spartac. Paul and I were staying at the latter and on going to my room I noticed that the double bed had no blankets. I assumed the bed was yet to be made, but when I returned late that first night, the bed had not been touched. There were pillows and a sheet covering the mattress, but above it lay what to me looked like a large white eiderdown. I examined it closely and as there was an opening at one end and the room was very hot, I decided to slide in and lie on whatever the inside was made of and just have the outer covering on top of me. I decided not to ring for help as the maid would most likely not speak English and I still felt a little nervous about spending my first night behind the Iron Curtain – I suppose I wanted to be as insignificant as possible.

Surprisingly, I slept well that night and at breakfast asked Paul about the bedclothes situation in his room, telling him of my experience. He was incredulous and astounded at my ignorance – the 'thing' on my bed into which I had climbed, was a duvet! Such quilts were barely known in the UK in the 1960s and I suppose Paul was only so knowledgeable because he travelled extensively, particularly to the USA. Whether or not my dislike of duvets to the present day is in any way connected to this rather humbling incident, I do not know but I rather doubt it. I like to be 'tucked up' in bed and to be in control of what is covering me.

That first visit was memorable, however, not only for the hospitality I was shown but also for one experience which could so easily have ended my Supraphon appointment. Paul and I had been invited to dinner by the top brass of Artia. We were taken to an exclusive restaurant that in bygone days had been a monastery, built on top of a hill overlooking the city. Tables were set on either side of a long-vaulted hall and we were seated against the wall at the very end – the only table facing down the centre aisle. We settled into a considerable dinner with drinks of all kinds helping us through the different courses. Coffee arrived and cigars were lit. You must understand I drink very little and while I enjoy an occasional cigar, I had never been used to the king-sized brands that Paul smoked.

As we chatted and laughed over liqueurs, I became aware I desperately needed to relieve myself. I held on as long as I could, but when I rose from my seat I realised that as I was sitting against the wall, to get out I would need to disturb two of our hosts. The moment I stood up I knew I was faced with a crisis. I was tempted to look down to check whether I had my legs with me, and as I groped my way along the table, holding on to it for balance, I noticed Paul looking at me with a quizzical smirk across his face. I managed to reach the end of the table and as the two Czechs moved back into their seats, I looked down the long avenue between the other diners knowing full well I had no chance of making it to safety. I could not just stand there indefinitely and decided therefore I had no option but to step out, collapse, and get it all over and done with as quickly as possible.

I took a deep breath and had taken no more than two or three strides when I felt a hand grasp my clothes at the small of my back and literally propel me forward, holding me upright at the same time. We covered the whole length of the hall without mishap and when we reached the entrance hall I was wheeled into the Gentlemen and then into a loo where I was violently sick. My saviour had disappeared. I waited for a few minutes, collected my coat and stepped outside. It was snowing and the darkness was white with snowflakes; I leaned against a wall and could see the lights of Prague below. Thankfully Paul and our hosts came out of the restaurant within a few minutes and I was able to apologise soberly for my departure from the table a few minutes earlier. I must have resembled a snowman but I think our hosts knew how well they had wined and dined me and were flattered that I had entered into the spirit of things so heartily! I never knew whose hand it was that rescued me from what surely would have been a fate worse than death. I suppose it could have been some kind of divine hand intervention that enabled me to cover the ground upright and steady to the safety of that little room. But no, I rather think it must have been a guardian waiter who had been watching this patently innocent young Englishman as he ate, drank and smoked himself towards perdition and had sprung to his rescue in the nick of time. I so much wanted to thank him but that was impossible because I wouldn't have known whom to thank.

On another occasion, in November 1965, Artia had asked Paul Hamlyn and senior members of his staff to visit Prague to celebrate the success of the business partnership. Some twenty-five of us flew over in a rather old and decrepit Russian aircraft and were relieved to land safely at the airport. The visit was great fun, highlighted by a dinner on the last evening at the Dobric Castle. As was the custom, official speeches were made and then anyone who had anything to add could jump up, say a few words and propose a toast. Paul had warned us this was likely to happen and expected appropriate members of his staff to do their duty.

As I was the only Hamlyn Supraphon representative, in due course I felt courageous enough to get up and suggest that Hamlyns and Artia would make a formidable soccer team. Hamlyns would provide the Inside and Outside Right, the Right Half and Right Back, Artia the Inside and Outside Left, and the Left Half and Left Back. The Centre Forward and Centre Half positions would be alternated between the two companies and we would ask the United Nations to provide the Goalkeeper. I felt such a team would be hard to beat. I am happy to say that these remarks produced great hilarity and the Czechs all sprang to their feet applauding.

When our visit came to an end we were each presented with an album of photographs taken at the dinner the night before. The first page of the album read

> In case you will ever want to remember
> This visit, the following photographs will bring it
> To your mind.
> No photograph, however, can show how happy
> We were to have you with us.

So do come again – you will always be welcome.
Bon voyage!

22nd November 1965   The staff of Artia

In 1968, Dubcek became First Secretary of the country and for a few short months he preached his gospel of 'socialism with a human face' softening the iron grip of Soviet Communism. His few weeks in office became known as 'the Prague Spring' but alas it was followed not by summer, but by a hard and cruel winter, for in the middle of August, the Red Army invaded Czechoslovakia and occupied Prague. Moscow accused Dubcek of 'heading a minority of a right wing group guilty of perfidious and treacherous activities'.

For many years we had had daily telex messages from our Artia friends and I treasure those I have in my possession, covering the first two days of the Red Army occupation. The first was transmitted via Hilversum on 22nd August 1968 –

'In these tragic moments of our nation, we appeal to all people of the world who love freedom. We ask you to influence public opinion by all means. We only want, and have only ever wanted, to live in freedom and realise a human type of socialism. Long live our free socialist Czechoslovak Republic. Signed 'All leaders of Artia – Your friends in Czechoslovakia.'

A line was then added, 'We ask in all telexes to Artia not to mention any names of Czechs over here.'

There then followed messages backwards and forwards on 22nd and 23rd August. There was little we could do except to let them know we were actively trying to influence public opinion throughout the world, but when we read 'there are tanks around us and no one knows what will be tomorrow' and 'women and children are being murdered here' our feeling of impotence was overwhelming. Paul Hamlyn and Philip Jarvis sent telexes of support and sympathy, and, at ten a.m. on 23rd, I sent this message: 'Whole world including China and Communist parties in Western countries condemn invasion. We are still receiving TV and radio reports from your country. We are doing all we can. We send admiration and regards to you all.' An hour later Artia telexed that their President Svoboda and Dubcek were flying to Moscow at their own request but soon after midday all telex and other means of communication ceased.

Eventually our partnership with Artia was resumed, albeit with more formality than before. Dubcek was removed from power and in 1970 was expelled from the Communist Party. In 1989 he supported Havel (who became First Secretary initiating 'the Velvet Revolution'), and was elected Speaker of the Federal Assembly. He was killed in a car crash in 1992.

Now of course, Czechoslovakia no longer exists, it has been divided into two countries, the Czech Republic and Slovakia, The people themselves chose this split and I hope that in the long term it proves successful for both countries. Czechoslovakia had had a troubled twentieth century. Names like Benes and Masaryk, not to mention the hundreds of thousands of Sudetanlanders, weigh heavily on our conscience but eventually, thank God, the Czech and Slovakian peoples have emerged from those sinister years of Nazi and Communist domination.

My memory will always be of friendship and I wish I could name names, but even after nearly fifty years, I think it is better not. If any of those friends read these words, they will recognise themselves and the events. They will, I hope, manage a smile.

John Mills

'Please Do Not Shoot The Pianist. He's Doing His Best.'

Oscar Wilde (John Mills loved this quotation)

WITHOUT DOUBT, ONE OF the most pleasing actors I produced on the LFP audio book series was John Mills. He died in his ninety-sixth year and was deservedly knighted in 1976. Few people realise that he was a song and dance man in the 1930s, appearing in such musicals as *Funny Face, Pelissier Follies, Jill Darling* as well as Noel Coward's *Words and Music*. Thereafter he became a 'straight' actor and must have made nearly a hundred films including *In Which We Serve* (Coward again), *We Dive at Dawn, This Happy Breed, This Way to the Stars, Great Expectations, Scott of the Antarctic, The Colditz Story, War and Peace, Dunkirk, Tunes of Glory*, and of course, *Ryan's Daughter*. His popularity grew decade by decade and he was greatly respected in the profession, not only for his talent but also for his integrity and his devotion to his family. He was still working shortly before he died despite being very deaf and nearly blind. His marriage to Mary Hayley Bell was remarkable for its tenderness and longevity. Mary developed Alzheimer's disease in later years and died only recently, some eighteen months after her husband. (I had a very distant indirect contact with her during the war when I was in the RAF stationed in Italy. I produced one of her plays *Men in Shadow* which had an all-male cast and was about an RAF aircrew shot down in France who were being sheltered in a barn. The play was running in the West End at the time, so how we got permission – let alone the scripts – I do not know!)

It was in 1978 I decided to record Paul Gallico's enchanting story

The Snow Goose for Listen for Pleasure. It is a long short story and is set in wartime, telling of the unspoken bond between a recluse, a young girl and a snow goose during the epic days of Dunkirk. At the same time I was able to get the rights to two other Gallico short stories – 'The Small Miracle' and 'Ludmilla' – the former about a young Italian boy and his donkey telling of their mutual devotion and faith, the latter about a frail cow in Liechtenstein called 'the Weakling'. All these stories needed sensitivity in the reading and I leafed through my Spotlight directory to try and find the right actor to approach. When I came to John Mills' name, I knew he was the right actor to try for. Both his image and his gentle voice were exactly right for the Gallico stories and I was delighted when he said he was keen to record.

It was to be a single-voice recording involving a relatively small amount of equipment and only the reader, the engineer and myself (as the director) involved. John was always a very busy person and didn't particularly want to journey into a London studio on what on his calendar was going to be a free day. He asked if it would be possible to record in his home – Hills House in Denham Village. My engineer paid a visit to his home and decided that, by using an upstairs room immediately above the study where John would read, we could record there adequately. Hills House is a lovely old regency house and the acoustics were surprisingly good.

It was the most enjoyable and relaxed day of recording I have ever had. John read well and took production advice gratefully. Mary provided a delicious buffet lunch and told us of the witch's stick in their Richmond home and her belief in fairies. At the end of a long summer's day, my car refused to start and was eventually push started down the village High Street by Sir John Mills and the engineer, Barry McCann!

A few months later, but this time in our studio in Hayes, I recorded John again – reading A A Milne's collection of poems *When We Were Very Young* and *Now We Are Six*. I had decided, however, that as these cassettes were mainly for children, it would be beneficial to spread the poems between male and female voices. I decided to approach Hayley Mills, John's younger daughter. Not only would marketing be enhanced by the father / daughter connection but Hayley was very well known and liked by the younger generations from her portrayals in such films as *Tiger Bay*, *Whistle Down The Wind* (written by her mother) and, of course, *The Parent Trap*. She readily agreed and recordings were arranged on different days. Hayley was the first to come into the studio and all went well. However, when she made mistakes – and they are always made – Hayley was inclined to use four-letter word expletives to express her irritation at her own errors. These were doubly effective set in the context of A A Milne's poems for children! Although of course we re-recorded, I kept the originals.

When John came to the studio a few days later to record his allotted poems, he asked me how Hayley had fared. I asked him if he would like to hear some extracts. He was keen to do so and thereupon I played him some of the unedited, more colourful highlights of Hayley's recording. He nearly had hysterics and asked me if he could have copies of the offending extracts. He said they would make wonderful Christmas presents for his close friends and relatives. Unfortunately I had to refuse his request. I didn't know Hayley well enough and there could be legal ramifications if such recordings fell into the hands of certain sections of the media. He chuckled his understanding.

It was to be twenty years before I met John Mills again and it was a complete surprise. Kim and I went on a seven day cruise to Spain and Portugal on Cunards's *Caronia*, now Saga's *Saga Ruby*. When we reached our cabin and read the ship's internal news sheet, we learnt that Sir John Mills was to be on board. I scribbled a note to him, mentioning the recordings of twenty-five years ago and adding that, if he remembered me, I should like to say hello at some point during the cruise. I left the letter at the purser's office and within an hour or so, I had a phone call from his nurse saying he well remembered the recordings and suggested we meet up on deck the following day. This Kim and I did and found him in his wheelchair surrounded by a small entourage – his nurse, his manager and a friend. I hadn't realised he was so frail – nearly blind and very deaf. He seemed genuinely pleased to talk about old times and again chuckled when I reminded him of Hayley's language in the studio. We talked of life in films and I asked him if he had a favourite among the hundreds he had made. It was no surprise to me that the first film he mentioned was *Great Expectations* – he played Pip to Alec Guinness's Herbert Pocket. At first, sitting beside this lovely old man, making considered, deliberate conversation to ease his inevitable loneliness within deafness, I wondered if I was intruding on his past. But no; he was an actor and to talk of Pip in *Great Expectations*, of his Colonel in *Tunes of Glory* (again with Guinness) of his village idiot in *Ryan's Daughter* with Robert Mitchum, Trevor Howard and Sarah Miles, was nectar to him. I could see he was being lovingly cared for by his nurse and, despite his frailty, he was enjoying the bustle and routine of a cruise ship. Relatively few passengers recognised this little old man being wheeled around the ship, into the large dining room where he sat with his friends at a corner table, and into the huge lounge at teatime to enjoy the deliciously thin cut sandwiches.

I was astonished, however, to read that he was going to appear on stage in the main entertainment lounge and be interviewed about his life in film and the theatre. He seemed so fragile and his voice so quiet in conversation, I could not imagine how he could cope in front of so many hundreds of people – even with a microphone. I need not have worried. He had been lifted onto the stage in his wheelchair and when he appeared before the audience, the place erupted. He beamed and waved until the applause subsided and for the next twenty minutes or so, he told stories and made jokes in a voice that belied his ninety-three years. Adrenalin was flowing and he brought reality to the old cliché 'There's No Business Like Show Business'. At the end of his performance, I called for ' Three cheers' and they were heartily given as he left the stage to a standing ovation. I don't know when last he appeared onstage in front of a live audience (I recall his appearance in Terence Rattigan's *Separate Tables* in 1977) but he was astonished and delighted at his reception. So many film and TV stars have never set foot on a theatre stage and have therefore never experienced the applause of a live audience. John Mills had grown up in the theatre and was reliving the magic of his early days and to witness his emotion was something we will never forget. We will never see him on stage again but we, and future generations, will be lucky enough to enjoy the hugely varied performances this lovely man gave us on film – for decades and perhaps centuries to come.

Harrods

'Being young is greatly overestimated…any failure seems so total. Later on you realise you can have another go.'

Mary Quant

I HAD LEFT MALVERN College at the end of the summer term 1937 and returned home to 23 Mecklenburgh Square for the holidays and to think about what I was going to do with my life. I had scraped through School Certificate at the second attempt but with only four credits. For the immediate future I was determined to get a job of some kind to earn enough money of my own to buy Christmas presents for the family and, as Tony, my elder brother and a medical student at Bart's Hospital, rightly pointed out, to contribute toward my 'keep'. There was family delight, therefore, particularly from Tony, when, in answer to an advertisement in the *Daily Telegraph*, I got a job at Harrods, the Knightsbridge department store.

I owned a dark green, three-speed Rudge bicycle and was able to cycle to work every day. I revelled in the journey and it was quick and free! Harrods had a staff bicycle store only a block away and there were hundreds of bikes parked there every day. I left home at 8.30 a.m. every morning, carried my steed up the area steps and set off up Guildford Street, through Russell Square, past the British Museum, down Shaftesbury Avenue, across Piccadilly Circus, along Piccadilly, round Hyde Park Corner and into Knightsbridge. I was removing my bicycle clips by 8.45 a.m. and ready for work at nine o'clock.

I worked for a Mr Buckingham who looked rather like Lloyd George. He had terrible asthma and was rather a grumpy fellow, having been in the basement all his life. We belonged to the Men's Ready to Wear department and we worked downstairs, packing the suits and jackets for delivery to the customers. There seemed to be an awful lot of paperwork even in those days, but Mr Buckingham obviously considered I was too young to handle it.

I have many memories of my short encounter with Harrods and on the very few occasions I have shopped there in the last six decades, I always walk through the Food Hall. The smell has not changed in all those years – an aroma of warm luxury. I am not able to revisit the warren of passages under the store but again, smells permeated the stockrooms and the alleys connecting them. Perfume, fish, furniture, clothes, fancy goods, jewellery all had distinctive smells, not to mention the staff who sold them. Whenever I pass Harrods, particularly at Christmas when the windows are dressed so lavishly and thousands of lights glitter over Knightsbridge, I remember three specific incidents during the three or four months I worked there.

Mussolini's Italian troops had invaded Abyssinia and Anthony Eden, Foreign Secretary, was calling for sanctions against Italy. There was considerable concern in the country and the press was demanding immediate action of some kind. Count Grandi (he was either Italy's Ambassador to the Court of St James, or their Foreign Secretary) had been into the store and bought a suit. It came downstairs for Mr Buckingham to pack. He was folding the jacket when he hesitated, unfolded it and handed it to me. He then pulled open one of the side pockets and spat into it before following his usual meticulous packing procedures. The suit was duly dispatched to Count Grandi.

For the weeks immediately preceding Christmas, staff were moved around to cover those departments more heavily involved in seasonal merchandise. To my delight I was posted to the splendid toy department on one of the upper floors. One of my allotted tasks was to demonstrate an electric aeroplane which was attached to a long projection which, in turn, was attached to an upright revolving bar protruding vertically from the centre of a platform about four feet square. By using two controls, the aircraft could be flown round and round the circuit, climb, dive, loop the loop and land on the platform. One morning, I was between demonstrations, when an authoritative male voice behind me said, 'Would you please demonstrate?' I turned round and recognised Sir Richard Burbage who, at that time, was Chairman of Harrods. Seeing him was quite enough to terrify me and had I turned straight to the task ahead, perhaps all would have been well. But in gathering myself together and stammering, 'Yes sir,' I noticed there were three people with him. I carried out what must have been the first 'double take' in my life when I realised that lined up before me was the Queen with the Princesses Elizabeth and Margaret Rose. I panicked as I grabbed the controls. The aircraft took off, went into a vertical climb, stalled and spiralled down, crashing on to the platform. I think the Queen smiled and said, 'How interesting,' as Sir Richard gently moved his royal visitors on.

The third 'incident' happened very soon after the royal encounter. Harrods sale started early in January and, again, junior staff were moved around to cope with the extra business in busy 'sale' departments. I was moved to the shirt counter which was immediately next to the 'ready to wear' department. The first two days of any sale are hectic and so far as I knew, I did well and earned a small commission. On the third day, a thickset and not particularly distinguished-looking gentleman came up to me and chose two shirts for delivery to his home. We bade each other 'good day' and I set about processing the order. Unfortunately, I sent the wrong size shirts – and the customer turned out to be Winston Churchill. He was, of course, in the political wilderness at the time, but nevertheless, it occurs to me in retrospect that it might have been this encounter, following the plane crash, which prompted the staff manager to send for me and suggest that Harrods' future and mine were not really compatible and that I might consider leaving at the end of the sale. I did – and I did.

Although I am not an account customer, I am still in touch with Harrods in a roundabout way. I have been a supporter of Fulham Football Club ever since the war. It was always known as the Actors Football Club and of course, the comedian, Tommy Trinder, was its chairman for many years. Occasionally I stood on the terrace by the river watching the games in the glory days of the 1950s and '60s when Haynes, Clarke and Hill were playing. The club then slid from the First Division (now the Premier Division) into the Second and Third divisions and for decades the club was the butt of comedians' jokes. Then in the 1990s, something stirred at Craven Cottage on the banks of the Thames and Mohammed Al Fayed became chairman, Kevin Keegan the manager hauling them swiftly from the Third to the First Division. For a month or two there was despair when Keegan departed to become England's manager but a Frenchman, Jean Tigana, succeeded him and within two years Fulham joined the elite again, this time in the Premiership. Ah yes, I nearly forgot to tell you the connection with Harrods. Mr Al Fayed, the Fulham Chairman, also owns Harrods – just up the road.

I have one other story about Harrods which concerns my late Aunt Ena, my mother's half-sister. She had been shopping in Harrods and as she left the main entrance, it was raining, so quite naturally she put up her umbrella. From it fell several knives, forks and spoons, clattering onto the pavement at the feet of one of the store's tallest and most formidable commissionaires. She was immediately apprehended and taken to the security office. Fortunately for her, all the pieces were engraved with the family initials and she was allowed to leave. How the family silver found its way into the umbrella was never known. It was all very strange.

Winnie and Vi

'To me old age is always fifteen years older than I am.'

Bernard Baruch

WINNIE AND VI! WHAT a special pair they were! How they loved each other's company and how, from time to time, they squabbled. (Vi was my mother, of course, though that is incidental; these lines are about their friendship.)

They first met when they moved into their flats at Hanover Mead in Bray in 1971. The City of London Haberdashers Guild had built a delightful development of homes for the elderly; residents are totally independent and have to fulfil certain criteria (income, relatives or close friends nearby, age, health, etc.) to qualify. A warden lives on site and is connected to each flat by an emergency bell. Winnie and Vi were amongst the first occupants when Hanover Mead opened its doors – they both had ground-floor flats, six front doors apart. Within a few days of moving in, they became friends – despite their very different backgrounds. Winnie was eighty-eight years old and came from Yorkshire. She had been 'a Tweenie' in one of that county's grand houses, and she remained 'in service' until she married. She was a very tiny person, but more than made up for it in personality. Vi was seventy-seven years old and came from the rural middle class. Her father farmed Shottesbrooke Farm near Waltham St Lawrence in Berkshire and was at one time Master of the Queen's Hounds in Windsor. Both had been widows for many decades and it may be that is why they were such strong characters. They spent many hours in each other's flats, cooking meals together, playing cards, drinking tea, and generally enjoying themselves. They went to church together every Sunday and participated in all the village activities, volubly expressing their different views on the way the world in general should be run. And when they did fall out, I am sure they made the most of it so that their reunion could be that much sweeter.

On one occasion I was planning a quick visit to Mount Pleasant, our cottage in Hartland, and asked if they would like to come with me. There was no hesitation and we drove down, stopping at Clovelly to show Winnie the picturesque cobblestone village sloping down to the little harbour. At the time, Vi was in her eighties and Winnie in her nineties and they insisted on cooking me the most delicious meals. I drove them to Spekes, Shipload and Welcombe bays and we had roaring log fires on the two nights we were there and played cards and Scrabble. When we went to bed at night, Winnie said to me, 'I'll leave my door open Dick, – just in case.' We journeyed back on the Monday. It was a beautiful day and Winnie pestered me to drive faster; I am ashamed to say we covered the 210 miles in marginally over three hours – I have never done it in less time.

Vi died in 1984, just before her eighty-ninth birthday and at the funeral Winnie sat in her wheelchair and wept. Not many months afterwards she had an entirely successful cataract operation and soon regained her energy and determination. On her hundredth birthday she received a telegram from the Queen and there was a splendid party in the village hall. Michael Parkinson, a Yorkshire man of course and a Bray resident, called in to congratulate her. Shortly afterwards she fell in her flat and was eventually moved to St Mark's Hospital where she died peacefully in February 1987 just before her 101st birthday. She would have relished all the tributes paid to her at her funeral and in the local paper.

Winnie and Vi! Their ashes lie side by side in the churchyard of St Michael's, Bray. That was what they wished.

Postscript

HARVEY, SOME TIME AGO I wrote a long poem and I called it 'Searching'. It was addressed to a young person, probably of the age you will be when you read this book and in it I tried to emphasise the importance of balancing the wonders of modern technology with the mysteries of nature and the miracle of life itself. Like most people, I suspect, it was not until I was relatively old that such thoughts entered my mind and it occurs to me that, having cobbled these memories together, I ought to come to some kind of conclusion by making a few observations. I am, therefore, ending with the last few lines of that poem.

> I acknowledge all the marvels of the present day,
> Pay tribute to the genius of man
> But ask you to remember the transience thereof
> And think of time's eternal span.
> And so young friend, midst all the wonders of the world
> Take time to ponder 'how' and 'why';
> Perpetual questioning is imperative.
> Absorb a vision of the sky –
> Its silence and immensity is frightening.
> But being old allows one time
> To wander round the numinous and secular;
> Is God mammon or divine?
> Journey on but always travel hopefully,
> Embracing faith or harbouring doubt;
> Rejecting raucous claims of exclusivity –
> Searching is to be devout.
> Do you believe in an omnipotent creator

And does he need an earthly shrine?
Call him God or what you will, it matters not,
For we are part of the design.

And so the future eases from my weary shoulders
On to yours; pray lose no sleep.
'Tis good to dream awhile but when you are awake,
A time for searching always keep.

Dabbers